RUGGED MERCY

A Country Doctor in Idaho's Sun Valley

RUGGED MERCY

R O B E R T W R I G H T

WSU
PRESS

Washington State University Press
Pullman, Washington

WASHINGTON STATE
UNIVERSITY

Washington State University Press
PO Box 645910
Pullman, Washington 99164-5910
Phone: 800-354-7360
Fax: 509-335-8568
Email: wsupress@wsu.edu
Website: wsupress.wsu.edu

Library of Congress Cataloging-in-Publication Data
Wright, Robert, 1948-
   Rugged mercy : a country doctor in Idaho's Sun Valley / Robert Wright.
      pages cm
   Includes bibliographical references.
   ISBN 978-0-87422-314-9 (alk. paper)
1. Wright, Robert H., -1980. 2. Physicians--Idaho--Biography. I. Title.
   R154.W75W75 2013
   610.92--dc23
   [B]

                                              2012040681

WSU PRESS
WASHINGTON STATE UNIVERSITY

To my sister, Pat

Rugged Mercy immerses the reader in the daunting medical realities of life in rural Idaho in the late nineteenth and early twentieth centuries, through the experiences of a country doctor, the author's grandfather. Structured around actual events as uncovered in written accounts and gleaned from family stories, the book is a fascinating recreation of the difficulties of medical practice of the time, from fighting through blizzards by dogsled to get to women in labor, to confronting deadly infections with only the most rudimentary medical tools. The narrative is packed with memorable characters in addition to the protagonist: the itinerant snake-oil salesman, the bawd running the local brothel, and, not least, the doctor's own formidable wife. This is a most enjoyable read.

James Whorton
Professor Emeritus of Medical History
University of Washington Schoool of Medicine

"In the spirit of the American West, *Rugged Mercy* succeeds as a story of family, faith, and hard work, sometimes in the midst of suffering. The lively dialogue, family photographs from the author's own collection, and transcribed letters turn this family story into a historical record that comes to life on the page."

—*Columbia Magazine*

Contents

Illustrations

Unless otherwise noted, all photos are from the author's collection.

Preface

This book is an attempt to capture what my grandfather experienced as a turn-of-the-century country doctor. Though written in literary form, it is based on actual events. Literary license is taken only when gaps existed in the chronology that could not be filled in any other way. Those gaps were bridged with events recorded in written accounts and dialogue gathered from oral histories and interviews with people who knew the specific characters and were familiar with the particulars.

Regarding the free use of dialogue and the employment of the omniscient author perspective, the question naturally arises, "How, as a nonfiction author, could I possibly know what went on in the minds of those specific characters?" And a fair question it is. As it happens, it's the easiest question of all to answer. Quite simply, I asked.

I began researching the stories of my family long before a first draft of the work was completed nearly two decades ago. In fact, my first efforts to explore the stories my family told were made when I was in high school, almost 50 years ago. The book always remained a goal. In 1978, when my aged grandmother came to Seattle for a visit, I realized it might be my last opportunity to interview her. I sat her down and plopped myself cross-legged on the floor in front of her, typewriter propped on top of a ten-pound dictionary, and let my fingers fly as she answered question after question about events, emotions, and personalities. What did things look like, smell like, feel like, sound like? I had similar opportunities with my grandfather when I picked his brain as well. How did he feel when he was a boy being asked to assist in actual surgery? "I wet my pants," he said. What did he think about when the avalanche almost caught him? "My honeymoon on the Overland Express."

The stories came from a quadrangle of oral histories: Mom, Dad, my grandmother, and my grandfather. And they came at various times throughout my life, up to age 44 when Mom, the last of my sources, died. Mom gave me the details about Count Schaffgotsch being at the accident scene described in chapter 20. My grandmother made only slight mention of the Count passing through Hailey on the same day, seeming more fascinated by the anatomy of the little girl's neck splayed open by shattering windshield glass than the appearance of the celebrity who founded Sun Valley.

The description of Jean Wright's emergency trip to Salt Lake City and the unfolding tragic events (see chapter 19) was a particular challenge to relate because, apart from my mother, none of my family would discuss it. I have taken the story my mother shared and expanded it out of necessity. As a part of the story she would always say, "—and they flew her to Salt Lake." It never occurred to me that in 1919 air travel was a rare novelty. What sort of aircraft would they have used? My description of the barnstorming Englishman and his plane described in that chapter is drawn from unrelated stories told to me by my father.

Keeping this account true to the times was challenging, and if I've succeeded it's because of people like Roberta McKercher. Roberta was a reporter for the *Hailey Times News* and a local historian, and was extremely helpful in providing details about the way the town looked, what it was like to walk down Main Street in the early 1900s, and Hailey's cultural qualities and values. My grandfather said nobody knew more about Idaho history than Bert McKercher. He was right. Bert was a damn good reporter, and a good writer who fell in love with the Wood River Valley and stayed, rather than pursuing journalism in San Francisco or New York. McKercher interviewed everybody from Averill Harriman to Ernest Hemingway. That ever-present smile of hers could warm the heart of the most adversarial of interviewees. The way her eyebrows would lift in lock step with that smile, that's how you knew Roberta was about to say something significant. She passed on in 1993 and Hailey's city park is named after her.

Another person deserving special mention is Dr. James Whorton, Professor Emeritus, Department of Bioethics and Humanities at the University of Washington School of Medicine. Jim was one of numerous medical specialists with whom I consulted to make the detail of medicine and surgery as accurate as possible. Dr. Whorton advised me on medical practice during my grandfather's era. Thanks also to Dr. Stanley Herschberg, Seattle EENT specialist; Dr. Isamu Kawabori, pediatric heart surgeon at Children's Hospital in Seattle; and Dr. Anita Connell, Seattle OB-GYN, for sharing their knowledge of medicine.

My greatest avowal of appreciation is extended to my first wife, Wendy. She continually urged me to write this book, and was fascinated by my grandmother's stories, tales of pioneer days in danger of being lost forever. Ten years after Wendy's death, and after many failed attempts to start this book, something magical happened. I got lost in its creation. The book began to write itself. Writing was no longer difficult—it was stopping the writing that took discipline. Wendy would be happy to know that I took her advice.

Another person deserving special mention is Laura Wright, my daughter-in-law. I thank her deeply for continued support and encouragement when I'd given up and put the manuscript on the shelf. It was at her suggestion that I submitted it to WSU Press—well, suggestion is a poor word, insistence is more like it.

I also need to thank my second wife, Christie. Knowing I was writing the book, she asked one day if she could read it. Her praise of the manuscript was just the encouragement I needed at that moment. She made a few suggestions, good suggestions, one of which was to reduce the length of the manuscript by about two thirds. The pile of papers I had dropped in her hands weighed as much as an armload of firewood.

Family member Lillian Wright was also extremely helpful in providing specifics to some of the stories where I had only scanty details.

There are many others that were helpful, crucial even, in helping me gather historical data. Most of them, I'm embarrassed to say, are faces and voices whose names are now lost to me. To all those people, please know that I am grateful. I would like to offer a special thanks to the following: Carolyn Ruby at the Idaho State Historical Society; Donna Voyles at the Family History Center in Hailey; Janet Hatch and Don Board of Hailey; Teddie Daley, Director of the Blaine County Museum; and to Sandy Hofferber of the Hailey Community Library.

And lastly, I'd like to thank the staff of WSU Press: designer Nancy Grunewald, marketer Caryn Lawton, copyeditor Kerry Darnall, director Mary Read, and editor-in-chief Robert Clark, who took the manuscript and rearranged its pieces with brilliance. The result is a story that truly does reflect the dramatic struggles of our forefathers in laying down the foundations of what has become the greatest civilization in history. Because it's not just my story. It's not just my grandfather's story. It's everyone's story, every grandfather's and grandmother's story.

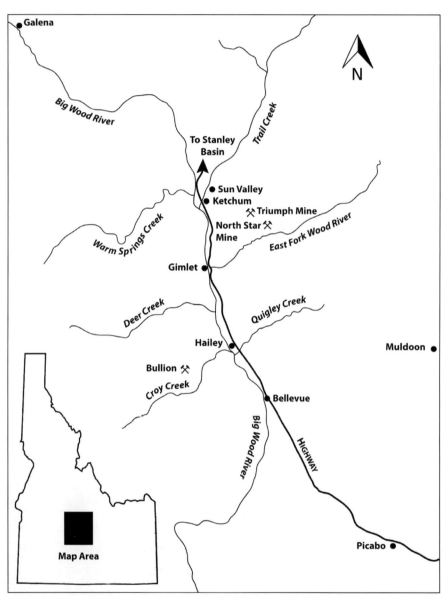

The Big Wood River Valley. *Map by Ed Sala.*

Chapter 1

The First Victory

Hailey, Idaho

1894

Two children strained high on a bench and peered through the window, shivering at the sight within. A young child lay upon a pedestal, draped in a shroud of white, encircled by fifteen to twenty coal oil lanterns. Above her stood a man holding a dagger dripping with blood. With it he was cutting out the child's entrails, and under each stroke the shroud grew more crimson. Shadows of the deed flooded against the rough timbered walls, and brought to mind a tale of terror: *"...and Abraham stretched forth his hand, and took the knife to slay his son."* There to guard the ritual was Sheriff Charley Furey, back against the wall and six-shooters strapped low to his hips.

The man with the dagger lifted his head and looked at the window, looked right at the children, meeting their eyes. "At the window!" he thundered.

The bench tipped to the ground beneath them and tumbled away. Before they could recover a heavy grip tugged at their collars. The chilly pre-dawn sky silhouetted a looming figure whose voice boomed. "I'm Charles Furey, Sheriff of Alturas County. Now you kids are going to have to answer to me." Warm urine ran down the older child's leg.

The sheriff hovered in front of them, looking down. The handles of the six-shooters poked out the sides of his suit coat. The coat was buttoned high up at his neck and hung loose to his knees; it made the tall man seem all the larger. His long mustache twitched. "You hombres here to rob these good folks?" He drove his evil stare at the older child, a boy, about eleven or twelve. "You there. You Billy the Kid? Is that who you are? Huh boy?"

"No, sir," squeaked the boy.

"You here to rob these people? Huh? S'at it?"

"No, sir."

Charley Furey then fixed his eyes on the second child. Both children wore oversized trousers held up by suspenders, but this child had strawberry hair that tumbled down the middle of her back. "How 'bout you, little missie?"

"No, sir."

"'Cause if you are, 'cause if that's why you're here, I know right straight away what I'm gonna do with you two."

The children shook their heads in denial again. Charley Furey said, "What do you kids think you're doin'? Comin' here like this. Sneakin' around. You're lucky you didn't get your fool heads stove in." He looked at the boy once more. "What's your name, son?

"Robert."

"Robert? Robert who?"

"Robert Wright."

Charley Furey looked surprised, then twisted up his mouth in a mocking expression of disbelief. "No. Not R. H. Wright's son. Tell me that ain't so."

"Yes, sir," acknowledged the boy shamefully.

"R. H. Wright? The stock grower?"

"Yes, sir."

"I know your daddy, boy. He's not gonna be happy about this. No siree. Not at all. You know your daddy came here in '81 during the gold fever? Friedman's store, it warn't no more than a tent. Came here, your daddy, because he wanted a better life for you and those brothers and sisters of yours. He worked the Minnie Moore before water filled her shaft. He worked up some savings and he went out and bought himself some livestock. Settled on that piece down by Bellevue. He did it for you, boy, you and those brothers and sisters of yours." Charley shook his head again twice before speaking. "No, sir. He's not gonna be happy about this. No, sir. That's for sure."

Charley looked then at the other child, the girl, fixing that awful stare on her, twitching his mustache. "And you, girl. What's your name?"

"Cynthia Beamer, sir." She looked down at the ground, shrinking from the stare. Charley Furey stepped forward, making two loud thumps. "Yeah? You Cynthia Beamer? Little Dottie Beamer?" He was looking straight down from the sky. She started to cry. "A woman's tears mean nothing to me, young lady. Now what I want to know is, I want to know who your pa is. I s'pose next thing you'll be telling me is that your pa is Al Beamer, Union Pacific station agent. Look at me, young lady, when I'm a-talkin' at you."

The child stretched her neck back. "Yes, sir."

"Yes sir what."

"Yes, sir. Al Beamer, he's my pa. Sir."

Charley clicked his teeth, turned his head, and spat. The children jerked. "Another good man. He works himself silly for you kids, for you and your brother and that baby sister a'yourn. Never seen a man who could work a telegraph key like your pa. He can talk on that thing faster'n most people can speak. Respected man around these parts. And I find his daughter chasin' around with the likes of an hombre like Billy the Kid."

"I ain't Billy the Kid, sir," the boy said. "I'm Robert Wright."

"So you say." Charley spat again. "—lucky thing I lost the keys, or I'd be throwin' you two in the hoosegow, lockin' you up good'n tight, is what I'd be doin'." The children turned their eyes down toward the ground once more, toward Charley's big boots.

A voice bellowed from inside the house. "Bring those children to me." The man with the dagger! Charley grabbed them, a hand behind each neck, and dragged them squirming and kicking to the back door. The door was heavy, made of logs hewn in half. It scraped across the rock-hard dirt floor as Charley kicked it open with the toe of his heavy boot. A stench permeated the room, scathing to the throat. The pedestal upon which the child lay was in reality a large dining room table with exquisitely carved legs. The man-with-the-dagger was wrist deep in the girl's abdominal cavity, like he was holding her together with something. "I need more light." He nodded toward the children, hanging from Charley's hands like coats on hangers. "And you two are going to help me get it." He directed the children and Sheriff Furey to hold lanterns high, and another person, a man, was asked to hold a mirror to reflect the light down. Then he spoke to a woman in the room. "Mrs. Thompson," he said. "You will help me." He continued muttering his instructions. He told Mrs. Thompson to take strips of towels and soak up the blood. "Don't be afraid. That's it. Keep it all soaked up so's I can see what I'm doin'."

The man was chewing on the stub of an unlit cigar, his face dirty with a heavy growth of whiskers, maybe two days' worth. "Tip that mirror just a mite more. There we go. Now let's see what we can find in here." Both his hands were swishing around the transparently pink mounds and nodules of tiny intestines. "He's a hidin'." The man reached behind something along the back intestinal wall, an organ about the size of an orange, and pulled out what he was looking for, the tit end of one of the intestines. "There he is. Come to poppa. 'At's it." It was about the size of a little finger, black and swollen. He grabbed it with pliers. Funny looking pliers, bent at the handles. "We need to tie this jigger off…" There was a thump on the hard dirt floor. Mrs. Thompson had fainted dead away. The man with the dagger seemed more annoyed than concerned. "She will be fine. You needn't worry about her." Clenching his teeth tighter on the cigar, he looked at the man holding the mirror and said, half with a grin, "Come over here and take up your wife's place, over here and start soakin' up this blood. It's flowing a mite heavier than I expected. It doesn't mean anything. I just need it swabbed so's I can see. But wash up first." Mr. Thompson didn't move. All that happened was that droplets of sweat beaded up on his upper lip. He shook his head as if to plead for another way, because he couldn't force his arms to move, or even compel his voice to utter a response.

The man with the dagger looked at Sheriff Furey. The tough lawman turned pale and quickly shook his head. "Doc. No. Not me." The doctor bit on the cigar and tipped his head forward and aimed his eyes at young Robert, almost as if it amused him to do so. "Looks like it's up to you, boy. How 'bout it, son? You wanna step up to the challenge? Help me save this wee child's life? If you do, it will be something you'll not soon forget. I guarantee you that. It'll be something that will change your life." Robert stared back at the doctor, reluctant to believe what he was being asked to do. "What do you say? I could sure use four hands right about now. The Good Lord only made me with two." Robert was shaking inside. The doctor's expression became more tender as he tipped his head forward in powerful reassurance. Robert put down his lantern and took three very slow steps forward. "'At's a lad. I want you to do something first, 'afore you go pokin' around in here. I want you to go over to the stove—" the doctor gestured toward the far corner of the single room log home "—and wash your hands. You'll notice that the water there has been set to boiling. Take that pitcher and scoop some up. And pour it in the basin and scrub your hands. Scrub them good, all the way to the elbow. Don't doddle about it. Go. Hop now."

Robert did as he was told, took steady, cautious steps over to the cook stove in the corner, dipped out some of the boiling water, washed, then took his place by the side of the doctor, his hands red and prickling from the sting of the lye soap. As he looked down into the child's abdominal cavity he realized that that was where the stench was coming from. The awful smell rolled up and hit him in the face like a slap, and when he sucked it down into his lungs his throat tightened with a jerk. He stifled the urge to cough and stood his ground. He found it was bearable if he took shallower breaths. In one hand the doctor was holding the still attached appendage with the odd-looking pliers. In the other he was dabbing up blood with the strips of cloth. "Quite simple. All you have to do is take these strips and press them against the side of the incision. Soak up the blood. Here. Just like this. Simple. You couldn't make a mistake if you wanted to. It's as easy as falling off a log. And young missie—" his eyes went to Dottie "—you bring that light a mite closer. 'At's a girl. Right there. Good girl. Hold it right there."

Young Robert was still shaking inside. But his hands did what they were supposed to do. And upon his face was frightened wonderment. He did his job superbly. He kept the area clean and visible for the doctor to make his ligations on the appendage and cut between them, two ties about a quarter of an inch apart, tight so that the bowl contents wouldn't spill and infect the abdominal cavity. The whole thing was over in a matter of minutes. The doctor rolled the cigar stub in his teeth in a gritty smile of satisfaction. "Not bad," he said. "Not bad at all. Halsted himself couldn't do as good." He looked at Mr. Thompson. "Your little girl will wake up soon. She will be fine. But I want her in bed for two weeks. Too much strain could tear the incision."

Mrs. Thompson, conscious now and on her feet, drew in a husky breath, as if she'd been holding it the entire time. Color flushed her face and she began to cry. The relief was overwhelming.

The doctor stitched and closed, and waited with the child while she recovered from the anesthesia. Then Robert and Dottie joined him in a hearty breakfast, supplied by the Thompsons. Bread, eggs, and dried beef.

When the two children walked out of that tiny log home with the doctor at mid-morning, things were different. A cool wind was blowing down from the north mountains, tossing their hair, and it carried about it a certain scent, a crispness drawn up from the good earth by the melting overnight frost. It was the same wind that blew every morning at this time, but it seemed different, better. Things were charmed, somehow, transformed. Colors were more vivid. Things seemed more alive. And the two children felt just a little closer to one another, as if the deed had bonded them in some unexplained way.

"Well, would you look at that," observed the doctor on the way home, shifting the reins to his other hand so he could point to the moon, still visible in a faint blue outline above the prominent span of Carbonate Mountain. "A hangin' there in Heaven, refusing to go away. A hangin' there like a silver bell."

The children squinted as they looked. Carbonate's steep hillsides, dotted in cliffs and sparse sprouts of evergreens, lay ornate from the sun that had by now fully crested the rolling mountains on the other side and was high enough to pierce the valley. It seemed to drape her crusted ridges in a kind of clean softness that left the cloudless sky behind her

Wood River Valley with Hailey in foreground, 1884. Carbonate Hill is across Wood River beyond the town.
A. E. Browning. Collier & Cleveland Lith. Co. Library of Congress digital collections, G4274. H3A3 1884 .B7. Courtesy Janet Hatch.

almost white. The Indians had a name for it. "Ee-dah-ho." Sun coming over the mountain. Idaho.

The wagon was tall to the point of being top heavy. It served as both home and office for the doctor as he meandered from town to town. The driver's seat was high up by the wagon's roof. The children, one on either side of him, leaned instinctively inward as he drove. They'd never been so high. A backpack containing their makeshift fishing gear, with a Birchwood pole sticking out, was lashed onto the back along with the doctor's pots and pans and a collection of high-backed chairs. Painted on the side were letters of silver and gold.

The Kickapoo Sagua Remedy Company
Dr. Joseph I. Durham, Proprietor
Surgery, Dentistry, Eclectic Medicine
Reasonable Rates, Fortunes Told

"Are you a for-real doctor?" asked Dottie.

Robert hushed her. "Mind your manners."

"It's all right, son. It's quite all right. Yes, my dear, I am a for-real doctor. Diploma from the Eclectic Medical College of Cincinnati Oh-High-Oh."

"Is that a long ways away?"

"End of the world, child. End of the world…"

Robert kept turning his head back to look at three riders accompanying the doctor, clopping along in back of them. One was slumped down, half asleep on his horse, an Indian, the oldest looking human being Robert thought he had ever seen. Long locks of dusty gray hair fell from beneath the wide brim of his hat, and his skin was pasty brown with white wrinkles. But the sight that kept drawing Robert's attention was the giant man riding the next horse, the likes of which he had never in his life seen, a real African chief. He seemed so tall his feet would have drug the ground had he not been holding them up. His fist alone was the size of a normal man's head, and his skin was the color of a starless night, so black it seemed unnatural against the contrast of his billowing feathers and war paint. Next to him rode a stunningly attractive woman, also with black skin, whose knees and thighs now and then emerged from the sides of a grass skirt.

"What's that Kickapoo thing mean?" Dottie asked. "That thing that's written on your wagon." Dottie was young, but she could read, having been schooled by lantern light with the Holy Scriptures.

Dr. Durham's chest swelled a bit. "The Kickapoo Sagua Remedy Company, my young friend, happens to be the trademark of a company born of pure genius." He lifted a smoky bottle about the size of the palm of his hand. "The name is a reference to a miracle elixir. Contained herein is a concoction good for both body and soul."

"What's in it?"

"Ah—that is a secret. A potion from the darkest of Africa. I've taken it upon myself to assume the responsibility of offering it to the good people of the Wood River Gold Belt, as a service, taking nothing for myself but a modest remuneration."

Robert started to speak, to ask a question, but lapsed into a coughing fit. His throat still hurt.

"From the chloroform vapors," offered Dr. Durham, half-laughing. "Chloroform is what we use to put a patient to sleep before an operation. It reacts with the open flame of a lantern to produce some rather unpleasant fumes. A body gets used to it."

"I thought it was coming out of the little girl."

The doctor laughed fully and heartily. "No, child. You just happened to be in a place where you got a good strong whiff of it. It'll pass."

Robert cleared his throat and began again. "What causes people to get sick?"

Durham clicked the reins of his one horse team and blew smoke above his head from his cigar. "What causes people to get sick? What do you think?"

"The headmistress at school says it's demons. My pa says there's no such things as demons."

"The schoolmarm's right. Tiny buggers. You could put a thousand of them on the head of a pin." The doctor slapped the reins again. His suit coat lay across his lap, and his shirt, stained in blood spatters, was rolled up at the sleeves to expose oversized fuzzy forearms and short fat fingers. The stub of his burning cigar was stuck between two of them. It seemed like he could barely hold it. Robert wondered how he could operate with fingers like that. "Microbes, we call 'em. Demons for sure. So small you can't nary see a one without the aid of a microscope. Even then you can only see the big ones." Dr. Durham tended to come across as a kidder, because of the way he always half smiled when he talked, so a person was never quite sure where the line was between fact and a tale. Truth of it, Robert was a little that way himself. "Invisible demons," restated Dr. Durham. "Demons so small you can't see them."

"If they're so small, how's come you know they're there?"

"Oh they're there all right. Like I say, some of them you can see, with a microscope."

Little Dottie had fallen asleep, head dropped against the doctor's shoulder. It must have happened quickly, because a minute ago she was wide awake. Durham stuffed out his cigar on the footboard and took his coat and carefully tucked it over her back and shoulders, then put his arm around her to keep her secure. Mornings are chilly in Idaho, even in the heat of summer.

"It wasn't too awfully long ago," he said, "that this fellow across the ocean concocted a notion that it was microbes that were causing patients to up and die after an operation. Some doctors believed him, some didn't. Fact was, the doctors who started washing and scrubbing before surgery started having fewer fatalities. So I figure, why take a chance? But I will tell you something. I never had a problem. Hardly ever lost a patient. Ever. Even back before I started washing and disinfecting. Because I got in and out fast. Tissues exposed to the air for too long a time don't heal right. If an incision is left open and exposed to the air for an extended period and coagulation occurs, when the wound is finally closed the tissues are no longer in the best state for quick healing. What takes those hospital doctors two hours to do I'll complete in fifteen minutes and do a better job to boot. You should see the way they operate in big city hospitals. It looks like something out of a Middle Eastern harem. Surgeons wear gloves. Masks, some of them. Sheets are draped everywhere, even on the surgeons. All in efforts to keep the patient and the wound clean from microbes. Those big shots back at Johns Hopkins—why, fiddle, I'll match my kitchen surgery skills against their high falutin' techniques any day. And I will have less tissue deterioration."

"What was it you did back there? To the girl?" asked Robert.

"The removal of an inflamed vermiform appendix. Doctors have been doing this particular procedure for nigh on ten years now. It's quite common."

"Weren't you scared?"

"A surgeon can't afford to be scared. Let me tell you something, boy, if you want to be the best at something, you can't be scared. You've got to have a cares-be-damned attitude. That's the truth of it. You must care without caring. Something to remember if you ever become a doctor."

"Not me. I'm going to run away and live a life of adventure."

"Oh? You don't say. When do you plan on doing this?"

"Soon, I expect. First I aim to go up into yonder hills and dig me a gold mine, get about a hundred dollars' worth, then I'll probably go hook up with Joe Snake and his river pirates for a spell. Then I'll join the circus. Tame me some lions and tigers. Maybe I'll scout some for the Army, like Rube Robbins."

Spoke up Dottie, from the drifting clouds of her sleep. "Me? I'm going to be a very famous pianist. I shall perform at all the concert halls in Europe. Kings and queens will invite me to play before them."

Robert said, "Maybe after I strike it rich, and after I'm done scouting with the Army, I'll come to Europe and see one of those concerts."

"That would be lovely," she said, speaking it as though she truly expected it to be so, and dropped once again into the soundness of her sleep.

"Dottie plays for all the churches, you know," said Robert. "She's the only one in town who can do it, except for the saloon players."

"What were you kids doing way out here, and so early in the morning?"

"We came out to go fishing. And look for beavers. Dottie hasn't ever seen a beaver."

"You both did a fine job in there."

"My brother Lester died when he was two," said Robert. "It was from derithia."

"Derithia? You probably mean diphtheria. Also caused by microbes."

Robert's mind gathered the courage to revisit the time his baby brother died. Little Lester had a pumpkin-round face and wide innocent eyes, trusting eyes. The elder Robert Wright thought himself worthy of that trust, at first, convinced that what ailed his son was only a slight case of the consumption. He was sure that the cool rubs and the elixir would cause the cold to pass. But the pain grew within the child, and the crying became louder and more desperate. A parent can remove a sliver, bandage a cut, calm hysteria, but there are some things none alive can fix. No one can reach into a tiny chest and deliver air. Even the doctor could do nothing but sit by the child's bedside and watch, helpless.

Diphtheria kills because a mucous membrane forms to slowly choke off air over a period of days. The doctor knows when the end is near, because the child stops crying. All its energy must be directed to the task of breathing. Finally, after torturous hours, the child stiffens, the face turns blue, the eyes bulge out, the little body twitches. Then goes limp.

The doctor at his brother's bedside spoke: "The Lord giveth and the Lord taketh away." It would have been better had he said nothing.

It was the only time Robert had seen his father cry.

"We've got an antitoxin for it now," Durham said.

"What's an antitoxin?"

"Poison. Poison for demons. See, what happens, the demons get inside a person and spit out poisons. We doctors call poisons toxins. So what we do, we give a person antitoxins. The antitoxins get rid of the toxins. Sort of. It's a bit more complicated than that, I 'spect. But basically that's what happens."

"Does it work?"

"Appears it does. Word is from back East that it does."

Dr. Durham still had the grin on his face, and Robert still wasn't sure if it was there because it was the way he was, or because he was spinning a tale. "I'll be telling you the truth, young lad, I don't quite know myself how it works, exactly. But I hear tell it does."

"Is that why your tonic works, is because it has those antitoxins in it?"

He didn't answer.

"Well?"

"Well what."

"How does your tonic work?"

The doctor made motions with his jaw as if he was chewing on something. He was thinking. That's what he did when he was thinking.

"Well?"

"Well what?"

"Well how does it work?"

Dr. Durham scratched his hatless head on his sunburned bald spot—he'd hung his beat up bowler on the end of the wagon's buggy whip—and ran his fingers through grey tufts of hair that stuck straight out. "Now mind you, it doesn't always work. But when it does I suspect it's because—" he leaned over and whispered it out of the side of his mouth. "I 'spect it's because it goes to work on your mind." He tapped his head. "In here. It works on your brain. Makes you think you're not sick. It fools you into getting better. The mind's a funny thing that way. Sometimes that's what you have to do. Sometimes you have to fool 'em into getting well."

"Oh." The answer satisfied young Robert, and with it he fell away into sleep, traveling in his mind to a different place, a different time, one in which he was a great surgeon, accomplishing many great things, helping many people.

Chapter 2

The Old Shyster's Big Show

Hailey, Idaho

1894

Y OUNG ROBERT WAS AWAKENED by the popping of firecrackers and the distant sharpness of a brass band bleating out "Camptown Races." The whistle of the Oregon Short Line on its way through to Ketchum echoed through the streets, and the wooden wheels of Dr. Durham's wagon clacking over hard packed streets mirrored the rhythm of high stepping horses. He'd forgotten. Today was the 3rd of July. Idaho observed two big days of festivities in the summer, the 3rd and 4th of July. Four years earlier, July 3, 1890, Idaho had been officially admitted to the union by proclamation of President Harrison.

Red, white, and blue buntings bannered Main Street, and flags fluttered from every building and street corner. Carriages were moving briskly about, but in a way suggesting they had no particular destination. One, driven by an attractive woman in lace and bows, was parked in the middle

Main Street in Hailey, late 1880s.
Idaho State Historical Society.

of the street while she talked to a man with his hat in his hand. The man jumped as some children tossed a string of firecrackers at his feet.

Two steam engines were clanking and puffing and flapping their way side by side through the city, their prideful operators unaware that at that very moment, somewhere far away, an unknown by the name of Henry Ford was fast at work on the development of a better machine. The mining boom and the allure of gold were changing everything. Each day more and more people were crowding into the Wood River Valley, coming to the towns of the Idaho Gold Belt—Bellevue, Hailey, Broadford, Bullion, Ketchum, Muldoon. Some came to work the mines. Some came to farm and raise livestock. Others opened businesses. Fortunes were made in the blink of an eye. A man might be sweeping a saloon one day and depositing twenty thousand dollars in the bank the next. Fourteen years earlier there had been nothing in the valley but a trapper's trail.

Now, in 1894, Hailey alone boasted four churches, nine saloons, three hotels, and seven attorneys. Dottie played at all four of those churches. They staggered their services so she could get from one to the next. Her little feet couldn't even touch the floor.

All eyes were on Dr. Joseph I. Durham and his wagon and entourage as he moved down Main Street. People were stopping conversations and coming out of businesses and homes to see the strange sight. Children began following after him. As soon as he had gathered the attention of most everyone in town he stopped at the intersection of Main and Carbonate, right in the middle of town. The Friedman stores were on the left, the McCormick Bank on the right. He gathered so many people, men in bowlers and top hats, women in dresses and lace, that the driver of the Ish and Hailey stagecoach had to fire a shot into the air just to clear a path.

Then, with the wagon as a backdrop and the dirt of the street as a performance platform, Dr. Durham entertained the townsfolk, just like he had done in Muldoon, just like he had done in Bullion. Part snake oil salesman, part surgeon, the good doctor made his living traveling the towns of the Northwest with his dancing Indians and Negroes, putting on his side shows, performing surgeries, setting broken bones, peddling electric belts, whatever he could do to serve the public and make a buck or two in the process. And of course he would sell his miracle elixir, a tonic good for all ills of body and soul, a potion that once gave fluid voice to the great orator William E. Borah, before a chronic stutterer. The noon sun was blasting down. Its heat shimmered off the red bricks of the McCormick Bank building and gleamed against the green trimmed white sides of the S.L. Friedman store, and gave a kind of mystic validation to the odd little man. Dust kicked up at his heels as he strode back and forth. Grasshoppers clicked as they flew to get out of his way.

"A time back I had no hair at all. None. Two tablespoons a day. That's all it took to give me this."

A dog was yapping, frightened apparently by the drums and the dancing. Durham removed the cork from one of the bottles and shook some of the liquid onto the animal. It stopped its yapping forthwith. He replaced the cork and continued, with no reference whatsoever to the amazing occurrence.

"Take a good look at Chief Momokimbo." He pointed to the African. "The chief is a giant of a man, an incredible physical specimen. And do you know how he got that way?" He held up the bottle. "Of course we can't be sure, but the fact is, the tribesmen across the river, the ones who *don't* have the elixir, are all pygmies, none over four feet tall. And have a look at his queen." The woman, her ink-black skin entirely exposed except for her breasts and loins, danced and twirled in a circle around Durham, her bare legs slipping in and out of the long grass skirt to the rhythm of the old Indian's drum beat. Some of the women in the crowd gasped.

"A specimen of health and beauty. And do you know how she got that way?" He held up the bottle again. "Of course we can't be sure, but I am told she is over a hundred and fifty years old. Fact is—she comes from the land wherefrom the potion originates." He held the bottle out further. "I have been partaking of this, two tablespoons a day, for nigh on three years now. And in that three-year period I have not had a single cold. A colleague of mine back east used to wear eyeglasses, until he began taking this twice a day. Now he has perfect vision. Twice a year I journey back to Africa, and return with a small quantity. The contents of this bottle could well sell for twenty dollars. Even then it would be a bargain. What I will do is give it to you for the cost of the bottle itself, One Dollar and Fifty Cents, a pittance considering the glass is specially treated to keep the essence from seeping through into the air. Why am I willing to do this? Because, my dear people of the Wood River Gold

Belt, I am a fool. I am willing to lose money, if it will benefit you. All I ask in return is that you allow me to be your doctor. That is how we will square things."

A man from the crowd put up his hand. "Here. I'll buy two. Right here."

Dr. Durham held his palm up. "Patience, my good man. Time enough for that."

Another man waved his fist, clutching in it a silver dollar and two quarters. "Here. I'll take one. Over here."

"Patience. You will all get your chance. We will get to you all. That I promise. First, allow me to draw your attention to the device the queen is holding before her, yet another miracle of modern medical science. The amazing electric belt."

The queen was prancing back and forth holding the belt above her head. It looked like an ordinary leather belt, except that it was thicker and wider in back.

"The properties of electricity are far reaching, immense, and are only now beginning to be understood. We are in the infancy of discovery. It is a marvelous age we live in, one in which the curtains of the unknown are being lifted, finally, slowly. Oh so slowly. Electricity has the power to destroy—" Dr. Durham waved his hand and brought forth an explosion of smoke. The people jumped back. "But it also has the power to heal. This device is charged with electricity. It will not be painful. In fact you won't feel it at all. But the electricity and its healing properties will be moving through your body, balancing your energies. The Chinese have known for centuries that the health and well-being of a human body is dependent upon the proper balance of its energies. Wear this belt for twenty-four hours and I guarantee you, you will feel a hundred percent better. For the low price of only two dollars and fifty cents." Then came more dancing. Then the queen circulated among the crowd and sold some tonic and belts. And the old Indian did some knife throwing and trick shooting.

At the end of the show, to the people who had any money left, the charitable doctor offered to sell a small book he'd written advertising his remedies. And last of all, but certainly not least, the old Indian, a Shaman, wise in the mystic ways of things, told fortunes for two bits, or for whatever else he could extract from a willing and gullible participant.

The show lasted most of the afternoon, and stole away the people from the other events of the picnic, the tree climb, the fishing contest, the pie judging, the horse show. Whatever medicinal value the tonic and the electric belts may or may not have had, the folks got their money's worth, at least in entertainment. It was better than the circus that had come to the valley the previous fall. The town purely sparkled with camaraderie. For an afternoon the people forgot their cares and struggles.

Dr. Durham stayed for a time, a few weeks, until he was arrested for boring a hole in George Shirley's head. Practicing surgery without having a medical diploma filed for record was the charge, brought by another of the town's local doctors. Dr. Durham was tried in Bellevue, where it was proven that he did in fact have a medical diploma, and that it was on record. He was acquitted, on the condition that he file his diploma in Alturas County, the county of residency, as required by law. But as quickly and mysteriously as he arrived, Dr. Durham vanished.

Only for a time, though. In less than a year he was back, this time without the wagon and side show, this time setting up an office in the *Daily and Weekly Wood River Times* building, with phenomenal success. And a funny thing had happened during his absence. George Shirley made a complete recovery. It gave people a celestial confidence in the town's new doctor. George's condition before Dr. Durham's strange procedure had been pronounced as incurable. He had been the victim of torturous headaches, memory loss, speech difficulty, even spasms of unpredictable violence. One of the local churches had proclaimed him possessed. Dr. Durham's simple diagnosis was mastoiditis, and he bored that hole in George's cranium and drained out what must have been two cups full of puss. George was cured. To the people of the Wood River Valley, Dr. Durham's return was no less than a divine event. They came to him in droves with their ailments, robbing the doctor who filed the original complaint of nearly all his business.

Then, on July 4, 1895, a beautiful woman arrived in town aboard the John Hailey Stage, from somewhere down in California, and married the eccentric Dr. Durham. In celebration he passed out bottles of his tonic, the Amazing Kickapoo Sagua Remedy Elixir. He gave twenty bottles to the driver of a triple freighter plodding through town with his 20-mule team, headed for the steep switchbacks of Galena Summit.

Barely a month after the wedding another beauty showed up, this one from Cincinnati, and, beset by an apparent jealous rage, aimed a bullet at Dr. Durham's head. It whizzed past and crashed into his diploma, shattering the glass and putting a hole in the middle of the "o" in the name Joseph. The hole was so perfectly placed no one would have been able to tell it was there, had it not been for the broken glass.

The next morning the town of Hailey had one less citizen, one less doctor. Dr. Durham was gone again, this time forever, with his wife and belongings, and diploma. Where he went was a mystery. No one ever saw him again.

And the tonic? The Amazing Kicapoo Sagua Remedy Elixir? Did it work? Yes. And no. It had no medicinal value, other than what might be carried in water, molasses, and corn liquor. But the future Dr. Robert Henry Wright learned something from Dr. Durham, healer, shyster, fortune teller. As the good doctor himself once put it, "Every now and then you can fool them into getting well. The mind's a funny thing that way."

Sometimes in his career, when medical science was not enough, when he had tried every possible thing, Dr. Wright would give the old shyster's method a try. "Fool 'em into getting well." And every now and then it would work. The mind's a funny thing that way.

But it didn't work on Robert's first patient. His first patient was doomed from the start. His first patient was the victim of a disease of a different kind, different than that wrought by microorganisms, different than that brought about by trauma to muscle and bone.

It began with a knock on the door. Barely out of medical school, newly married to Dott, his childhood sweetheart, and living in Walker, Missouri, he had gone into business with his brother-in-law, Dr. Stanley Love.

It was a weak knock, barely to be heard. A humble tapping, almost like the scratching of an animal. Dott put her hand on the octagonal glass knob, and hesitated, then turned it and swung the door open.

Standing there, looking up, face distorted in fear, was a child, a little girl no one would help, not even compassionate people, for her skin was the wrong color, and she was in the wrong part of town. The child tried not to cry, but tears came anyway, streaming down her pearly black cheeks. She tried to talk, but it came out in hard to understand gasps. "My momma is dying," she finally choked out, pleading with her eyes. "Will you help me find the doctor? Will you please? My momma is dying. She's having a baby and she's dying. Please, please, please—"

"Whoa, slow down there," said Bob, appearing in the doorway with his coat half on. "Doctor Love won't be in for another hour. But I'm a doctor. Let's you and I go see about that momma of yours."

The door shut hard and Dott heard the running of footsteps down the stairs, the little black girl's footsteps followed by Bob's. She watched out the window as the child ran down the street, Bob following in wide strides, coat tails flying, medical bag held out to one side, half breaking into a run to keep up.

Cynthia "Dott" Beamer Wright said a prayer for her new husband—the man who had been her best friend pretty much her whole life—a prayer that things would go well. She then busied herself about the apartment with the tasks of the morning: emptying the wash water, drawing and carrying new water, heating it up, cleaning the tub and wash basins, emptying and cleaning the porcelain bucket by the bed, gathering and folding clothes from the line out back. Once her tasks were complete, she began composing an answer to the letter from her mother that had just arrived.

Hailey in winter. The Friedman stores at left were directly across the street from the office of Dr. Wright.

Chapter 3

Getting the Office Ready

Hailey, Idaho

1952

I HAD MY OWN SNOW SHOVEL, and every time Dad would lift a shovelful out of the path I'd shovel it back in. "Makin' her summer, Dad," I would say. It was sound logic to my four-year-old mind: why make a single pathway when you should be getting rid of the whole bunch of it? Never mind that some of it happened to fall back into the path Dad was making. Necessary collateral damage. The world at 5:30 in the morning, after a fresh snowfall, is full of wonder and adventure to a busy child. "We need to get this done afore O'You comes to the office. Right, Dad?"

"That's right."

They tell me that when I was a baby my grandfather would poke at me and say, "Ohhh you!" The name stuck. But most people called him "Doc," because that's who he was—a doctor. His office was in the same building where we lived and where Dad worked in his shop, on Main Street, and I would help Dad shovel out the walks and driveways when it snowed. O'You's real name was Robert Henry Harrison Thornton Hix John Brown Wright. But no one could remember all those names strung together.

"We got to get things ready for him. Right, Dad?"

"That's right."

The town still slept. There were no sounds except for the drone of road graders crisscrossing the streets, piling up ten- and twenty-foot banks of unspoiled clumps of white. And that made me and Dad special. The two most important people in the world. By the time the sun was up and O'You came down the hill in his '51 Studebaker, riding the clutch with a half-idle roar, we had cleared the paths to the building, front and side, parking lots and sidewalks. And the hopper was filled with coal and the furnace stoked, and the office warm. We'd done our job. Dad shook

The McCormick Bank Building, with its new owner Dr. Robert Wright, soon after he had purchased it in 1909.

his head as O'You slowly roared to a stop. "Your granddaddy burns out a clutch a month. But you can't tell him anything."

"Nope, Dad. You can't tell him anything."

The old McCormick Bank building still had the stenciled name painted on the south side. O'You owned it now. The front half was his office, the middle was the "Workshop," where Dad and Mom made things out of wood and sold them to people who came to Sun Valley, and the back half of the building was storage O'You rented out. Underneath it all, supposedly, was a tunnel that ran to the alley where they used to bring gold shipments into the bank. I was never allowed to go there.

The Workshop must have been a famous place, because Dad's creations—*Beavercut* was the name he and Mom had for them, a trademark for glass-smooth swirls of wood they'd find in the riverbeds and fashion into bowls, ashtrays, cigarette lighters, vases—were featured in magazines that sold in newsstands in places as far away as New York and San Francisco.

The Workshop in the McCormick Bank Building. Glenn Wright stands at the doorway.

We lived upstairs. "The Apartment," we called it. I did my best during the day not to "run wild" while O'You had patients. But a certain amount of thumping was just something that had to be accepted. Sometimes I would smash my face against the heat register and peer down at the astonished people below. When the patients finally left, it was my turn. I'd trot on down the stairs, thump, thump, thump, and a whole new adventure would begin. O'You would be sitting at his roll top desk reading the *Twin Falls Times News* or the *Boise Statesman*. A black desktop telephone was always within reach. A framed photograph of a baby in a crib was on the left hand side, in the same spot every day, in a place all by itself with nothing cluttered around it. A picture of me, I had always assumed. O'You would show me my bones through the fluoroscope, and let me listen to my heart. He'd show me the jar of formaldehyde with the tapeworm he'd taken out of Mrs. Leopold, and he'd let me feel the weight of a jar of mercury. Then he'd read the newspaper out loud and talk about the day's events, just like I was one of his patients, a regular person.

"What do you know. Ol' Jersey Joe got himself beat. Rocky Marciano is the new heavy weight champion. Who'd have ever thought it."

"Hmmm. Says here someone invented a heart lung machine. You know what that means? That means we can operate on the human heart now. Makes you wonder what's next."

I remember him talking about a place called Vietnam. I remember him talking about it because he told me it was close to a country where

Siamese cats come from. We had two Siamese cats, Little Baby and Monkey Puss. "They're having a civil war over there," he said. "The north and the south, like in Korea. Doesn't make much sense to me, us sending guns over to a place all the way on the other side of the world, but if it helps fight communism, I guess it's OK." I always knew our visit had come to an end when he'd read the funnies. "What do you say we see what Major Hoople is up to?" Then—"That'll be three dollars." Three dollars was the price of an office call. "Give it to my bill," would be my stock answer. It was hard for me to imagine O'You as anything but powerful and blessed with wisdom, or that there was ever a time when he doubted his own abilities. I didn't know about his first patient—the little black girl's mother, the placenta previa case, back in '06 right after he graduated from medical school. I didn't learn that story until I was an adult when I overheard my wife having a conversation with Nanna. Girl talk, while Wendy was doing Nanna's hair. They were in the bathroom. I just happened to be in the bedroom, one door down, and could hear clearly everything that was being said. I was particularly alert because Nanna was giving her advice on how to handle men, about how women are stronger than they realize in helping to shape their husband's careers and destinies. "You want to know how he proposed to me?" she said, in a sudden burst of amusement. "He wrote me from St. Louis right after he graduated and said, 'I've met a girl back here, and unless you marry me right now I'm going to stay here in St. Louis and marry her.'"

"Why, I had half a mind to tell him no!" she said. I couldn't believe she was laughing about it. Maybe because she didn't believe it. I didn't believe it either. I believe it even less now, after reading his love letters to her. There was no girl in St. Louis. There never had been anyone but her. The threat to marry another woman was nothing more than a wacky marriage proposal…one that worked.

"Good thing you didn't say no," I whispered to myself.

And then came the story of the first patient, one of the times when she was the powerful one…

Chapter 4

A Powerful Woman

Walker, Missouri

1906

THE BEGINNING OF A DAY always brought a softness to Dott, a peacefulness, because while she cooked she could hear her husband shaving and dressing in the other room—the sounds of a straight razor slicing through stiff overnight whiskers, the splashing of the water she had heated earlier on the stove top, the slapping on of cologne, the snaps of suspenders. On her face was always a purposeful look, as the flapjacks and the salt pork sizzled. A strand of reddish blond hair would invariably fall over her brow, which she would blow aside. Now and again she'd scratch an itch on her forehead with the back of her wrist. At 7:20 every morning—you could set your watch to it—would come the chugging of an automobile.

"For eight hundred smackeroos we could own one of those things," Bob would joke, as they'd watch the dark green machine from the window, with its shiny brass headlamps, making its way through the crowd, the carriages and horses stopping to let it pass. Nearly forty thousand automobiles were registered in the country, but most were seen on major city streets. The sight of one in an outlying town like Walker, situated between Kansas City and Springfield, was rare. "The Stanley Steamer, now there's a machine," Bob would say. "One of those I wouldn't mind owning."

Passing by her second-floor window, she could look down at the sign extending above the door one floor below. It announced "Drs. Love and Wright." A week ago it carried only Dr. Stanley Love's name. She laughed as she wondered how it ever happened that she ended up here, a place where she once swore she'd go only if the devil chased her there with a switch. She'd been bamboozled. "I've met a girl back here," he had said, "and unless you marry me now I'm going to stay here and marry her." Bamboozled by the woman that didn't exist, and by her husband, the

25

Dr. Robert Wright, 1906, upon graduation from medical school.

Dott (Beamer) Wright, 1904, upon graduation from the Collegiate Institute, Salt Lake City.

doctor. "Husband." It was a new word, a beautiful word. And he'd actually done it—without a dime to his name her husband had worked his way through school and married her, just like he always said he would. Since they were kids he had always said he would marry her. And his older sister's husband, Dr. Stanley Love, had offered them a partnership opportunity in his practice in Walker. And it *was* an opportunity. She knew that, and felt humbled by it, and appreciative. But she so wished that it was a little closer to her Idaho home. And she so wished that someday they would be able to go back. Even if not in Hailey, just somewhere in Idaho, somewhere close. It was in her prayers.

Bob had been gone for three hours when she finally sat down to read the letter from her mother. She took up the brownish envelope upon which was scripted the ovular swirls of her mother's handwriting and withdrew the thin pages.

My Dearest Cynthia,

Was so pleased to receive word from you and Bob. I just finished putting up chokecherries. There are so many jars that I'm going to send you some. I have no room for them all in the cellar. The ice cage is almost full as it is, which reminds me—Harry Purdham delivered ice today. He says hello to you and Bob.

As we've said many times before, your father and I are very proud of you for everything, your music, your graduation from Westminster with such high marks—it's an achievement that will never be wasted—the experience gained and the discipline incurred in college from rising to meet a challenge will prove invaluable whatever your path in life.

We're proud of Bob too. If we didn't express it clearly it was because things happened so fast. We had no time to prepare ourselves. My heavens! You could have given us some notice! Instead of practically eloping. I know we haven't always been supportive of you and Bob, in days gone by, but we truly are pleased. I have to admit, in the beginning, I would have preferred you to choose someone like Tom Bailey, if I'd have been given the choice. A mother wants the best for her daughter. You'll be the same when you have a daughter of your own.

Dott smiled so hard she burst aloud in laughter. "So that's why Tom Bailey was so persistent. Mother put him up to it!" Tom would be waiting for her after her last church service on Sundays and at the end of every Wednesday night choir practice, standing at the bottom of the steps by his expensive team and fancy buggy, a Whitechapel no less, rimmed yellow wheels spinning in elegance, hoping to be able to persuade her to let him drive her home. What girl wouldn't be proud? She always declined, sometimes forcefully, because she wanted to walk home with Bob, her childhood pal.

One day Bob had had enough. She came walking out of the church with Della Delano, dressed in sunset pink, pink hat, white ribbon, pink skirt, long sleeve white blouse, and found *two* suitors with carriages waiting, Tom with his Whitechapel, and Bob, standing on the other side of the street beside a four-passenger surrey he'd rented using an entire week's wages. The surrey was a beauty. It put the Whitechapel to shame. Deep blue body, scrolled cream molding, powder blue dusters and seat panels, fringe topped canopy. Bob was like a king on a throne, driving his lady home in that surrey, in his dirty miner's clothes and hobnailed boots. On the way they stopped and bought rhubarb and flowers from Vegetable Charley, plodding along as he always did carrying his rich smelling fruits and vegetables in two deep baskets hung on a pole across his aging shoulders, ever flashing his infectious Chinese grin and barking his sales pitch. "You want letticy, raddishy, you want a bean? You want a pea? Belly good. Belly good."

I suppose it was because I didn't really know Bob or his family that well. Heavens—here was a young man, penniless, who worked in the Minnie Moore in summertime, with all those rough and tumble miners, then he'd be on that sheep train working his way back east so he could go to college. I suppose we all thought that if he had any sense of responsibility he'd be out there on that farm helping his father make ends meet, like his older brothers...

She finished the letter, then picked up pen and paper and began a response.

My Dearest Mother—

Always so good to hear from you.

I'm on pins and needles right now. It's all I can do to sit still. Bob had his first patient moments ago, a little colored girl that came knocking at the door looking for Stanley. Stanley—bless his heart for giving us the opportunity to go into business with him—fixed up the attic above his office as an apartment for us. He wasn't in, so Bob took the call himself—

Dott didn't notice the door open. She didn't notice her husband standing there until she looked up from her letter. He was soaked in blood, staring at her, his eyes begging for help. As God was her witness, she would never forget the look he bore that day.

The breath rushed from her chest.

"...I couldn't save them. I lost them both. I just couldn't save them."

When he had arrived, the woman had been unconscious and hemorrhaging. There was no pulse, the labor had stopped. He had to pull the child so hard to get it out he thought he was going to dismember it. But it didn't matter. The baby was gone too. It was a boy. It would have been their only son.

This was his first case, his first two patients. Inexperienced though he was, he knew exactly what was happening because of his flawless knowledge of anatomy. He knew that the placenta had pulled away from the uterus, and that the bleeding had to be stopped. He knew that he had to get the baby out fast because oxygen was no longer being channeled to the child. The child was suffocating, trapped within the membranes of an airtight bag for five, ten, maybe fifteen minutes.

The little one was warm when Bob pulled him free, and seemed so close to life. The struggles of those last moments were frozen on his face, and his fists were tightly clenched, tiny fists, no bigger than Bob's thumbnail.

Bob tried to resuscitate the mother, to force air into her lungs, using arm lifts, chest pressure—all the textbook methods. There was no response.

Then he went for the child. When he had pulled him free it was like popping a cork from a bottle. Blood had gushed from the vaginal opening, much of it in huge clots. The life-giving substance that should have been running through the mother's veins and arteries had instead been backing up uselessly inside the uterus. For the mother there was no chance. At least the child still had blood in his body. Bob had to somehow induce respiration, get the diaphragm to work. He applied the Prochownick method, the most commonly used, suspending the newborn upside down by the ankles and squeezing the chest, while resting the head on the flat of a table. Nothing. The baby's fingernails and lips were black. He tried again. And again. Still nothing. Thoughts were racing through his mind in fragments of seconds. All he could think of was to suck the mucus out with his own mouth, carefully, so as not to damage the fragile lungs.

Still there was no breath in the child's body.

Perhaps if he blew his own air into the baby's body, used his own air to fill its lungs and stimulate the diaphragm, perhaps then he would find his miracle. But mouth-to-mouth insufflation had yet to be recognized by the medical world.

Bob held the baby's tongue with his finger to keep it from sliding down its throat. He felt the rise and fall of its chest with each breath. He even thought for a moment there might have been a response, a loosening of the facial muscles.

It was not to be. A human life without oxygen for that length of time is not a life, no matter the effort.

Now he sat with his wife, despondent over the loss. All Dott could think of to say was, "He's with Our Lord now." Dr. Love explained later, "It's the luck of the draw. You had a bad draw, that's all. These situations happen. One in a hundred, I've heard it said. It was just your luck that it happened on your first time. Mostly, in confinement cases, all you do is stand there and let it fall into your hands. Those people should have summoned help long before they did."

"They tried," spewed Bob, his anger directed not at his brother-in-law, but at the people who slammed the doors to the little girl's pleas.

"Even then it may not have turned out any differently," said Dr. Love. "Even then we may not have been able to do anything. That type of condition is usually always fatal, regardless of the birth precautions, regardless of whether or not a physician is in attendance. The best of physicians lose mother and child when that happens."

Some days later Bob sat alone in the darkened kitchen, long after midnight. Dott, waking to find his side of the bed empty, got up and came to him. He spoke to her across the room. "I struggle through high school, getting up at five for chores, working the fields past sundown, studying until the moon itself is tired, so I can go to college. Then, when I get to college, I work the mines so I can pay my way. I work the sheep trains for passage, all so I can be a doctor. So I can help people. And live a good life."

He was in his night clothes, arms folded, his chair-back tipped against the table, looking out the open window. The curtains were lifting themselves inward from the chill of the night breeze. "I was thinking about my days at American." Moonlight was shadowing his face in lustrous shades of gray compassion. "American Medical College is one of the finest schools in the field of medicine. I never thought I had a chance of even getting in, let alone graduating. But I did, and somehow I figured out how to pay for it, and somehow or another I got that diploma." He waved in the direction where his graduating class photo was hanging, framed and encased in glass out in the living room, which was really the far corner of the kitchen, living room and kitchen being all one room. "I was counting the days, the months, the years. I knew that if I could just put on that cap and gown and cross that stage and shake that man's hand, the struggle would be over."

He thought of those days now, in fondness. Those most difficult of times now seemed pleasant in comparison, the lack of sleep, the below zero temperatures that rolled right through the paper thin walls of his dormitory, the terror of exam time, the hellish anatomy exam in particular, a walk in the park compared to this. It caused his mouth to curve into a smile, the memory of that exam, of how up until a certain day, a certain point in the middle of a cold February night, he had been convinced he would fail. The complex names for bones and body parts had been jumbles in his brain, their impossible definitions floating loose, unassociated. The study of medicine as it passed into the twentieth century was difficult at best. A student could depend on only one thing, that most of what was learned today would be disproven tomorrow. Textbooks were practically useless. Medical science was emerging from the shadows of quackery and magic overnight. Ironically, the facts coming forth seemed in themselves mythical—mechanisms within the body that clone themselves against invading micro forces, the intentional infection of microbes for the purpose of healing, the almost daily uncovering of newer and different strains of microbes. The discoveries and the theories were overwhelming, and were stacking themselves one on top of the other: x-rays, aspirin, the blood groups, chromosomes, messages of heredity, yellow fever, amino acids, on and on. Twenty-four hours a day was not enough. The young surgeon-to-be had to somehow pack all that information into his brain, then discard it and pack in new information. Failure, as close as it was, was so unthinkable, so terrifying, that his mind dared not entertain it, not so much as a fleeting ghost.

He remembered a playful kind of day when the sun was shining off the afternoon snow in sparkles, a day whose beauty only served to deepen the hopelessness he felt. He was struggling to memorize anatomy. Jumbles. Unconnected jumbles. Definitions, names. All jumbles. The glowing filament of an incandescent lamp revealed the complex diagrams and wordage of Henry Gray's 1858 text entitled *Anatomy: Descriptive and Surgical*. Later editions would simply be called *Gray's Anatomy*. Next to it, shaded in shadows, was a worn leather-bound version of Metchnikoff's *Immunity in Infectious Diseases*. Beside them both was an uncapped dark green fountain pen and furrows of papers upon which had been written notes from his classes and labs, where he'd scribbled out each one of those long Latin names, after viewing and touching the actual body part, thanks to a cadaver named Uncle Josh. The names blurred before his eyes. He decided to take them one at a time. Just one name at a time. He decided to forget about the time squeeze, the fact that there were only ten days to exam time. That way he'd at least have one body part that he would know. Maybe by exam time he'd know a dozen. Maybe a hundred. However many, at least he would know them flawlessly. He might fail the exam, but at least he would know those specific body parts as well as the Good Lord who made them.

He could see Glenn Smith, his roommate, from the window, out having fun in the snow with Oliver Mitchell and the boys, throwing snowballs, laughing, tipping their hats to the ladies. No exams for them; they were on different schedules and had already completed theirs. Watching his friends made his emptiness grow, a fathomless thing that was beyond loneliness, and his fear of the future deepened.

The snow was white and smooth. Another four or five feet of it and Missouri might have been Idaho. Except in Idaho the snow was dry, and there were mountains. He especially loved the mornings in Idaho, right before the cresting of the sun, when the jagged tips of the Pioneer and White Cloud range turned themselves into a kind of lavender glow. It seemed like he'd never see home again. Or, if he did, it wouldn't be with Dott by his side. Would she wait for him? Some days he thought she would. They had decided—*she* had decided, more accurately—that they should wait another year before getting married, so proper preparations could be made. Dott was the practical one, but was she having doubts? Demons flooded his mind.

Exhausted, his mind fell into sleep, an unwelcome savior, and his head flopped back against the wall. His thick black hair was flyaway and loose, having just been raked by frustrated fingers. Clutched in his hand, even in sleep, were the pages of a letter he'd penned. It somehow seemed just as important as the exam.

St. Louis, Feb. 7, '06

My Own Darling—:

I expected a letter from you yesterday, but as it didn't show up—I just knew I would get one today—"but nixie"—not for Bob.

I don't know whether you are entitled to a letter tonight or not after treating me in such a way. What do you think about it?

Smith says his girl loves him more than mine does me—and the main point of his argument is the "letter question"—he gets three letters per week rain or shine and he knows exactly what mail they will be in on— He certainly has me bested in that regard—but I tell him I have him skinned in every other way. You would certainly have a good laugh if you could hear us discus our future plans etc and again you might hear some things that wouldn't make you smile so much. Ha! Ha! I suppose girls get into some pretty interesting conversations at times—as well as the boys, don't they?

Dearest, I wish I could be with you this eve. I am sure we would have an interesting talk—but what good do those wishings do? As you say—fly away vain thots. I am almost the busiest fellow in St. Louis I do believe—the profs are sure working us plenty— They thought they were not giving us enough to do by keeping us in school all day—so they added a night lecture three times per week to the schedule and one of those is in Chemistry—so you see where I stand. I have to arise at the early hour of five o'clock in the morning and go out to one of those packing houses after some "beef eyes" to be used for anatomical purposes. We are going to have an exam on the eye next Friday.— I will be awfully glad when it is over for it is one of the hardest branches in our curriculum. I know all this "shop talk" will be interesting to you, [___]. The weather here has been awfully cold for the past few days, our stove seems to have gone on a strike and we are almost froze out—the mercury is down to zero—and we feel that dreadfully here for it's so penetrating. I am shivering right now like an Arkansas squirrel that has the "Ague". I suppose you and Della and your escorts go skating occasionally—skating is fine on the different park lakes throughout the city—but somehow or other I have lost all desire for such sport—presume it's because I am getting old.

Darling, I am lonesome tonight. What can you do for me? If I could just have one of those sweet kisses I am sure it would act like a panacea—I don't see how I am going to stay away from you all next summer—it almost makes me sick to think of it, darling. I love you more than my own life and before I can be real happy I must have you with me. I must close by giving you an imaginary goodnight hug and kiss, and with the hope that I'll get a letter tomorrow.

Truly Yours,

Bob

A startling rush of cold jerked him awake. There was laughter and the clamoring of feet as Smith and the boys entered the room. He took a moment to breathe, like people do when they forget where they are, then walked over and put a piece of wood into the stove's crackling red belly, and closed it up quickly to keep from getting his fingers singed. The tiny stove, its pipe crooking upward into an iron plated patch in the ceiling, was glowing around its bulging edges, but didn't seem to be doing much to stop "Ol' Jack Frost" from creeping through the wall in back of him. It had been invading his sleep, chilling through into his dreams, dreams of Dott. The boys stayed for a time, rescuing Bob from his fears, talked some, studied, then left, and Smith went to bed. And the demons came back. The sun had gone down, leaving now the moon to shine off the snow and shame him for his ineptness.

He put in another piece of wood.

And somewhere beyond that, in the middle of the night, by the light of a single incandescent lamp and the escaping glow from the stove fire, something very strange happened. Something incredible. It all fell into place. All of it. Everything. Not a hundred names, but a thousand. More than he'd ever need for the exam. It must have all been in his head, all that information, all those names. What must have been needed was a trigger, a catalyst to bring it together—the step-by-step approach, one name at a time, something for his mind to wrap itself around. It was as though his mind had been instantly organized, with each name and definition categorized and cross referenced. The burst of knowledge, like enlightenment itself, so enlivened Bob, so rushed through his veins and arteries, that to sleep was impossible. To sit was impossible. His mind was repeating names and definitions, reading them off inside his head like a sergeant at roll call. He was afraid to stop or even slow down. He was afraid if he did he might forget it all. He threw on his wraps, coat, gloves, scarf, hat, muffs, and went for a stroll, speaking the names as he walked, reciting the definitions. *Lateral palpebral raphé—eyelid ligament, attached to the zogomatic bone, much weaker than the medial palpebral. Medial palpebral—eyelid reference again, can be arteries or ligaments, two of them, encircling the eyelid. Posterior peroneal septa—separates the lateral compartment of the leg...* Hundreds. And hundreds more. The air was clear and cold and the moon high, and its light streamed over the purity of the night like something sent by God to say congratulations. And as he walked, he realized his perception of reality had changed. The emptiness had been filled, the loneliness transformed. And his vision of the future no longer held fear. Dott no longer seemed distant. The design of his future was now ordained. In a few short months he'd have the letters M.D. after his name. He'd be in partnership with his sister's husband, a doctor in a small town in western Missouri between Springfield and Kansas City. There was, however, that one slight problem, that part of his life that wasn't carved out in chronological certainty. His Idaho darling. She was less than excited about living in Missouri. They hadn't even settled on a date for the wedding. These things can't be rushed into, she kept saying. They needed the summer, she kept telling him, so he could get settled into his practice, and then they could start planning things. But in the meantime Tom Bailey and his Whitechapel would have more opportunity to court her.

He walked some, up Euclid, down Forest Park, down Market Street, and then rode a ways in a taxi—the fare was free because he once tended to the lame leg of the driver's horse. He walked some more, and stopped when he came to a postal station. Lights were burning in the back. Men in aprons and caps were stamping and sorting letters. He sauntered in as if he owned the place and gave them his letter. It was so important that it shouldn't be delayed for so much as a single day. He watched as it was stamped—*St. Louis, MO, Feb 8, 12:30AM, 1906*—and thrown into a heavy bag and tossed into one of the waiting wagons for the trip to the train station and the journey westward. Then he walked down past the Rosebud, where even the police were afraid to go, where music rolled out like billows from a furnace, where raucous shouts and laughter came roaring into the night.

The struggle was finally over, and he did indeed get the girl—the one in Idaho. They were married in Bellevue less than six months later, on June 30, their foolish plans to spend another year apart vanquished, blown into oblivion by his brilliant threat to marry the nonexistent girl in St. Louis.

"How ironic," he said, coming back to the brutality of the present in the darkened kitchen. "I now have everything I dreamed of, but it appears the struggle is just beginning. I have you, and I'm a doctor all right, but my first two patients are dead. And I'm poverty stricken. The new doctor has rent to pay, food to buy, a business partnership to buy into, and no patients. Except the two that died. Thirty-five men and three women graduated with me that day. They're all doctors too. And I'll wager their patients are still among the living."

He collected his thoughts with a deep breath, then held it and blew it out. "Dott dear, I've made a decision, a very difficult decision. Remember that land my father said he would give us? We could irrigate it from a portion of his Wood River divergence. He'd set us up with some cattle, start us off with some seed. We wouldn't have to start paying him back until we—"

"Quit medicine?" screeched Dott. She stormed over and stood squarely in front of him, so that he could see the fire in her eyes.

"I've been farming my whole life," he said, "Longer than I've been studying medicine. Farming is something I understand."

Dott stomped her foot so hard the pots hanging on the wall rattled. One fell to the floor. "I will not let you do such a thing. I absolutely will not. You are a doctor! You are a smart man and a caring man, and you are a doctor!"

His reply came softly, no more than the whisper of the wind at the window. "I can't even feed my family…"

"I will starve and live in poverty before I will let you defeat yourself!"

He grumbled something unintelligible and looked away from his powerful wife, out the window at the moon. Several times he moved his mouth like he was going to speak. Finally he said, "No bull-frogs."

Dott slapped her hips and shook her head. Laughter spilled from her mouth. "What in Heaven's name are you talking about?"

"I hear crickets, but no bull-frogs. I never noticed that before. There mustn't be any bull-frogs in Missouri."

She smiled with forceful affection and kissed him, snaring his head between her two hands. "What am I ever going to do with you?"

"You want to hear a funny story? I was walking across the street the other day with my bag and my new Prince Albert suit, and this old man asked me for a nickel. I didn't want to tell him the truth, that I didn't have a nickel either. So I just said no."

Bob was smiling now, a little bit, a barely noticeable twitch of an expression. "When was the last time your doctor stopped you on the street and asked you for money to buy food? A cigar, now that's a different story. I never have a problem getting a good cigar. People give them to me for no reason. Why? Because they think I do have money."

He was still morose, but with a lighter touch to it. "Yes indeed. It is an odd world out there, my dear wife, for a doctor. A farmer, mind you, a farmer whose crops have been destroyed by a flood or a tornado, has an abundance of help. The church comes with baskets of food. But who would ever guess that the doctor is hungry?"

Dott moved through the moonlight to the ice box. "It so happens that the church did provide." Bob pierced her with an angry look.

She soothed him with her eyes. "Relax. I said not a word about our money woes. It's Hazel Burnett's preparation, from the buffet last night. I tricked her into giving me a good two days worth." Bob's frown of disapproval left as she laid two big platters out onto the table. "I told her that I simply had to have the recipe, because for this food my husband would die."

"*Without* this food your husband may die."

"Each time I opened my mouth to rave about how good it was and how much you'd like it she gave me another scoopful. Finally I had to quit talking, because I couldn't carry any more."

Every sound, every sight was making Bob feel better. The whispering of Dott's bare feet across the floor. The rustle of her long nightgown. Her nighttime hair long down to the middle of her back brushed to a golden strawberry sheen. The thick clunk of the ice box handle. The clink and rattle of dishes and silver.

The food, cold though it was, threw its flavor into the air with such an essence that he could taste it before it touched his mouth. That simple meal in the moonlight, of chicken, crusty bread slices, and rice, was one of the finest of his life.

Dott was right. Things did get better, as the days passed into weeks. Business began to come. But the guilt remained.

Thirteen months later in the mountains of south-central Idaho he'd get a chance at vindication, when next would come a call from a mother in crisis during labor. To answer it would mean traveling avalanche-torn canyons by dog team in whiteout conditions, at midnight. A suicide mission.

Leona (Bridge) Wright.

Chapter 5

Twelve Minutes to Sun Valley

Hailey, Idaho

1951

Sometimes in winter, while Dad was working in the shop, Mom would pull me on long rides in the snow up to see Nanna and O'You, all bundled good and tight in a wooden sled Dad had made. A crisp wonderland of white would peek in at me on those days, along with a black Lab I named "My Dog" that would slather my face with affection. And Mom would tell me about her childhood in Texas, a place that was warm all the time, about Momma Lou and Daddy Earl—they were my other grandparents—and about her little brother Tommy, and about the family's colored cook Lizzie who practically raised her. It was like I knew them—if I wished hard enough I was sure I could fold back time and help Lizzie make those pies and chocolate chip cookies, play with Tommy, and maybe ride his donkey called Barney. Tommy would always come home crying, dragging his saddle behind him, because Barney had a habit of scraping him off against trees and fence posts.

At bedtime Dad would sit on the edge of the bed and talk to me, and pat my leg, and speak of things a young man should know, like not teasing Old Blind Bill. "His name is Mr. Scharf, and whenever you see him, you be sure you always stop and say hello." And he'd tell me stories of the jungle, where he was in World War II, of the Marmoset monkeys that would throw things down from the trees, and of the army ants, and of a time when a vampire bat bit one of his men. And of a sergeant that was smarter than he was. Dad was a second lieutenant in the war. A second lieutenant was higher than a sergeant. "Nighty night, McTight," he would finally say. And, with the sour-sweet smell of beer lingering, he would tiptoe away and I would drift off into dreams, anxious for another magical day.

Somewhere around midnight the "Sun Valley Stage" would stir me awake, blowing its horn on its way through town with guests bound for the Sun Valley Lodge and the Challenger Inn. The bus's loud horn blast was a signal to the telephone operator in the building next door to phone up the bellhops and let them know they had twelve minutes.

The summer of '52 was particularly memorable. It was a time of discovery. One cloudless morning a crowd was gathering outside O'You's office, looking up, pointing. The entire dome of the sky was vibrating with a high pitched rumble, and a thin, white line was drawing itself right to left across the sky, as though atop a huge blue fishbowl. "I think it might be lightening," Mom postulated.

Del Panning smiled. He knew what it was. "It's a jet," he said, and stretched out his thick arm tattooed with a navy eagle. "See that little silver glint? That's a jet. It's like an airplane, only it hasn't got a propeller. It's a cross between an airplane and a rocket."

That same summer a crowd had gathered outside of Harris' furniture store. People were pointing through the big window at a tan box with a gray circle in the middle. Del Panning said, "It's called television. That there picture comes through the air just like radio waves. That man there? In the television there? That's what Milton Berle looks like. That's him. That's Milton Berle. Right there."

Dad lifted me up and sat me on one shoulder so I could see too.

And Mom squeezed his hand and put her arm around him. To me it seemed as normal as sun in summertime—Dad and Mom were a unit like that. But some folks had to wonder how a proper southern lady like Mom ended up with a square-jawed cowboy like Dad, who only had one suit he'd dust off and wear with a bow tie whenever we could drag him to church. On Sundays he preferred instead to sit and sip coffee and read one of his historical novels. "Dad, don't you want to go to heaven?" I asked him once. "Nope," he said. "Can't stand harp music."

The hardest thing for Mom to get used to, she always said, was the Idaho cold, but she came to like it, the clean quality of the winter air, the quiet of the snow, the serenity of it. She walked in it every day while I was growing inside her. Doctor's orders. Every evening she'd bundle up and crunch her way through six blocks of snow up Carbonate Street to the white house on the corner where O'You would check her over, blood pressure, heart rate, the baby's heart—mine—and pronounce her fine, then poke at her bulging stomach and talk to his grandson. Mom almost died when I was born. She used to talk about how she was floating above her body listening to the shouts of the doctors and nurses, but that's another story.

O'You and Nanna finally bought one of those television sets. Every night Dad and I would go over and lose ourselves in the stories of the heroes of the Old West, men and women who'd fight on the side of what's right, men and women with extraordinary courage who would risk their very lives to save others, the men and women of *Rawhide, Have Gun—Will Travel, Wagon Train, Wanted: Dead or Alive, Annie Oakley, Roy Rogers*.

During commercials Dad would smoke his pipe—I loved that cherry wood smell—and I would go tromping off into O'You's bedroom and we'd read the funnies, "Ally Oop," "Little Orphan Annie," "Gasoline Alley," "Major Hoople." Sometimes he'd start to tell me about the old days—but I'd stop him—no time—the commercials were over. Had to get back to the TV room and the heroes…

Leona and Glenn in the Workshop.

Chapter 6

Sunshine Over Baldy

Sun Valley Hospital

1948

I N THE SANCTITY OF THE WOMB a child's heart lay beating.
Floating, suspended in warmth, life surging through its limbs, the child waited, unaware that any other realm existed.

The sounds coming to its ears from somewhere unseen gave familiar comfort.

In his life-giver, he had complete trust. He could hear the whooshing and thudding of her heart, the filling of her lungs, the various and muffled sounds she made. Trust—he knew not the word, having nothing in the vacuum of his memory to measure it by—was nonetheless a thing he experienced. And it was unconditional.

But the child's absolute environment would not, could not last. Soon it would collapse, and in the chaos to follow he would be overwhelmed by a barrage of catastrophic sensations—horrific pressure, shocking waves of cold, blinding light, a violent ripping deep within his chest as he struggled to find his first breath, and a stinging pain on his backside that shot out into his arms and legs.

And the one sound he had come to depend on for his ultimate comfort could no longer be heard, the voice of his mother. Instead, the child could hear other voices, shouts, urgent commands. He couldn't understand their meanings, but the power being conveyed made him cringe and jump. The child's mother heard the voices too, though for her they were more distant, having a surreal quality, because she was hearing them as she was floating up and away from the fury of activity.

She floated to the ceiling, then through the ceiling, and it all seemed perfectly normal, like in a dream, the way unusual things seem perfectly normal.

And the pain had transformed itself. It was, in a very strange way, now pleasant to experience.

The further away she floated the more pleasant it became, and the less intense it became...until finally it was gone altogether, replaced by a wonderful type of peace, an indefinable ecstasy.

She could look over and see Baldy, its ridges fanning the aura of the rising sun, still hidden behind its rounded treeless peak. Its summer mountainsides, packed with evergreens and chiseled in grassy ski trails, smiled at her as she floated toward them, then above them, following the dotted line of the chair lift towers to the top, dozens of towers in a single row, tiny orange pyramid-shaped trestles. "Too bad the President can't have *this* view," she thought. President Truman had wanted to ride one of the chairs up Baldy, to make his short visit memorable, but the secret service dissuaded him because the forested hillsides that folded around the tower line could be foliage for an assassin. So what Sun Valley did, to the amusement of all, was to take one of the Baldy chairs, the only ones with footrests, and install it on the smaller and barren Dollar Mountain. Hence the popular photo seen in newspapers worldwide, confusing to skiers familiar with Sun Valley, of the President of the United States riding a chair lift that didn't exist.

Now she knew what it was like to die. How pleasant. How extremely wonderful it was. Yet—in the most significant of ways—it wasn't wonderful at all. The child was being left behind, the child with the irrevocable trust, the child who was reaching out with the power of that trust.

Also breaking through death's veil, through its blinding shroud, were thoughts of her husband, the handsome man with the mysterious past who came out of nowhere two years ago and swept her off her feet. Courteous, romantic, sensitive, he showed up one day in her San Francisco art studio, in the upper offices of Nathan Dohrmann's Department Store, because he had taken a wrong turn. Then once a day after that he'd stop by, just to chat, and talk of dreams. He worked as a salesman there. Her heart would beat a little faster whenever she'd hear footsteps in the hall, and would stop completely when she'd see it was him, when she'd see that spiffy straight-back walk of a soldier. "Someday I'm going to Idaho to open up a gift shop," he kept saying.

"Someday I'm going to open up an art studio in Carmel," she would say.

The signs she painted at Nathan Dohrmann's, the loose and powerful brush strokes, had an artistic flair that reflected her personality—strong but carefree, conforming yet fiercely independent, positive to a fault because of a Christian Science up-bringing. They brought to the store windows a touch of class none of the other stores had, an expensive look, a sophisticated flare that refused to reach beyond the everyday person, the average shopper.

Then there came a time when he didn't come by for an entire month. And it left her terribly unhappy, to her complete surprise. Then, one day, as she sat staring at her work trying to figure out why it mattered so much, why she had become so dependent on a simple ten- to twenty-minute conversation with her secret visitor, he burst through the door. "I'm going to do it," he said, out of breath, excitement burning in his eyes, sounding like he'd run the entire stairwell instead of using the elevator. "I'm going to do it. I'm going to open up that gift shop in Idaho. I'm leaving tomorrow." He looked straight at her with those deep-set eyes and said, "Come with me. Marry me and come with me. You can sell your art and I can sell my woodwork. We'll make a terrific team. An unbeatable team."

To her own bewilderment, she was actually considering it.

"I'm leaving tomorrow. If you want to come with me you have to tell me now."

But words wouldn't come.

"Be at the Shining Star Cafe at five tomorrow morning, if your answer is yes," he said.

So—the funniest thing—she did it. She actually did it. At 4:59 the next morning she came walking up the street lugging a suitcase. It was the only time in the forty-one years of her life she had ever done anything foolish, purely from the heart.

Robert Glenn Wright and Leona Spencer Bridge were married October 12, 1946, in Minden, Nevada, on their way to Sun Valley.

So strange for her to be there. She came from an aristocratic southern background. Servants and nannies. Her family was close, and very formal. When anyone in the family addressed her it was either as "Miss Leona" or "Leona Dear." Her mother was "Mother Dear," her father was always "Father Dear." Every morning at five she'd swim with her father in the San Antonio River. Then she'd make him breakfast. At night she'd press his suits. When they moved to San Francisco she would swim with him every morning at the Y, then make his breakfast, and lay out his clothes she'd pressed the night before, even at age 41. Then one night she didn't come home.

She was floating, getting closer and closer to the top, to the sunshine on the other side. The urgent voices of the doctors were now no more than hushing sounds, nothing more than the rustle of the wind in the grass. And the calm inside her was now a firestorm of bliss. The world she knew was almost gone, but the memories were staying strong, memories like the enchantment she felt when they crested Timmerman Hill and for the first time saw the Wood River Valley open up in fall majesty—reds, shimmering yellows, huge rolls of white drifting across the sky, the blue peaks of the Sawtooths high in the background. And she remembered the nervousness she felt when they pulled up in front of the big white house on the corner, and the warmth she felt when her father-in-law embraced her, though he must have been terrified at his son's impulsiveness. His first reaction had been shock, speechless shock, when his son had proudly announced, "Mother and Dad, I'd like you to meet Leona, my wife—we were married yesterday." Then came a welcoming smile and the embrace. In her mother-in-law's face she saw a mix of emotions—but mostly she thought she saw acceptance, and maybe relief, because in his own words Dad in the early days had been "the black sheep of the family," a bit of a troublemaker.

Her own father though—his acceptance didn't come for some time. She was remembering how she cried when her father first came to Idaho with hurtful words, wanting to take her away from this "God forsaken place." And she was remembering how her mother had softened things by apologizing for him and scolding him, and how she had hugged her daughter's new husband and said, "Welcome to our family." And how she had marveled at the beauty of their creations, the "Beaver-Cut" wood found at the bottom of stream and river beds, shaped and smoothed by years of sand and water, enhanced by artistic hands into bowls, cigarette lighters, lamps, vases, with just enough of the chiseled beaver portion left to add a touch of the wild to the otherwise refined pieces, a little like Dad, wild yet refined, refined by the southern lady who once yielded to an impulse. Several of the pieces found their way onto the glossy cover of *Good Housekeeping* magazine. Some ended up on the desks and tables of statesmen and movie stars.

Floating. Floating. Up toward the top of Baldy, toward the sun on the other side. And such a beautiful sunrise it was. The closer she got the warmer she became, and the greater became the ecstasy. Each escaping ray rolling over the mountaintop was quite literally tingling through her body. Ee-Da-Ho. Sun Coming Over the Mountain. Idaho. Of all the scenery she'd seen, from Texas to New York to California, nothing compared to the beauty of an Idaho sunrise, this one in particular. It was so bright it was beginning to obscure the entire mountain. And when she finally did crest the top and see the sun on the other side, its brilliance exploded and swallowed up everything. It must indeed have been the source of her euphoria, because it was also exploding *inside* her, in an indescribable way, in a very wonderful way.

And she was moving toward it. Right into it.

But she couldn't go. The Sun Valley side was her home. And the child was waiting. Her family was waiting.

She couldn't go, as empty and sad as it made her feel.

Someday.

But not now.

Not today.

She didn't realize it at the time, but it couldn't have been a sunrise, because Baldy was to the west. The sun rises in the east.

The faint mutterings and whispers of the doctors grew louder. "We're getting her back," she heard one of them say.

And everything was fine with the child, suckling at his mother's breast, secure. He could hear his mother's heart beat once again. He could hear the comfort of all the familiar voices again.

One of the doctors, mask hanging from his neck, a smile on his face, weariness in his eyes, kept poking at him and saying, "Oh, you!"

Another victory. Among thousands. Except this time he had a special connection with the child. One of these days he'd have to tell him about the Stewart baby up Warm Springs, back in ought-eight…

Dr. Plumer and Dr. Wright, with an unidentified man at right, outside their Hailey office, 1908.

Chapter 7

The Placenta Previa Case

Hailey, Idaho

1908

T HIS TIME THE OUTCOME WOULD BE DIFFERENT. In the valley the night snow was floating to the earth in huge flakes, in magical silence. But in the canyons it was fairly screaming out of the sky, up where the mountainsides narrow and the slopes steepen. Tiny ice pellets. Stinging bullets driven by a furious wind. The wind bore deep into the side of his face, into the bones of his skull, the nerves of his rugged jaw and forehead. It was the devil himself up on that mountain ridge, trying to keep him from his chance at redemption. An unborn child was losing its lifeline—the very same emergency he'd faced back in Missouri. The placenta, the coupler to the blood supply, was beginning to detach from the uterine wall. Soon, the baby's only source of oxygenated blood would be spilling uselessly elsewhere, leaving the trapped child struggling for breath while still in the womb. And its young mother, also deprived of blood, would die.

The call had come an hour before the January storm took down the phone lines. It had come from Leff Shaw, the ranger up at Warm Springs. "John Stewart just snowshoed down from his place," he reported. "Says it's his wife's time. I don't know, Doc, this one don't sound right to me. Says she's bleeding. That normal, Doc?"

"Let me talk to him."

John Stewart came on. He said that the contractions were coming, and that there was blood.

"All right, here's what I want you to do. I want you to get back up there and make sure she doesn't get out of that bed, not even to pee. Now you go do that. I'm on my way."

John was out of breath, probably from the wide leg trot required to make good time on snowshoes. "What's wrong with her Doc? What's goin' on?"

49

"Well, John, bleeding isn't good. I'm going to need to get up there right away."

There was the dull acceptance of misfortune in John's voice, also a pleading. "Doc, you ain't gonna make it. Ain't nobody can make it up here in this storm, now that the sun's goin' down and the wind's a startin' to kick up. I barely made it, and I had the light of day."

"I'll make it."

"Doc, in two hours you won't be able to see your hand in front of your face..."

"Now you listen to me, John. I will make it. I'll use the light sleigh. I'll have the livery rig it with a four-horse team. And Leff there can outfit me with his dog team for the second half of the trip, have it ready and waiting at the ranger station. Believe me John, I will make it."

"Doc, hug the creek. Stay away from them mountainsides. Slides are comin' down."

"John, I need you to hold yourself together. I'll be coming up there by myself and I'm going to need some help. I can't have you falling apart on me."

"Be careful Doc. Hear? I'll put a lantern out."

"Now John, here's what I want you to do. You go back there. You tell her I'm coming. But you tell her in such a way that keeps her calm. I want you to hold her hand, tell her things are going to be fine, tell her whatever you have to tell her, just keep her calm. If she's calm the bleeding will be slower. And don't let her get up out of that bed. Whatever you do, don't let her get out of that bed. John, one more thing. I want you to boil strips of rags for me and dry them before the fire. Long strips. Long cloth strips. New clothes, old clothes, I don't care. Just boil them. And have some water boiling for me when I get there." Bob always stood when he talked on the phone, when there were urgent things to be said, holding the thin bronze stand in one hand and the black ear piece in the other. He paced back and forth the distance of the cord, ten or twelve feet from where the phone normally sat on the corner of his desk, by a stack of books and papers upon which lay his derby hat.

The office was small. Outside there was a sign tipped with a wedge of new fallen snow that read "Dr. Plumer and Wright." A similar cap of snow sat on top of the iron hitching post in front of the snow-covered

Dr. Wright in his office.

boardwalk. Jim, the boy who helped out, had begun to shovel again. Four more inches had accumulated. It had been snowing since noon. In all, including previous snowfalls, five feet lay on the valley floor.

The move back to Idaho had come quickly. First they moved to Meridian, a small town outside of Boise. Two weeks later, with the paint barely dry on the sign outside Bob's new office, a cable came from Dr. Plumer in Hailey offering a partnership—a gift from God with built-in patients, guaranteed food on the table, and 30 percent of an existing business.

It worked for Dr. Plumer as well. Bob quickly established himself, tripling the business. Bob had a gift for healing, particularly when it came to children. He was continually traveling back east to the Mayo Clinic for post-graduate work in the diseases of children, and to Chicago's Cook County Hospital for surgical residency. Cook County was staffed with the best in the field of surgical medicine, and had a continual inflow of trauma patients. It was like a processing plant—construction accident victims, surgical emergencies, gunshot wounds, knife wounds. This experience, combined with his mastery of anatomy, gave him a reputation no other doctor could match. Whenever there was a child with a broken bone, Bob was almost always called, even by other physicians. When an appendectomy was needed, Bob was the one they summoned. He was known as the doctor who never lost a patient. No one knew about the Missouri tragedy.

It would not happen again. He was wishing it was tomorrow, because then he would be looking back on his victory.

"I'm on my way John."
"You really are gonna make it, aren't you Doc?"
"You bet I will. Your Mary's going to be fine…"

He slapped the reigns again, to drive the lead horses through a barrier of drifting snow, and pulled his high collar further over the side of his face…and shivered way down deep, not from the cold, but from having made such a promise.

The bobsleigh jerked as the lead horses finally broke through. The sleigh's skis had been forged from foot-wide strips of metal. The rear runners had been detached so that it could move about with the ease of a two-wheel buggy balanced by the yoke and horse. Up ahead, he thought he could see what might be the flickering lights of the ranger station.

He'd already come about fifteen miles, he figured, following the railroad tracks to Ketchum where Sid Venables had been waiting with a fresh team, then veering off into Warm Springs Canyon. Each one of those miles had become more difficult to travel, more impassable, each one buried deeper in blowing and drifting snow. And with each passing minute the sky was growing darker and the air colder. He was well-shielded—thick clothes and gloves, woolen hat with earflaps, horsehide coat—it gave him a feeling of power against nature's onslaught. Ahead of him was the protection of four massively muscled and loyal beasts, relentlessly pushing forward, pulling, protecting. Nothing could stand before their awesome strength.

But as the minutes went by the horses began to struggle. Their sides were heaving brutally, their nostrils flaring as they sucked in the cold air. The ranger station would be their limit. The light he thought was from the ranger station was gone. Soon it reappeared, then was gone again, then came back, then gone again.

Eventually the light split and became two lights, then three, each from one of the windows. And carried upon the screaming wind came the barking and wailing of the waiting dogs.

The snow had drifted up to the windows, all the way up to the roof on one end. One window was half covered by a drift. The wind was fearful now, with an empty sound, a roar that couldn't be silenced, rushing with merciless speed through the evergreens and the naked aspens, breaking at times into a scream. The edge of the ranger's roof was flapping against the side of the building, and suddenly flew off into the dark. The roof was single sloped and steep, with the back wall inset into the hillside like a bunker, and covered with a good two feet of unshoveled snow. The dark outlines of two larger buildings, unlit, were silhouetted on the other side.

Two figures emerged from the warmth inside, Leff Shaw and his wife Mary-Ellen, wearing sealskin parkas and fur hide mittens and mukluks. "Come on in and warm ye' self, Doc." In the old days Leff used to run a team in and out of the Hudson's Bay Company, carrying mail and freight. There was nobody better at driving dogs than Leff.

"Can't spare the time, Leff," said Bob, shouting through the wind as he climbed down from the front seat of the sleigh. "This one's urgent, real urgent."

Leff looked up into Bob's face with concern. "Doc—ye might want to think about letting this one go. Plain truth is, yee're not going to make it out there. Ye'd need to be half wolf to survive out there in this storm. To tell you the truth, Doc, I haven't convinced myself I want to risk my dogs either, on something that can't be done."

Bob spoke loudly, through the rigidness of his wind-shorn jaw, and stared so hard at Leff that it frightened the little man. "With or without your team, I'm going," he stated. Then, after seconds of only the sound of the wind, he said in a gentler voice, "Leff—it's just something that has to be done."

"OK, Doc, I'm comin' with ye then. Mary-Ellen will board down and water yeer team. I'll take ye as far as Board's Saw Mill. While I'm gettin' yeer bags hitched onto the sled, ye go ahead and go inside and get a swaller or two of coffee. Go on now, hear? It's on the stove. Ye go do it. Yee'll want to dry those hands and gloves out a bit. The worst of it lies ahead."

"All right, Leff. Five minutes. There's three bags there. I need them all."

The shoveled out pathway to Leff's front door was drifted over, visible only as an indentation closer in to the building; the two sets of fresh footprints were already beginning to disappear. The door was made of thick beams of timber covered with canvas. Bob had to kick snow from its base to open it. Inside was refuge. Two coal oil lanterns burned on a rustic table that had been hewn from the trunk of a tree. From a cast iron cook stove emanated a wave of heat that flushed Bob's face. On the stovetop beside the hook-handle used for lifting the lids was a coffee pot. He poured some into an iron cup; its heat was euphoric inside his belly.

Before the ice on his turned-up collar could melt he was back outside, cradling the steaming cup, sipping its magical brew. Leff was pulling the last strand of rope through the sled, tying it over the bags, throwing it into a final half hitch. The sled, of flexible birch wood, was about ten feet long. Its parts were lashed together with rawhide thongs to give it flexibility when moving over bumps and around curves. A bendable u-shaped piece was fashioned over the brush bow in front to give the trailbreaker

A dogsled team from the early twentieth century.
Courtesy Frank and Frances Carpenter collection, Library of Congress. LC-DIG-ppmsc-01979.

a handle while kneeling for a ride, or for enclosing a passenger within a canopy, or, for night travel, a place where a lantern could be lashed.

They were ready. "Maw-Shaaaay," yelled Leff, a word resembling the French word for go, and the team rose. The lead dog jerked against the tug lines, the signal for the other five dogs to pull. Leff was anchor and push man. Bob ran ahead on snowshoes to break down the deep snow for the lead dog, slapping along at a fast walk, an awkward trot. Two fools. Two courageous fools, disappearing into the night, the lantern bouncing, twinkling, the last thing to be seen.

If Mary-Ellen was worried for her husband's safety, she didn't show it. As the sled broke into a glide she simply continued unhitching the horses, barely looking up. Surely though, terror must have gripped her, for a moment at least, upon seeing them blend into the blackness, upon hearing the wind swallow up the sound of the dogs.

Back at home, in their small two-bedroom home on Main Street, Dott was preparing dinner, to be served whenever Bob returned. She was melting snow in a big tin bucket on the stovetop. The pump outside had been frozen for days. On their oval kitchen table, the same table they had back in Missouri, was a cup of sifted wheat flower and a half-cup of sugar, and an empty mixing bowl. She was making Poor Man's Pudding. Then she'd make hot biscuits and dried sweet corn, then panned chops. Or maybe brown beef stew. That would be easier to keep warm until Bob's return. She knew Bob could always stop in at Fat's Chinese restaurant down on River Street on his way home, have Fat fry him up a steak. But this was something Dott needed to do. It kept her mind occupied. Her thoughts tended to form their own patterns, diabolical scenarios of what could happen to a man out there on a night like this, everything from wolves to snow slides to just plain freezing to death. The mind seems to move that way, creating mechanisms for its own misery. In that misery, strangely, it seems to find comfort.

"The Good Lord watches out for our doctors," Mrs. Plumer had told her. Dott and Mrs. Plumer had become close friends.

"Be careful, I'll pray for you," Dott had said when Bob flew out the front door. "I'll have a hot meal waiting…"

"Pray for Mary Stewart," he called back. "She's the one who needs a miracle."

She prayed for both.

Bob and Leff were traveling the edge of the creek bed, using its smooth expanse of snow and ice as a navigational highway. They could see steam rise from its center, could feel it as it came spiraling up. Warm Springs Creek was the size of a small river, really, thirty to fifty feet across in spots, and had enough of a flow to keep it free of ice in the middle. "Best way to move about in winter," Leff always said.

The dogs were finally running in precision. For the first mile or so they snapped and snarled at each other, stopping, starting, and tangled themselves in the lines. Then they settled down and began to pull, heads low, tails arched, muscles straining beneath their sheltering fur. The dogs were a mix of breeds, all large dogs—a couple of bird dogs, a collie, a hound, even a half wolf. The half wolf, Jake was his name, looked more like a floppy eared black lab than a wolf. He was the wheel dog, the first in front of the sled, the most important position on a team, responsible for the first tug, responsible for the initiation and steering of a turn, responsible for keeping the first length of line tight and the other dogs moving. The dogs were hitched single file, six long, connected by tug lines threaded on each side through a harness similar to the yoke of a horse, fitting over the shoulders and around the front legs.

The journey was uphill, and though the grade was for the most part gradual, imperceptible to the eye in most places, its rise was significant, almost a thousand feet in the ten remaining miles of the journey, and it was exacting its toll on the dogs as they slogged through the deep snow. Bob and Leff chose to run and push. Perhaps they could have ridden, driver and passenger. Perhaps the dogs could have pulled them, but it wasn't worth the risk. There is a point of refusal beyond which a team will go no further. They simply lay down and quit. When that happens, all a driver can do is rest them and wait.

Their travel was mostly through deep snow. Sometimes the freezing drifts were crusted over, and then Bob and Leff could both ride. At one point they came to a backwash—Bob thought he recognized it as one of his favorite fishing holes, too deep underneath to trust the ice—and had to leave the streambed through a narrow cliff-like passage between two stands of thick trunked cottonwoods and aspens. They had to unleash the dogs and help them along one by one, then, with Jake's help, rope the sled up.

"A horse would die out here," boasted Leff. "Smaller and weaker a dog may be, but out here a dog is the most powerful thing there be. Especially this one." He ruffled Jake's head.

"The creek, she's a windin' in closer to the mountain, Doc," Leff observed. "Best stay off her for a time. Best stay clear a' them slides. Otherwise they won't find us until the spring thaw. Best travel the brush awhile." Leff couldn't see the mountainside but knew it was there, cliff-like in some places. He knew exactly how far they were from the mountain at any given time by the twists and bends of the river, and by the size and types of trees that grew on its bank. "If'n we head straight yonder we'll meet up with her again 'bout two mile down." Leff pointed into the snow, to somewhere, as if he had vision that could pierce the storm. "Then, quarter mile more, where the creek crosses to the north, we should come to the saw mill."

"Ye need to spell me awhile Doc," he said. "I'm not as young as I used to be."

Bob was a respectable driver himself. He'd made at least a dozen trips using Leff's team, though never under conditions such as these. He rattled the drive bow and shook the sled. The dogs came to their feet. "Maw-Shayyy!" he yelled. The dogs jerked forward obediently. When a smooth glide was established he yelled, "GEEEEE!" to steer them to the right and toward where Leff promised was the correct course. They were traversing the canyon rise and the snow was crisp, so the sled ran easy, and when the dogs were up to speed Bob rode the runners and Leff kneeled on the brush bow.

"Now steer 'er a might that way," said Leff, pointing, as barren aspen trees began to appear around them.

"HAWWW!" yelled Bob, and Jake and the lead dog pulled to the left, and the team dogs followed.

"Best damn wheeler on the continent, that dog be," said Leff.

Soon the security of the creek was behind them and they were alone in the confusing maze of the valley, thick with trees, evergreens, cottonwoods, and aspens. Minutes seemed frighteningly like hours. The sagebrush and rocks and fences that in summer made the land recognizable and habitable were all slumbering beneath six feet of snow, twenty or more at the apex of the drifts—tree top level. Finally they saw it. Steam. They were once again at the creek. They bore left onto the creek bed, and twenty minutes later they came to lights. Board's Saw Mill.

Minnie Board was gracious. She knew they were coming and had hot coffee and sandwiches waiting. Someone had phoned her before the lines went down. She'd put lanterns in every room of the main house to guide them in.

Minnie was a young woman, nineteen or twenty, and pretty. She was so bundled in clothes and scarves her eyes were barely peeking out. She offered a room. "You should stay the night, Doctor Wright. And go on in the morning."

"Thanks Minnie, but I gotta keep goin'. Leff will be taking you up on your offer, I expect."

Said Leff, gobbling the sandwich and gulping coffee, "Doc, listen—what we've been through—a Sunday picnic compared to what's up ahead. Yee're not going to be much good to that woman and her baby if'n you end up lost and froze to death."

"Leff, if I wait and go tomorrow you just as well send Ralph Harris in my place." Ralph was the undertaker.

Offered Minnie, "Least ways, Doctor Wright, you can come in and warm yourself a spell."

"—I suppose I do need to put some feeling back in these fingers of mine. Working fingers are something I'm going to need up there."

Minnie's place was wrapped almost entirely in snow. It was a long log house with barely the tip of it showing. Sliding snow from the roof was packed to the eaves on the south side, and on the north side drifting snow sloped all the way to the roof's apex. A path deeper than a person's head had been hewn down to the door. It looked like an entrance to an underground potato shed with steps sculpted into the ice so perfectly they could have been done by an artist.

Flames roared inside a large floor-to-ceiling stone fireplace. Bob pulled off two sets of gloves and rubbed his hands together, and held them before the wonderfully warm fire.

Five minutes was all he could spare. Even that might be too long. Seconds could make the difference.

Minnie gave him a large set of cowhide mittens to put over his own gloves. "These here'll keep you so toasty you won't never need a fire again," she said. She wrapped one of her wool scarves around his face. "You keep this on too. You're gettin' one a' them spots." He'd once treated her for frostbite on her nose, a white spot the size of a dime, a circular dot of frozen flesh.

Leff instructed, "Back track to the creek, then follow it westward up the canyon till you come to a cottonwood. Big cottonwood. Trunk the size of a polar bear's chest. That'll be Warfield Hot Springs. Cain't miss it. Then ye turns left to the road. Ye can tell you're at the road because of the tall sticks John has put up to mark it. Ye should be able to see the tops of them, and the lantern he's hung there."

Leff followed Bob out to the sled to talk privately. "If anything happens to any of them dogs, if'n one comes up lame, I want you to use your piece. Ye got a piece in there? Right Doc? Doc?"

"Your dogs will be fine, Leff."

"Doc, ye promise me. I don't want no lame dog comin' back here. A lame dog ain't no use to me. Ye promise me ye won't bring me back no lame dog."

Bob turned toward the sled without responding.

"Second thought, Doc, don't shoot it. The sound will bring a slide down. Use that big knife of yourn. Cut its jugular real quick, so's it won't suffer."

"Nothing is going to happen to your dogs, Leff."

"I'm just sayin'—"

"I'll take good care of them."

"It's hard goin' out there. They could get hurt. I don't want any lame dogs comin' back and I don't want you to leave any of them out there to get froze."

"I'll be fine. Your dogs will be fine."

Bob seemed powerful as he pulled away, and Leff and Minnie were believing he would make it.

He moved faster than he expected he would, once the dogs stopped their bickering and augured in, traveling along the creek bed snowfield once again, running, pushing, gliding when they could.

The pounding in his chest made him feel strong, the thrashing of his heart, its powerful flexing as it sent blood surging through his limbs, tingling them with warmth. His hands were so warm he didn't need the mittens anymore. He felt a bead of sweat begin to roll down his right cheek. The body provides its own heat, if worked vigorously enough.

Then fear electrified him.

He yelled, "HO," for the dogs to stop, and he set the snow hook.

A warm wind was hitting his face.

A Chinook!

The ghostly blow from the north. A thing that cannot exist. The devil wind.

Legend only, some would have you believe, Indian folklore, the tales of the midnight wind, a blanket of heat rolling in out of the north in the ice-dead of winter.

Most of the falling snow had stopped. What was left was whirling about on bits and pieces of leftover sky, dying formations of low, fast moving clouds, black clouds, drifting air behind which lay the withdrawn storm system. It was a fury that was now locked within a massive, dormant cloud dome.

It was a wind that no longer howled, a wind that was deceptively quiet, that sifted through the treetops with a muffled roar, a wind warm enough to turn the bulletproof ice beneath his feet to mush and the mountainsides to butter.

"GEEEE," he yelled, and rolled the dogs to the right to get them off the creek bed. He cracked the whip and yelled for them to run.

The dogs perceived the danger also, for they ran furiously up the embankment. Beneath their movement could be heard hollow cracking sounds.

In minutes, perhaps seconds, the creek bed would be a death trap of slush. Frozen quicksand.

There was just enough light—snow reflects light off the sky of a snowstorm, somehow, from somewhere—for him to see the creek bed in back of him. It was rolling like it was in some kind of earthquake.

He'd made it.

He thought.

He heard the whipsaw of trees and the breaking of timber from the slopes of the mountain. At first it wasn't a concern because the mountainside was several hundred yards away, a half-mile maybe, and across the creek. But a look in the direction of the sound stopped his breath. A smoky white cloud was consuming the entire side of Bald Mountain, swallowing trees and blowing their crushed bits into the air like so many sticks of kindling. He'd never seen anything like it.

His mind froze. The dogs sensed his confusion and stopped completely, losing precious life saving seconds. He rocked and pushed the sled to jar it free; loose snowpack tends to grab the runners during even the briefest of stops. "GO! MAW-SHAY! GO! MAW-SHAYYYY"

The start was hard. The snow was excessively heavy and wet from the winds of the Chinook. The dogs strained and yelped and whined. With Bob's help they managed to lurch it forward.

He reached for the whip and began cracking it above their heads— "MAW-SHAY, YOU CRAZY HOUNDS. MAW-SHAY."—and pushed—and pushed—.

The avalanche, massive, a forty-foot wall of snow, was sweeping across the entire valley.

He and the dogs were gliding now, moving fast, but he could feel the monster behind him, gaining. It was like trying to outrun a locomotive.

To his right was the crest of a ridge. Safety. "HAWWWW," he yelled. "HAWWWW. COME HAWWWW." If they could just climb it in time.

The turn was so abrupt the sled tipped and the two lead dogs tangled themselves in the lines. Bob unsheathed his knife and cut them loose and righted the sled, and yelled for Jake and the remaining three dogs to pull. "PULLLL. PULLLL. PULLL. MAW-SHAY."

At the top of the ridge was a wind blown cornice, itself a recipe for a slide. The avalanche would follow the contour of the land. If they could get high enough it would pass by beneath them.

Somehow the dogs broke through the cornice, and it held stable.

First one dog made it, then another, then another, leaving only Jake to keep the weight of the precariously balanced sled from coming back and crushing Bob. Jake strained. His muscles surged beneath his skin in efforts to obey his demand that they perform beyond their abilities. His claws scratched and tore at the snow for leverage, and the creaking sled rolled its way over the top. It was part of what a good wheel dog does—he pulls the load over as the other dogs relax.

As Bob lay wondering whether he would live or die, crumpled in exhaustion beside the sled on the far side of the ridge, a hundred tons of snow and ice roared by behind him. Sprays of rock, ice, and pine branches fell from the sky. He had made it.

But all was not well. The unbraked sled had rammed into Jake, had trapped the faithful dog beneath it and crushed his hindquarters.

The best damn wheeler on the continent, useless, probably permanently. "Well, guess the wife and I have ourselves a dog," said Bob. "If that crazy Canadian thinks I'm gonna put a bullet in your head for saving my life, he's got another thing comin', sure as shootin'." Jake was in pain and panted all the harder because of it, in a pitiful sort of way, the way dogs do when they're vulnerable, in a way that almost seems like they're smiling.

Bob fashioned a splint and tied Jake to the sled.

Then he sank to his knees. Rest. He needed rest. Five minutes maybe, just enough to allow his heaving heart to slow, just enough to let his terror-stricken mind calm itself. He sat against the sled. His feet slopped themselves out in front of him, and he trembled with a wetness that sank far beneath his skin. His mind began to seek shelter, began to give way to the need for sleep, began to wander to a better place—to thoughts of his honeymoon journey on the Overland Express, when he traveled with Dott to their new life in Missouri, a gift of luxury presented to the bride and groom by the bride's father…A melting clump of ice negotiated its way inside Bob's coat to jerk him free from the deadly daydream, to remind him of where he really was. He shivered as it slid down his bare skin. How long had it been? Five minutes? Fifteen? Maybe fifteen minutes too long.

With the strength of Samson he pulled himself to his feet, and in less than a minute he was skimming over the crust, on his way once again to Warfield Hot Springs, the final leg, five dogs in the string now. The dogs were working well, in spite of the trauma, in spite of the loss of their wheel dog. Jake was wrapped in a blanket and tied in next to the bags, his hip all trussed up just like he was a person, and Bob was talking to him like he was a person. "Yes sir, Jake, we're gonna make it. We're gonna get up there and deliver us a baby. Nothing to stop us now. No way in hell am I going to go through all this and not have a baby at the end of it.

"Know what, Jake ol' pal. Me and you, we're goin' fishin' as soon as the snow melts, right when the first crocus breaks through. Fly fishing. Yes sireee.

"Right now though, we've some business to attend to. We have a baby to bring into this world, this big ol' changing world."

Jake responded with a whine, like he really was listening.

The dogs were still able to travel on top of the light crust. Bob helped when he could by running instead of riding. A time or two he lost his footing and ended up face flat in the snow with the dogs running on out ahead until he could "HO" them to a stop. Once they broke into a run because an animal crossed their path, a fox or a rabbit, jerking the sled forward so hard it nearly pulled his arms from their sockets.

Eventually the light John had promised to set out appeared. Bob had heard the stories of the hallucinations, the snow mirages that plague the long distance drivers up north, and wondered if this was all he was seeing, something made up out of his mind, because his mind wanted it so desperately.

But it was a lantern all right, hanging on the top of a pole stuck in the snow. It was real.

The relief Bob felt must have measured insignificant alongside John Stewart's when he realized Doc Wright had actually made it. John heard the dogs long before he saw the sled. Dogs have a tendency to begin yelping and sprinting when they sense that a journey is at an end.

The Stewart place was a quarter mile further in, a large one-room house with a barn and a snowed under corral out back. John came running out the door in shirtsleeves and with fear burned into his eyes. "Doc, she's in an awful way. She's bleedin' Doc. She's bleedin' somethin' awful. She's bleedin' like somethin' I ain't never seen before."

Bob set the snow hook and strode toward the door, exhausted, emotionally drained—to face the beginning. "How long has she been that way?"

John followed behind him. "Not long. Couple a minutes maybe. The worst of it happened just after we heard your team comin'."

Bob walked over to the bed without removing his coat, in long, purposeful strides, and sat calmly by Mary's side, like a father would do to a child, and took off his gloves. "How we doin' here, Mary? John, bring me my bags in from off the sled." In times of a crisis, when critical seconds demanded his best, he always remembered what Dr. Durham said those twenty years ago during that high-perched ride in the morning sunshine. "To do your best you've got to have a cares-be-damned attitude." He was right. One has to care without caring.

Mary was rolling her head back and forth on a sweat soaked pillow. The bunched up bed sheets and quilts around her feet were crimson, absorbing the growing flow from her still living body. Mary's breathing was shallow. She seemed not to feel pain, even as a contraction rolled across her exposed and stretched abdomen.

"Mary, I want you to pay attention to me. Mary. Mary. Keep awake. I'm going to help you now. But I'm going to need *your* help. I'll tell you every step of the way what I'm going to be doing. Hear me Mary. Concentrate on what I'm saying." Bob's voice came smooth and with self-assurance. It was his way. In the midst of a crisis his fears dissolved. He became a player in a game, an actor in a play.

"John," he said. "Set those bags down there on the floor. Bring a table over. And an empty pan and boiling water. Quickly now."

A midwife was there to help, a neighbor. Bob hadn't seen her at first. She knew what she was doing. She began setting up the table, pouring hot water, laying towels out, taking from his bags pre-sterilized instruments, forceps, scissors, clamps, unwrapping them from their linens and laying them out on the towels.

Bob was sitting on the bed as though he was unaware of the building pool of blood surrounding him, soaking into his clothes. He still hadn't taken off his coat. There wasn't the time. Nor was there time to wash and sterilize. He removed the glass stopper from a bottle of carbolic acid and splashed it on his hands and instruments, unconcerned about where it spilled or what it soiled. Its smell instantly permeated the air and gave confidence to those watching. "Mary, what's happening here, is you're about ready to have your baby. We have a bit of a problem though. It seems the placenta has slipped down and is blocking the baby's entrance into the birth canal. What that means is, we're going to have to get your baby out a little faster. And to do that I'm going to need you to be awake and helping me. All right?" As he was speaking he was forcing his fingers into the membrane of the placenta, ripping it apart and pulling its pieces out so he could secure his hands around the child's head and guide it into position.

"OK little one," he whispered. "I've got you now. I've got you. Here we go."

When the tip of the head began to clear open air he gripped it with the forceps and pulled. "All right Mary, the next contraction is going to have to bring this child into the world. When you feel it you have to push. Push real hard."

Mary screamed with the force. A good sign, that she was conscious enough to feel the pressure, and to react to what he was telling her.

One more contraction was needed. "Almost there, one more time."

Again Mary pushed and screamed.

"Aaats my girl. Good girl."

The child was out—motionless and blue, with the soft sides of its head pushed in from the grip of the forceps.

He clipped the umbilical cord and calmly, swiftly inverted the stillborn and performed the Prochownick maneuver, holding the ankles with one hand, squeezing the diaphragm with the thumb of the other.

The child's pursed lips fell apart and fluid drained out.

It remained lifeless, free from fear and pain—for the moment.

Soon however, within seconds, its terror would be reawakened and it would be pulled violently into its new and unfamiliar world. A touch from the doctor's lips would bring the miracle. The Breath of Elisha. Still discounted by most. Fallacious hocus pocus, according to modern medicine. But here, high in the mountains of Idaho—a miracle.

Soon the infant boy's sensitive skin would be reacting to temperatures thirty degrees colder than that of the womb. Soon his arms would jerk back and he would begin his fall into another existence.

The midwife took the precious baby boy and wrapped it in linens, and held it close to her breast. She herself was a mother; you could tell.

Bob was folding pieces of gauze and packing them up into the uterine cavity to press off the blood flow, reaching easily through the still fully dilated cervix, at the same time massaging her stomach so the muscles would loosen, so the saucer sized opening would close. Once the bleeding was stopped and the cervix closed, he could slowly pull the gauze out, strand by strand, and Mary Stewart's weakened body could begin the incredible process of mending itself.

"She's all right," said Bob in reassurance to John Stewart, as the poor disheveled man stared helplessly down at his unconscious wife. "She's sleeping. She's weak, but her pulse is strong. She'll be fine. And your baby, looks like he's going to be fine too. Don't be concerned about his head, about the indentation marks. That won't last."

The time was a little after midnight. Bob fed and bedded the dogs, then changed into a spare set of clothes he had in one of the bags. He stayed until five, just before the crack of dawn, sleeping a little, checking on Mary, removing the uterine packs, helping her with breast feeding, sleeping some more, checking on the baby, testing its reflexes, sleeping some more.

"Remember—" said Bob as he was readying himself to leave, speaking both to John and to the midwife neighbor. "She needs plenty of fluids. Soup. Lots of soup. Custard pudding is good. If the bleeding starts again, use the sterilized cloth strips that we boiled, and get word to me. She's got to stay in bed. I'll be back out next week, in five days, on Thursday."

The breakfast the midwife fixed him, eggs and potatoes fried up in a big iron skillet, over a stove stoked by sweet smelling cottonwood, was immensely satisfying as it lay in Bob's stomach, washed down by strong coffee.

John Stewart's husky voice was spotted a bit with proper Scottish tones and inflections, a rich man's way of speaking, like he was well educated, though to Bob's knowledge all John had ever been was a farmer. John was grateful beyond his ability to articulate. Perhaps that's why he said so little. "Doc. I, I don't know when I'll be able to pay—"

Bob put a strong hand on his shoulder. "John. Times will get better. You pay me when you can. I know you're good for it."

And times did get better. And the Stewarts did pay, two years later when Mary had her next baby. Then they paid for that one when the next one came, and so on.

The storm had passed, and the air was cold and the sky blue. The Chinook had left the snow cover crisp and hard, glistening before the mountain sunrise, like it was water, smooth and white. Bob had to reach down and touch it, run his hand across it, to make sure it was real. The tops of the mountains, above yesterday's temperature inversion, were dusted in sugar. They touched the powdery sky with majestic serenity, touched the remnants of empty clouds drifting slowly upward to blend into the blueness. The sides of the mountains were torn by the jagged pathways of the snowslides that had lacerated them to bare rock and dirt. The largest of the slides had buried the creek and created an arctic lake from the backed up water. It must have been the one that nearly cost him his life, three lives, nine lives including the dogs.

The down hill journey was smooth and fast. He rode the runners and seldom had to push, and closed his eyes when he could to protect against snow blindness. And the peace of his accomplished task rode with him, transforming each moment into something incredible. Thoughts of his honeymoon came again to mind, the burnished black and bronze engine, nearly twenty feet tall at her stacks and four times as long, and her lengthy line of palace Pullmans stretching a mile to the rear, sleek and dark and green. He was remembering the way she sat idling on one of the dozen or so tracks and sidetracks and switch-lines at the Ogden station, obediently containing her power. "Serene, she was, Jake my boy." Jake lifted one of his floppy ears. Who knows how much is understood by a loyal dog. Bob was convinced Jake understood it all. "Engine 1849, stamped right there on her nose. Steam rolling out from underneath her wheel beds. Flexing those mighty muscles. Quite a sight, Jake my boy, quite a sight.

"I was a mighty proud man, walking along that platform with that pretty wife of mine in her Queen Mary dress. I remember she had this large-brimmed flowered hat that was kind of tilted to one side. How'd I ever get so lucky, to get a woman like that? It's not just that she's pretty, but smart too, and damn loyal. Damn loyal. A lot like you.

"That trip on the Overland, I sure do remember that, sure do. Before we boarded her we bought these fresh baked rolls from a bakery nearby. You could have smelled 'em all the way to Timbuktu. Just out of the oven. So warm the butter and the frosting was dripping off the sides onto your fingers. Ummhh. Like heaven.

"The Wellington. That was the name of our car. The Wellington, Vestibule Sleeping Car. They couldn't just say sleeping car. It had to be *vestibule* sleeping car. It was written in solid gold on the side. And inside—it was the damnedest thing you'd ever seen—dark green leather upholstery, gold transoms, gold scrollwork, a bath for Dott on the left, one for me on the right, with hot and cold running water.

"I was awake when we eased into Cheyenne. It was nigh on about midnight. I was watching Dott. I do that sometimes. Just watch her sleep. There was a full moon out. It was small, hanging inside this hazy ring of ice-cold softness. The reason I remember it, it was shining its light right through the window onto Dott's long hair. Red hair. Light red, almost blond. It turned it kind of silvery. Lord almighty I love that hair of hers. You'll be meeting her pretty soon. You'll like her.

"Next morning, sooner than we would 'a liked, we saw the Missouri River Bridge. The end of the journey. Now that's a sight to see. It's this huge iron span connecting Omaha and Council Bluffs, double-tracked. And way up high, way up at its highest point, is this massive copper buffalo head. The unofficial gateway to the west, they call it. Some say it's a guardian, for the people that pass beneath it on their journey into the new land, casting down good fortune."

"Surprise for you," he said to Dott when he walked in the front door carrying Ol' Jake, cradling him like a baby, Bob's unbuttoned and blood-stained horsehide coat falling on both sides of the animal. "It appears a retired sled dog's coming to live with us."

Dott had a couple of surprises of her own, dinner kept warm and moist for twelve hours, and an announcement that sometime in July or August, she was pretty sure, she also was going to have a baby. "Hopefully you'll be able to find the time to deliver it," she said, the side corner of her mouth lifting slightly to show it was said lovingly, but nonetheless with absolute seriousness.

Chapter 8

Ol' Scotty

Hailey, Idaho

1908

JAKE NEVER PULLED A SLED AGAIN IN HIS LIFE. In the spring, when the sun brought forth the first patch of matted grass and the tiny bloom of the sturdy crocus, he and Bob went fishing, a promise fulfilled. Jake chased butterflies and romped through the dirt-tinged leftover snow with barely a limp, and Bob stood knee-deep in the water casting into the swirls of the Big Wood's deep green back washes, more muddy than green at this time of the year, swollen from the heavy April runoff.

And Dott became more beautiful each day as her belly grew with the precious life inside her. It brought her and Bob very close. In the evenings, when Bob wasn't at the bedside of a patient, they would sit on the porch together, or they'd walk. Occasionally they'd have dinner at Fat's down on River Street, one of the two Chinese restaurants jammed in amongst the bunched-up homes and laundry houses of Chinatown. Bob and Fat were great friends.

Bob delivered sixteen babies that summer, set a broken bone, sewed a man's toe back on, removed an ovarian cyst the size of a cantaloupe, and for six weeks from June into July traveled back east for more surgical training. His reputation was holding firm: "the doctor who never lost a patient."

At summer's end, during a sweltering mid-morning in August, their baby decided to come, just when Ol' Scotty tottered into the office, blanched to the eyeballs on his homemade potato whiskey. Things always seem to happen in multiples with a doctor. Never just one crisis at a time. Scotty would always come to Bob to get sobered up. He'd make a ritual out of it. After draining the last drop from his stone mason jugs, he'd dress up in his Sunday suit, dust off his bowler, and head on down to Doc Wright's place, cane in hand, zigzagging along the wooden sidewalk, trying his best to keep the cane tucked beneath his arm and not use it for support.

"Evenin' to ya Doc," said Scotty, even though it was morning, tipping his bowler. One pant leg was hiked up, giving him a bit of a tilt when he walked. A double gold watch chain hung from his vest.

"Scotty," acknowledged Bob.

Scotty negotiated his backside into one of Bob's white low back office chairs, same as always. Bob leaned back in his own, a swivel high back roller, and clasped his hands behind his head.

"It happens that I'm a wee bit under the weather, Doc."

"Zzat so."

"A case of the consumption, I do believe."

"Hmmm Hm." Bob continued, "Scotty, your drinking, we have to talk about it."

Scotty stiffened and picked up his bowler and patted it down on his head so that it tilted over one eye. "Might I say, I may have had a sniff or two, wetted me tongue a bit, in honor of His Lordship the Prince of Wales. His birthday you know."

Bob leaned forward and picked up a pad of paper from his desk and a fountain pen—everyone was using fountain pens these days—and drew some crisscross lines. "Scotty, I want you to listen to what I say here. There are wires in your body that carry messages back and forth to your brain. They're called nerves. This is how your brain can tell your body what to do, how to move and talk and breathe, everything you do. Look at it this way. These wires are hooked together with glue." He drew round circles and connected the lines. "Alcohol dissolves this glue, so that the nerves are floating around unconnected. All of a sudden your brain can no longer properly tell your body what to do, how to walk or talk correctly. So what do we do? How do we fix it? Thankfully, the Good Lord realized there'd be a few of you badger-heads out there foolish enough to get themselves in this pickle. So he made a thing called a liver. What the liver is, it's a factory that makes extra glue. Problem is, you work the boys in the factory too hard, they might just up and quit on you. When that happens, well, you buy the farm. And believe you me, Scotty, the boys in the factory *do not* like that potato whiskey of yours."

Old Scotty lowered one of his eyebrows and squinted out from underneath it. "Sooooo. Now yer insultin' me whiskey."

Bob said, leaning further forward, "That rot gut you call whiskey, a drop on a cat's tongue will bring it up stiff as a board. Truth."

"Now you've said enough Doc." Scotty was on his feet. The line had been crossed. And swish swish came the cane, same as always, sword play in the air with Bob as the target. "Now you've said enough Doc. I'm a fightin' Scotsman. You've said enough." Same as always, like it was scripted. Scotty's hopping and jumping efforts to keep his feet planted on the floor would finally fail and he'd trip himself backward onto Bob's large leather sofa, fast asleep. Bob always tried to arrange the sofa on the days of Scotty's visits so that it would be close enough to catch his fall.

Scotty's fancy bowler toppled off onto the floor. His eyes were half open slits showing only the whites. Except for his snoring he would have been mistaken for dead. Bob picked up the hat and cane, put on his own hat and top coat, and scooped up old Scotty. He slung him over one shoulder like he was a sack of potatoes, and strode off down the sidewalk for home. Other than the round little belly, Scotty wasn't much bigger than a sack of potatoes.

Bob nodded his head to the amused and amazed passers-by as if nothing at all was amiss. "Mornin'. Hello. Nice to see you."

He walked in with Scotty and flopped him down on the drawing room davenport, in front of astonished friends and relatives who had gathered to celebrate Dott's pending delivery. Her labor was in its early stages, and they were there cooking, playing cards, singing songs, making a party out of it. The house was buzzing with activity. Bob's mother, Mary Frances, had to move from the davenport to make way for the snoozing object falling from her son's shoulders. Scotty grumbled and rolled his face into the high-backed stiff cushions. And Dott, bless her sainted soul, waddled over with her protruding stomach and covered him up with a quilt.

Then, as though what had just happened was normal as hot dogs on the Fourth of July, Bob turned to Dott with arms open, an afternoon flower fresh in his lapel, and boomed, "Well, where's my hug?"

Then he turned to Mary Frances. "How about a big smackaroo from my mother, too." He drew them both into his arms, one under each. "The best two mothers on the face of this earth."

"I'm not a mother yet," said Dott.

He placed his hand on her abdomen. "You think that's a puppy in there? You've been a mother for nigh on about nine months now."

Dott winced and bent forward. Another contraction. Bob could feel it under his hand, rolling, tightening. It swelled quickly to its peak, making her stomach as hard as a brick, then faded back to normal.

He took her into the bedroom for an examination, to check for cervical dilation, to check blood pressure, to listen to the baby's heartbeat during contractions, make sure it was getting proper blood flow. "Everything is fine," he pronounced.

Then he walked out to the sofa with his bag and stethoscope and listened to Scotty's chest and took his blood pressure. "Alcoholism with Scotty, with his advanced age and in his weakened condition, could be very serious," he said, for the benefit of those who clearly did not understand, like Mrs. Leopold watching from the kitchen doorway, tapping her foot, the kindly neighbor next door who had taken it upon herself to be Dott's protector during her term and who would continue to help the family through the years.

"Land sakes but that man can snore," she acquiesced, walking back out to the kitchen where she had been preparing dinner, shaking her head from side to side.

Dott, meantime, had walked over to the piano, her long deep-blue dress fanning out to cover the entire stool. Her hands barely reached the keys over her stomach, and her feet barely touched the pedals. Beautiful music came forth. "Old Folks at Home" and "Auld Lang Syne," Bob's favorites. He sat in a stuffed wing back chair, his ankle hooked on one knee, head cocked to the side. The other folks stood beside the piano and sang along, when words were appropriate. "America the Beautiful." "The Old Rugged Cross." "Pomp and Circumstance." The piano was three days new, a present for her upcoming 24th birthday.

"If it's a girl we'll call her Jeannie," she said.

Mrs. Leopold came in from the kitchen to listen, wiping her hands on her apron, swaying from side to side.

The piano was in the living room against the wall just beyond the front door, below a large photograph of Red Fish Lake framed in dark brown. The door was open, an artistically crafted door with an oval window pinpointed in frosted etchings of maple leaves. A cool breeze was ruffling its sheer curtains. And beside the door, on the outside attached to the door's light yellow molding, was a round brass fixture with a black button in the middle. A door bell. It was installed only yesterday. Now they had almost all the conveniences: electric lights, telephones, a doorbell, all except for plumbing and a water closet. Someday maybe. The Friedmans had plumbing, including a water closet. So did the Fulds. Someday.

After a quiet afternoon they gathered for the dinner feast. Like Christmas, only with Dott as the guest of honor. "Heavenly Father—" began Bob after Mrs. Leopold had taken her seat. "We give thanks for this meal, and we ask your blessing on the hands that have prepared it. We know, Father, that you will always provide, even in these hard times. In return we pledge to you our service. And Heavenly Father, allow our child a safe delivery into this world, and help us to guide his development." Bob opened an eye and caught Dott's glance. They both smiled at each other. "—or *her* development, as the case may be. A-Men."

The dinner conversation had Dott as its center point, but then politics and the election took over, how Taft didn't stand a chance against Bryan, at least that was Bob's opinion. Then they talked about sports, and about the weather, and about the various and "new fangled" ideas and gadgets that had been popping up, like the guy who claimed to have invented a substance hard as steel but light as a feather, plastic he calls it. "Poppycock," burped Scotty from the davenport, then fell back to sleep. But no one talked about Dott. Or the baby.

Finally she exploded into tears and ran into the bedroom.

Bewildered, Bob followed her, stumbling to the conclusion that it may have been his fault. "Dear, can you forgive me?" he asked. "I'm afraid we ignored you. I'm very, very sorry. It was insensitive of all of us."

Actually, to be so emotional was uncharacteristic of Dott. She sniffed back tears, cutting a striking image of beauty in the blue dress, long to the ankles, covering her feet like a blanket as she lay curled up on her side. "You seem more concerned about Scotty than me."

"Don't be ridiculous. You know I had to bring Scotty home. If we turn him loose when he's like this, he may not survive. He'll sleep in some doorway, or on the ground next to that sheep wagon of his and catch his death. With the fluid in his lungs and with his body focusing its energy on his liver, he just wouldn't make it. You know that."

"I know. I know. I don't know what's the matter with me."

Bob smiled. "You're pregnant. That's what's the matter with you."

"You know what I want to do tomorrow? After the baby is born?"

"Anything. Anything at all. You name it."

"Lula Fuld told me Joe had a nickelodeon put in at the back of the store. I want to go down there tomorrow. Motion pictures. Can you believe it? Can we do that?"

"Done. We'll do it."

The evening calm was broken by a sudden pounding at the door, an awful sound that made it seem like the door would come tearing off its hinges and plunge inward.

It was Thaddeus Benson carrying his son in his arms. He must have been kicking at the door with his feet. His face was a wreck from worry. "I'm glad I caught you home, Doc. Something's wrong with the boy. He can't stand. I think he's done his back out somehow."

Bob kept the tension to himself, the violent urging of his own needs to attend to his own family. The world should stop, just this once, just once, just until his baby was born. "All right, Thaddeus. Let's have a look at him." He took the child in his arms. He'd take a quick moment to examine the boy, then get back to Dott. He walked with the boy toward the sofa but remembered that Scotty was there, so went to his favorite chair instead, the wing back. Dott was up, standing behind him. "Bring him into the bedroom," she suggested. "He'll be more comfortable on the bed. Poor thing." She stroked his forehead. "Oh, he's burning up."

So Bob took him in and set him on the bed. "Say there, little man." He spoke tenderly, in his loud yet comforting voice, sitting on the bed beside him. "Suppose you tell me what's wrong here."

The boy shrugged.

"Does your back hurt?'

The boy responded by curling up on his side. In the better light of the bedroom Bob could see that there was perspiration beading up on his forehead.

Explained Thaddeus, "The boy woke up crying. Said he couldn't stand up."

Bob listened to his chest and felt his pulse and his forehead, with reassurance in touch alone. "How was he feeling earlier?"

"He's had a touch of something. Nothing serious. Threw up some."

Bob placed his hand on the boy's stomach and thumped it with two fingers of his other hand.

The boy jerked.

Bob moved his hand to the boy's right side.

He cried out.

"Thaddeus, would you say he's been sick for a week or more?"

"Well yes, sir. I suppose so. A week or more. Yeah. But not like this. Nothing serious."

"Has your tummy been hurting for awhile, right over here?"

The boy jerked again under the touch. "Yes, sir."

"How long?"

"It's been a spell."

"A day?"

"Longer."

"Two days?"

"Longer."

"A week?"

"I 'spect. Longer maybe. It comes and goes."

"A lot longer?"

The boy nodded.

Bob patted the boy's leg. "Don't you worry son, you're gonna be fine. Just fine. I tell you what. I'm going to go out and talk to your daddy. I'll be right back. OK? That OK?"

"Yes, sir," said the boy.

In the kitchen, away from the boy's earshot, Bob lowered his voice to a whisper. The boy heard most of it anyway. "I'm going to draw some blood, then go back to the office to do a few tests. You take him on down home. I'll be along shortly."

"What is it Doc? What's wrong?"

"Thaddeus, I may have to remove his appendix."

"When? Now? Does it have to be now?"

"If it's inflamed, yes, it needs to come out. I'll know more after I take a look at his blood under the microscope. While I'm gone, why don't you set yourself to putting some water to boiling. Just in case." Though he was an exceptional surgeon, Bob was not one to operate frivolously. Surgery was always a last resort.

Another person was there, watching—twenty-year-old Earl Fox. "Earl, my boy, looks like you have your first patient. My wife." Earl was half way through medical school, another native son with a passion to be a doctor. He looked up eagerly at his mentor. He was almost a head shorter than Bob. During the summers when Earl was home from school Bob would take him on rounds, use him as an assistant.

"You'll do fine," reassured Bob. "No different than the other confinement cases we've been on. Just keep an ear to the baby's heartbeat, like we always do. I'll be back long before her time. And check on Scotty now and again. I'd have Plumer do it, but he's out on a confinement case up Galena way. You'll do fine."

Forty-five minutes later, in his own home in his own bed, the boy heard the doctor's voice again, whispering once more with his father, out in the hall, out of earshot, they both thought.

"Well? Does he need the operation?"

Bob nodded his head. "The alternative is to wait for the appendix to burst. If that happens his body will be filled with toxins." Bob looked at Thaddeus in earnest. "...it is a very dangerous alternative."

"Does it have to be right now?"

"I don't know when that danger point will come. It could be a few days, it could be another week. But given the fact that his body has been fighting this infection for some time, we really shouldn't chance it. Waiting even an hour could be too long. It may have ruptured already."

Bob looked at Thaddeus for an answer, and could see the helpless fear in his eyes. This was his only child. Mrs. Benson had been taken by tuberculosis a year and a half after the boy's birth. The child was Thaddeus' only and entire world. "All right Doc. All right. Go ahead. You know best."

"I could be wrong. It could be that I'll get in there and find it's something else. But the risk—if it is the appendix, which I believe it is—well, it's better to do the operation."

"All right, Doc. Go ahead."

Bob's next words were heard clearly by the boy. "I'm going to need that hot water now. And I'm going to need as much light as you can get me, more light than that one electric globe out there in the kitchen can provide. Round up as many coal oil lanterns as you can find. Twenty of them, if you can get them."

"Doc—I don't think I have more than one. Just have that one out in the shed, for choppin' wood."

"We're going to need more light. Thaddeus, let me use your telephone."

"On the wall in the kitchen. Through that door there."

Bob's voice came loudly, telephoning first to check on his wife, to say that he would be away a bit longer yet—her labor was progressing safely and evenly—then calling down to Dot Allen, owner of one of the region's best-known houses of prostitution. "Have your girls bring their lanterns over. As many as you can." Thaddeus was deacon at First Baptist up on Croy Street and strong in the way of the Lord, but if he had any objections at all to having as houseguests the ladies of Idaho's most infamous business establishment—of the oldest sort—he didn't show it. At that point he would have taken aid form the devil himself, if it meant helping his son.

Bob may have thought he was whispering, in conferring with Thaddeus, but it was all clearly audible to the frightened boy, the frightened but protected boy, protected by something in the way Dr. Wright's voice sounded, the confidence it carried. "Now. Set some more water boiling. Then we're going to go talk to your son. We're going to make him feel good. Make him feel happy. That's important. It's a big factor."

"Doc—you have done this before. Right?"

"Appendectomies, broken bone surgery, bullet wounds, knife wounds. I once removed a cyst from a woman's abdomen that was as big as a pumpkin."

He grasped Thaddeus firmly on the shoulder. Bob was taller than Thaddeus, by a good three or four inches. "It's going to be all right. You've got to believe that, and you've got to allow your son to believe it."

Bob preferred not to operate on a frightened patient. He believed in the mind's power to heal. Unproven. Unseen. Yet he believed it.

"How's your copperosity sagaciating?" he said to the boy, sitting on the bed, patting his leg.

"How come your name is Doc?"

"That's not my real name. They only call me that because I'm a doctor. Doc is short for Doctor."

"What's your *name* name?"

"You'd never be able to say it."

The boy was still curled up. It made the pain bearable. He was still perspiring. "Yes, I could. Tell me what your name is."

"Robert Henry Harrison Thornton Hix John Brown Wright."

The boy giggled. "Nuh uhh."

"Yep. That's a fact. Robert Henry Harrison Thornton Hix John Brown Wright. Doc for short."

"Am I going to be all right?" The boy asked the question knowing he would be, but looking for reassurance just the same.

Bob looked at him with a powerful smile and nodded his head. And while activity buzzed in the other room, while the water was boiling and the girls were bringing over the lanterns, he told him the story of how Pecos Bill tamed the tornado that carved out the Wood River Valley. "Big John Timmerman told me this very same story back when I was about your age, at a barn dance, while the adults were dancing up a storm, while Mike Brown was drawing fire out of that fiddle of his. I remember well the tune he was playing. 'The Irish Washerwoman.' Ever heard 'The Irish Washerwoman'?"

"No, sir."

"How about 'Old Folks at Home'?"

"No, sir."

"Some call it 'Swannee River.' Ever heard 'Swannee River'?"

"I think so."

"Songs from long, long ago."

"Ain't no tornadoes in Idaho," said the boy.

"Well 'a course not, not now, now that Pecos Bill tamed the big one."

The boy listened with eyes full of wonder, to how Pecos Bill, the wildest, meanest, ropenist bronc buster this side of the Pecos, was up in the Sawtooths looking for gold, when the big one came. "Well sir, Ol' Pecos, he climbed right up on top of that beast. Yes, he did. He sure enough did. Ol' Pecos, he never had as rough a ride as he did that day. He'd had some experience taming tornadoes, back on the plains, but this one was a tough one. The first thing he did, he sucked all the water out of that storm cloud and spit it out onto the ground. And that water channeled itself and became what we now call Big Wood River."

The boy looked at his father for confirmation.

Thaddeus shrugged.

"Even with all the water gone out of it, the critter still had fight in it. Well sir, Pecos Bill rode around on that twister for two solid weeks. By the time he had it tamed it was black and blue, and 'ol Pecos, he had about the bloodiest nose you'd ever seen in history. Why, he had a bloody nose so bloody it was running by the gallons. And he couldn't let go 'a that twister to do anything about it."

"Why not?" the boy asked.

Bob looked at him like he was being foolish. "Well because, if he'd a let go it would 'a started to buck again. He couldn't take that chance. He had to keep ridin' her. And he still rides her, to this very day. Most folks, when they look out at an evening sunset with colors of red and orange and blue, they think it's just that, a sunset. But I know better. And now you know better. We know it's Pecos Bill walkin' that black and blue twister across the sky, his nose still bleeding by the gallons. And most folks, when they see the Northern Lights, they think it's just that, the Northern Lights. Some call it the Aurora Borealis. But me? I know the truth. And now you know the truth too."

Bob leaned forward to practically touch his nose to the boy's. "What is it really?"

The boy gulped and whispered, "Pecos Bill with his bloody nose, a walkin' that twister across the sky." The pain was all but gone, so enthralled was he.

Bob left to sterilize his instruments.

A clean sheet was placed over the kitchen table.

"Now here's what we're going to do," said Bob to the boy, when coming back into the room, sitting on the bed again. "We're going to put you to sleep, and once you're asleep, when you can't feel anything, we're going to make a little cut right here and take out your appendix. It's a little thing about yeah big." Bob showed him his little finger. "That's what's been making you sick."

"I won't feel it?"

"Nope."

"What will it be like while I'm asleep? Will I have good dreams?"

"I'll tell you exactly what it will be like." He held up a rolled newspaper. "I'm going to put this over your mouth and nose, and when I do I want you to count. Can you count to a hundred?"

"Uh huh."

"Can you count backwards from a hundred? One hundred. Ninety nine. Ninety eight. Ninety seven. Can you do that?"

"Uh huh."

"Good. Well, when you get to one it'll be over with. That's all there is to it. Honest injun."

When the boy was comfortable, ether was dripped onto a towel that covered the other end of the newspaper, in measured drops, carefully, slowly. If done too quickly, anesthetizing with ether has a tendency to leave the abdominal walls rigid, which makes grasping for an internal body part difficult.

The boy went under smoothly. He was carried out into the kitchen and placed on the table. Encircling him were expensive lanterns with etched glass and gold basework, some on the table, some being held high by Dot Allen's girls. Flames burned bright and threw light at every part of the kitchen, bouncing it off the walls and ceiling and cupboards and reflecting it back onto the table top.

He saw angels, the boy thought, come to protect him, holding stars in their hands.

The antiseptic smell of carbolic acid permeated the room, and gave comfort to Thaddeus, watching from behind.

The Benson boy was thin and his stomach muscles defined. His skin parted smoothly under the steady and confident stroke of Bob's gloved hand.

Blood beaded up.

Bob caught it with rolled up gauze.

In ten seconds he was through the abdominal wall. In sixty seconds he had the appendix between the prongs of his clamps. The offending body part was no more than the size of a string bean. Bob's strokes and movements had been ordered and systematic, swift, careful. His fingers had been as adept as a magician's, as artful as a pianist's. Unassisted, he clamped the vessels and tied the ligatures, and put his instruments back in the same sterile bowl, and was careful never to touch them on unsanitized skin.

The closure took ten minutes.

Twenty minutes after that the boy was conscious, with strong breathing and a solid pulse. By 11:30 Bob was home. He could hear Dott's cries as he walked in the door. Ol' Scotty was still snoozing. Jake was curled up in front of the bedroom door, worried, whimpering.

A contraction had just passed when he arrived at Dott's side. He took her hand. "—looks like we're finally going to have that son of ours. How you doin'?"

She smiled. "Daughter." Her legs were spread and elevated, propped up on pillows that had been tied to the foot-board. Earl had fixed it that way so he could easily reach over for the birthing. "I'm glad you're here," she said.

Bob put a firm hand onto her bulging stomach, and used the other to listen with his stethoscope. "Everything is going to be fine."

"Did everything go well with your—." Dott never finished her sentence. Her face twisted in pain, and she tightened her grip on Bob's hand.

"I'll tell you a little secret here," Bob said, moving his free hand to the tops of her legs. "Relax. Right here." He shook the flesh and muscles with his fingers. "If you relax here, but push with your tummy, this thing will be over with so fast you'll think it was yesterday, and we'll be able to look at our new baby."

Dott gripped Bob's hand harder, and gulped air with short high pitched cries…then collapsed when the relief came. She filled her lungs and moved her head to the side to look at the wall clock.

11:34.

Another deep breath, and a pause while she waited for the next contraction.

Bob gave encouragement. "You're doing fine. Just fine."

"The baby's fully positioned in the birth canal," said Earl. "The head's almost there."

Earl had placed two bowls of hot water on a table by the bed, along with fresh towels and linens. Bob threw off his suit coat and rolled up his sleeves and scrubbed, then moved down to stand at the foot of the bed, bending over, positioning himself. Earl moved around to assist from the side.

The muscles surrounding his soon-to-be-born child involuntarily leapt into action once again, tightening, pushing, forcing that tiny human life with all its newly awakened senses from its floating sea of effortless existence and contentment, forcing it into a new and frightening world of confusing sensations.

The renewed surge of labor brought an autonomic response from Dott's diaphragm muscle, and her lungs filled themselves in desperation, taking the first breath with a low wheezing sound, and then following the pain with gulps and short gasps. She reached for Bob's hand again and dug fingernails into his skin. And through her clenched teeth came whispers of what she surely didn't mean, that she wanted to die.

"No, sweetheart, no." Bob pressed his lips to the back of her hand. "Hang on a little longer. A little longer and we'll have our baby girl."

Earl dabbed a cool rag on her perspiration-beaded brow.

Bob pulled away from Dott's grip and with four fingers from each hand inserted them on either side of the vagina, not so much to assist, but to wait, to be ready.

A flat surface with a dark, twisted, wet knot of hair became visible— stopping, pushing, then stopping again.

"We've got the head," Bob said in a businesslike voice. "Come on now, Dear. Relax your legs and push. Just like you were having a bowel movement. Come on. Push." The baby's head moved closer to the front of the opening, widening it more. "That's it. Relax your legs and push."

But the further constricting motions of labor brought her legs to stiffen and more painful gasps.

"I don't want you fighting for air like that. Breathe deep. Slow, easy, and deep. And relax your legs."

The contraction left, though, and the baby's head retreated.

Dott had been gripping the sides of the featherbed mattress. Her arms and hands now lay loose.

The relief was short lived this time, and Dott's relaxed countenance twisted in pain once more as she felt that awful belt tighten again, this time worse than before, from the middle of her back all the way around in a complete circle, pushing on her insides, squeezing until there was nothing left anymore to squeeze, and still squeezing tighter anyway, swelling her abdomen with such intense pain as to make her think its walls would surely burst.

"One more."

"I can't."

"Slow your breathing now. Deep breaths. At's a girl. Aaaat's a girl. Good."

"I can't."

"Come on now."

"I can't."

"Yes you can."

"No, I can't."

"Come on now, try again. One more time."

Bob was smiling, because it sounded like in the midst of her gasps she had spoken the absurd: "Changed my mind," it sounded like. "—don't want to do this quite yet—not ready yet—maybe tomorrow—"

"One more. That's all. Just one more. I promise."

Her face showed all the anguish she was experiencing, but a strange thing—he'd seen it before on the faces of other women in childbirth—in that anguish there was a naturalness. It was an expression that, though contorted in pain, carried beauty, an unsoiled beauty of innocence.

And a new born baby's head eased its way slowly into waiting hands, upon which Bob promptly and proudly announced, "It's a boy."

He clamped off the umbilical cord and smiled reassurance to his wife, and inverted his son by the ankles, and, with a gentle swat, helped him fill his lungs with air.

Dott looked over at the clock on the wall. The stroke of midnight. Exactly.

Her face had undergone an instant transformation, from an expression of unbearable pain to one of radiance, not relief at having been freed from the pain, but pure radiant joy, as though the pain never existed, as though the memories of a few seconds ago had been entirely wiped from her consciousness.

Earl brought the baby over for Dott to see, now bright pink and wailing, its tuft of reddish blond hair quivering.

"We're naming you after your daddy," she said to her baby boy, happiness streaming down her face. She reached for a tiny squirming leg. Funny, throughout the entire labor not one tear fell. Now look at her. "Robert Glenn Wright." The middle name was in honor of Bob's good friend and roommate from medical school, Glenn Smith, now a doctor in Tennessee.

Bob sent Earl down to check on the Benson boy.

A few hours later, as day was beginning to break, Bob asked Earl to go to the depot to pick up a young nurse, scheduled to arrive from Los Angeles, who was going to be caring for Dott for a few weeks. She was from Children's Hospital in Los Angeles, well recommended. She held a high position there and was quite successful. She couldn't stay long, just long enough for Dott to get back on her feet. Or so the young woman thought. She ended up staying until the day she died. She married Earl and together they opened up a hospital down in Carey, a ten-bed facility converted out of an old farm house.

Almost three years later a second child was born to Bob and Dott, a girl, on June 25, 1911. Jean Eleanor tumbled out of the womb in a burst of sunlight. Bob remembered that part of it particularly, a ray of afternoon sunshine piercing the bedroom window at the moment of birth. A gift from God.

Chapter 9

Trouble Down at Dot Allen's

Hailey, Idaho

1911

T HE RINGING OF THE TELEPHONE jerked them both awake, raising such a clatter that neighbors on both sides up and down the block could hear. There were clappers the size of silver dollars on the wall above the phone box. Outside in the back was a second set, as big as salad plates. Both sounded whenever the telephone rang.

"Hello," answered Dott.

There was screaming. A woman. Screaming for Dr. Wright.

Dott always had to stretch to reach the mouthpiece. She was on her toes trying to speak, to ask questions, but couldn't because of the screaming.

Bob had his hand out to take the call.

There was silence when he put the piece up to his ear. The caller had hung up.

Dott was shaken. "Something dreadful has happened down at Dot Allen's Place."

"What did she say? Who was it?"

"I couldn't understand her. All I know is, that it was one of Dot Allen's girls. I've come to be able to recognize their voices."

Bob rang the crank and shouted into the mouthpiece. "Yes, Central, this is Doctor Wright. Connect me with Dot Allen's place." Calls came regularly from the houses down at the Red Light District, a stretch of River Street north of Chinatown—fights, shootings, suicides. There were no actual red lights. The term might have originated in Dodge City, Kansas, from a custom among the early railroaders of hanging their red lanterns outside the door of their favorite lady to show that she was predisposed for the evening.

There was nothing but the unanswered staccato of the other ringing telephone.

"Call John Hart," he said. John Hart was the sheriff, having just replaced Wood Taylor. "Tell him to meet me down at Dot Allen's."

The mantle clock chimed out the hour. Midnight.

Dott watched with pride from the window as Bob crossed the street in what seemed like two enormous strides, his Prince Albert coat tails flying, a medicine bag in each hand. And she watched with apprehension. Whenever there was trouble in the Red Light District—Dot Allen's Place, Mabel's House, Tina's House—there was danger. Guns and knives were almost always a part of it. She'd have worried less if it had been a mid-winter blizzard he was heading into. One time, while down at Dot Allen's Place, he told her he wasn't sure he wouldn't take a knife in the back while he was attending to someone.

But she knew he had to go.

River Street was uncommonly quiet. The laughter and the rinky-tink piano melodies were absent, even from the saloons up on Main, except for way down at Daddy Fowler's Box Ball Parlor. But that was because it was so far away—Daddy Fowler's was on the outskirts of town, nearly as far away as the closest farmhouse. The Daddy Fowler piano player was pounding out a ragtime tune. They were distant sounds from another world, far removed from the pall that hung over the town. The bullfrogs and crickets and thrushes must have felt something too, for they also were silent. It was almost as if nature itself could sense the evil.

Two figures appeared from the alley between River Street and Main. John and his deputy, was Bob's first thought, because of the fast pace of their walk, but he soon saw that they were men he didn't recognize. They walked so quickly with their shoulders so far back that they looked like they were fleeing secretly from a swarm of bees. One was tall and stocky, the other short and slim. They looked over their shoulders, right, then left. One of the men held something down at his side with his arm straight.

They nearly bumped into Bob before they saw him. For a brief moment Bob was nose to nose with the man with the arm down at his side. And the face Bob saw was terrifying, not so much the face itself, but the countenance it bore—surprise, fear, desperation.

Not a word was spoken. The men walked on past. Bob hurried on.

The men stopped. The sounds of their footsteps were replaced by whispers.

Bob held his breath in expectation of the strike of a bullet, but there was no pistol crack.

The stars were brushing the earth that night. But their brilliance couldn't illuminate the solitary door he was approaching, shrouded as it was in the black shadows of the trees that surrounded Hailey's most notorious business establishment. A veranda wrapped the house. Porch swings and rocking chairs sat empty.

Bob climbed ten steps and passed between a set of stone columns onto the veranda. The front door was ajar.

He reached out to touch it, and slowly, ghost-like, it swung aside.

The unmistakable taste of spent gunpowder gushed into his mouth. He paused, and listened to the motionless silence, and thought for a second he may have heard the sound of someone whimpering.

He fumbled along the wall until he found the round object he was looking for. He turned the protruding spring-switch until it clunked.

Nothing. No lights.

In his vest pocket were stick matches. He pulled one out and struck it on the bottom of his shoe and saw that the electric light globes and coverings had been shot and broken.

The flickering match cast unsteady and disproportionate shadows onto the walls and ceilings, through the haze of the gun smoke, until it burned against his fingers and had to be shaken out.

Blackness swallowed him. He called out. "Hello. Helloooo. This is Doctor Wright. Hellllooooo."

Bob's voice must have given the girls courage. They started screaming his name from somewhere in the house.

There was the sudden smell of cigar smoke.

A voice came from the doorway. "That you Doc?"

Bob turned to see the silhouette of Wylie Blair, city marshal, cradling a shotgun in his hands.

"Doc? That you?"

"Here, Wylie. I'm here." Bob struck another match. "Over here, Wylie." He wasn't sure Wylie could hear him over the screams of the girls.

"Crazy assed women—" grumbled Wylie, cigar stub smoldering in his mouth. "I'm the marshal. You'd think they'd be a hollerin' for me, 'stead a you." Marshal Blair was a lawman straight out of a Bret Harte story, a pair of six shooters slung low and tied to the rumpled pant legs of his three piece suit, handles protruding backwards from underneath his coat jacket. He had a thick bush of a mustache covering part of his aging face, Teddy Roosevelt style, and a wide brimmed felt hat that must have been twenty years old. "I was over at C.T.'s workin' away on a slice of rhubarb pie—who'd ever guess that a Chinaman could make the best rhubarb pie this side of the Mississippi. You ought to try it Doc, the best—and Violet Young, she comes a runnin' in screamin' so loud folks in Texas could 'a heard."

Bob shook out the match and lit another, and put it to a coal oil lantern he found on a table.

Wylie spit between his boots onto the hardwood floor. "Get behind me, Doc. And hold that light up so's I can see where I'm goin'."

They walked down a hallway, brushing through its elaborate decor, tapestries, chandeliers, then through leaded French doors to the open area of the lounge and card room—chairs and tables were overturned—then into another hallway. In that hallway was a body, its lifeless head pointed toward a partially closed door, the door to Dot Allen's room. It was the body of a man, face down in a pool of its own blood. That had been where he was running, it seemed, from the parlor, to find sanctuary in Dot's room. Or perhaps to protect her?

It was obvious that Bob and Wylie were looking at an empty human shell, the way the head and arms were skewed, as if the life had been expunged in mid fall and the limbs had just folded beneath the weight. The man was older, sixtiesh it looked like, with stately snow white hair. But no—when Bob turned him over it was clear that he was far younger. The haze of the smoke had distorted his features, made sandy hair look white, made smooth skin seem wrinkled. He couldn't have been any more than thirty-five. He was in an unsoiled white shirt pulled up at the sleeves by green arm bands. A white straw hat with a green band lay off to the side. A set of spectacles sat crooked upon his nose. Nowhere on earth was there a gentler, a kinder man, spoke this picture of innocent death.

Bob knelt and felt for a pulse. There was none. "Rag Man Mickey," said Bob, still kneeling, resting his hands on his knees.

Wylie knew who he was. Rag Man had been playing piano at Dot Allen's for nigh on six years now. His real name was Crowley, M.J. Crowley, Mickey for short.

Bob said, "He could be out there playing with the best of them. In St. Louis. Chicago. Never could figure out what he was doing playing in a brothel way out west.

Wylie was standing with his back to Bob and the half closed door, holding his shotgun steady and chest high. The girls were no longer screaming. The only sounds now were the voices of Bob and Wylie, and a dime rolling across the wooden floor from Bob's watch pocket that had fallen when he'd reached in to check the time. 12:17.

"Relax, Wylie," said Bob. "No one's here. I passed two men crossing the street on the way over here. They were in an awful hurry. Those are your men, I suspect."

"I think I might know who they are. A couple of drunk drifters boarding over at Rorem's. I chased 'em out of Georgia's house earlier. They were makin' like they were gonna shoot up the place there." Wylie lowered his weapon. "Come on out ladies," he yelled. "It's OK. The doc and I are here. It's OK."

"You gals can come on out," repeated Bob loudly.

The saloon and show room area was like a large living room, about forty feet across with a fireplace on one end and the French doors on the other. Food and spirits, tonics expertly mixed, imported ales and expensive liquors, were served from a polished bar top and an adjacent kitchen. An observer unfamiliar with the nature of the establishment would think he had walked into a restaurant of the finest order. The chairs and tables were situated circularly around the piano. Fitted along the arches of the coved ceilings, just below the crisscrossing of large mahogany beams, were ornate fixtures of what some said were gas lights. Bob had never seen them in use. Encircling the showroom from the second floor above was a walkway railed in carved and shiny wood. Another closed door, on the far end of the bar, was the door to the wine room. It slowly began to open. Wylie tightened his grip on the shotgun, finger close to the trigger, within a hair's breadth of it but a safe instant away at the same time, in case a blameless face emerged. Indeed it did. It was the terrified face of Sing Kee, Dot Allen's Chinese bartender. Sing's voice was babbling as he inched toward Wylie and Bob. "Mickey, he put hands up when the man say hands up, but the man shoot him anyway. Mickey, then he start to run but the man shoot Mickey again. The man shoot Miss Allen too. Miss Allen, she dead too…"

But Dot Allen wasn't dead. The half closed door opened up completely. And there she stood, frightened, confused. The diamonds that graced her firm neckline sparkled in the haze, even though the only light shining on them was from a single lamp. Doors began opening upstairs as well. Footsteps sounded on the staircases. One by one the girls came, carrying lanterns. Dot Allen was like a parent taking a head count, checking to make sure everyone was all right, before anything else was done. No one knew exactly how old Dot Allen was. Most folks figured her to be around thirty. She was tall and had jet black hair, and a strong face and a mouth that had a way of smiling without really smiling. She had a little turned up nose which didn't at all fit with the rest of her face, giving her a girlish type of charm in the midst of the powerful femininity her countenance carried. But her appeal to men probably came from something deeper, a quality of mystery that seemed to shroud her appearance, something hidden, something inside for a man to conquer.

Every once in a while she could be seen strolling, always on the other side of the street from decent folk. She was always richly dressed in the latest fashion, ostrich plumed hats, fancy parasols, exquisitely styled dresses. When the "sheath" look came stateside from Paris, the narrow skirts that hugged hips and legs, Merry Widow hats, dotted veils, boned fishnet stockings, Dot Allen was the first in town to showcase it.

Bob tipped his derby hat. "Miss Allen."

Wylie grumbled and made a motion to do the same, but never quite completed it.

Then Dot Allen saw Rag Man Mickey. "Oh, noooo," was what came out of her mouth. She said it quietly, with the expelling of her breath, and with a look as if the very life were draining out of her.

She walked over to him, and drew up her skirt and knelt. There is a look of humility about a dead person, a type of helpless humility that seems to be reaching out to the onlooker for pity. Rag Man's arms, the way Bob and Wylie had propped him up against the wall for examination, were down limp at his sides, and his head was flopped back against the wall, like a dummy laid to rest for a time. His body appeared unmarked. At first, anyway. Closer examination revealed a number of entry wounds, the most notable being a splotch of red on his white shirt on the upper left side of his back, staining it crimson, pasting it to his skin, just on that one side from where the blood had flowed, now half dried. In the midst of the red stain was a hole the size of a fountain pen. Bob had twisted the body to that one side, so he could better see the wound. Dot touched the hole with a quivering finger, then pulled the dead man's head into the shelter of her breast and started shaking, like she was breaking apart from the inside out, and stared straight ahead, with eyes that focused on nothing.

Tears streamed down her face, silently, in unabashed purity.

The uncharacteristic display of sensitivity from the infamous Queen of River Street touched Wylie Blair. The crusty lawman put his cigar out on the bottom of his boot and stuffed the shreds into his suit coat pocket, then removed his hat and bent one knee down to the floor. "Miss Allen, I'm pure sorry," he said. "You have my word. We'll find the men who are responsible for this. We truly will."

It had been a robbery, nothing more, a brutal cold-blooded robbery perpetrated by men without a conscience. Sing Kee had been a witness, and told Bob and Wylie exactly what he had seen. He told how the gunman leveled his Colt 45 with purposeful intent to kill the musician, even though he had put his hands in the air. The gun had a rusted barrel, said Sing, and a brass screw that didn't seem to belong, like it had been stuck there in a makeshift way to hold something together. After the strike of the first bullet into a nonvital part of his chest, Mickey turned and ran. The gunman chased him into the hallway and fired again, the shot that felled him, then two more times into the prone body. He had fired at Dot Allen too, presumably because of the expensive necklace she was wearing, but the bullet had missed, grazing her head and rendering her momentarily unconscious. They had been after the sheep money, speculated Bob. To the Basque sheepherders who couldn't speak English, Dot Allen was like a mother superior. "She holds their money, then doles it out to them so they won't spend it all in one place. Not many people know about it."

"Don't that beat all," said Wylie.

Bob checked Rag Man with his stethoscope, just to be officially sure, then put a hand on Wylie's shoulder. "Come on Wylie. Let's leave her be for a time."

"All right, Miss Allen." Wylie was still holding his hat. "You take some time. But as soon as you're able I'm going to need to talk to you. The doc and I'll be outside talkin', in case you need me. And I'll need to be speakin' with the girls too."

"I always figured her for John Donnelly's woman," said Wylie, lighting up another cigar, pulling in the smoke, looking out over the porch railing at a distant and dispassionate moon.

"Hard to say," said Bob. "Hard to say." John Donnelly, six-foot-four and "handsome as the very devil," as Dott would phrase it (to Bob's jealous chagrin) was Dot Allen's right hand man. No one really knew what John Donnelly did, exactly, or whether his involvement with her was personal or professional. Both, most folks figured. John was regularly seen in her company. On Sundays at the race track one could always count on John being in attendance with Dot Allen and seven or eight of the other girls, sitting way up in back, away from the general crowd. "Don't stare at her," Bob would whisper, to which Dott would chuckle and respond with as much charm and grace and beauty as the illustrious madam herself, "How do you expect me not to stare, when she's so beautiful?"

Bob gave Wylie a description of the men he saw in the alley, then reached in the inner pocket of his jacket and handed him a fresh cigar, Cuban, worth ten of the one Wylie had in his mouth.

"Hmm. Thank you kindly, Doc. The good kind."

"I had a couple in my pocket from back when the little one was born."

"What, you've got two ankle munchers now? And you didn't tell me? Well, congratulations." Wylie took the cigar and gave Bob a hearty hand-shake and slapped his shoulder. "Yeseree. Congratulations. Boy or girl?"

"Girl, the cutest little thing you've ever seen. Hair the color of her mother's."

Wylie hollered up to the second floor. "You men up there. The doc and I are out a kabitzin' on the porch. If you happen to come down, and if you happen to go out the back way, we won't be lookin'. We won't be able to see who you are. You just git on home."

Multiple footsteps came creaking down the stairs. Wylie squinted a wink at Bob, then rounded them up and questioned them all. Afterward he picked up the phone to have the operator ring Sheriff Hart. No answer. "I had Dott call him before I left," said Bob. "I suspect he'll be along."

"Well Doc—I'm gonna have to go find him—you be all right here for a spell?"

"I'll be fine, Wylie." He wasn't quite sure why he said that. He didn't feel fine. He felt more like he was in the pits of Hell itself, like the lingering gun smoke wasn't gun smoke at all, but the rising up of smoldering brimstone, and that soon the devil himself would be making an appearance. He looked at his watch again. 12:28.

Bob was tall and strong, an intimidating figure, oddly more so than Wylie, but he didn't feel very much like he was, and was relieved immeasurably when both Sheriff Hart and Deputy Somers walked in, mere moments after Wylie had left. When Wylie returned they all moved Rag Man's body out into the parlor onto one of the card tables for further examination. By then more people were beginning to congregate. Wylie and Sheriff Hart dug a .44 slug out from behind a picture on the wall in Dot Allen's bedroom—it had been the one that grazed her head—and dug another out of the wall in the parlor, a .38 caliber.

Bob looked at his watch. 1:44. He guessed he'd be getting on home. "If you don't need me anymore, that is, for anything," he said to John Hart. "Nothing more I can do here, it doesn't appear." Dot Allen was fine. He'd taken the time to check her over, her eyes particularly, in case of a concussion, and pronounced her fit, frightened but healthy. "You're a lucky girl," he told her. The girls were all OK too, and Sing was uninjured. "Good fortune," commented Wylie, "considering all the lead that was flying around."

He'd be home in plenty of time to get a good night's sleep. But sleep was not in fate's future, not that night at least. This time it wasn't a call from a patient in need. This time it was his wife. She wasn't ill, only talkative. They lay in bed and talked until the Thompson's cock crowed, which always meant that the early dawn was glimmering in blue-grey on the tops of the mountains and would soon be melting away the blackness of their bedroom. He told her about what he'd been through. They used it as a springboard to philosophize about life and its complexities. They did that from time to time. Just talked. Even argued some. About what was unimportant. They had the unique ability to be able to argue vastly different viewpoints without getting angry, just sharing ideas, just connecting. A remarkable woman, his wife, always understanding whenever he was called down to the houses of red light row, never questioning his duty to go, never questioning his loyalty. The calls were for various reasons: a fight, illnesses ranging from the common cold to the feared and deadly constitutional syphilis, occasionally an attempted suicide. One 21-year-old killed herself by drinking a bottle of chloroform. The lives of the girls on the line in the late 1800s and into the turn of the century varied widely. Typically, they were lives of sorrow and grinding poverty. For the women fortunate enough to become associated with the more prestigious houses, such as Dot Allen's Place, life was a bit easier, for a time. But soon enough their lives were likely to descend from the luxurious brothels to the poverty stricken "crib" houses, where prostitutes were forced to live in single dwellings under the most unimaginable of conditions, often with children, where the overhead was high and the income low.

Wylie Blair was good to his word. He kept his promise to Dot Allen. He worked through the night, along with John and his deputy, interviewing again Sing Kee, all the girls, the men who had been visiting their favorite ladies, and anyone else that may have seen or heard anything on that fateful night. The following day four drifters were arrested—they'd been working out on Harry Smith's ranch—a man named Charles Allen, no relation to Dot Allen, and his brother Reece Clevenger, also known as Battle Ax Jack, both in their mid thirties, and a seventeen-year-old orphan named Charles Crawford and his twenty-year-old friend Lorenzo Swift, nicknamed "Babe," and charged them all with murder.

A week after that, following a trial that extended far into every night, a trial that gathered so many spectators there remained barely standing room, Allen and Clevenger were sent to the Boise State Penitentiary for life. Crawford and Swift were given one to ten years for their roles as accomplices.

Chapter 10

The Kilpatrick Ranch Case

Hailey, Idaho

1912

BOB HAD JUST RETURNED from a two-day confinement case up into the Stanley Basin, past Galena Summit where the snow had been chest high to the lead horses. It had been an exhausting trip. The journey to the summit itself took six hours. He'd taken a driver and a thirteen horse team. On some of the narrower switchbacks the horses had to be uncoupled and driven up in sections. At one point a mountain lion crossed the road and spooked the horses, almost overturning the sleigh. But then, on the other side, upon cresting the summit, lay a world of splendor, the basin ringed by the towering, smoky crags of the White Clouds, serene peaks untouched under their cover of snow. As far as the eye could see there was snow, with the only sign of life being a hawk riding a wind current out in front of them, hanging in the air almost close enough to touch, barely beyond the cliff-like edge of the summit. The outline of the road, switching back down the other side, was etched in the snow of the mountainside, untracked, probably unused since the time of the first snow. Folks on the other side just didn't travel in winter. They dug in with their supplies and there they stayed. Bob was thickly dressed and the sun was warm. A strange phenomenon of winter in Idaho is that the air can be cold and the sun warm at the same time. And in that warm sun, after they'd passed down through the switchbacks, after they'd reached the basin floor, as they continued on toward Stanley, he slept. He slept with a spiritual-like tranquility, the freshness of the virgin air vitalizing him, the jerks and glides of the bobsleigh entrancing him. It would be one of those remembrances that would follow him for the rest of his life.

When he arrived home, though he was tired, he was also refreshed in spirit. The sleep in the bobsleigh had only lasted a few hours, but it had been pure, uncontaminated by thoughts from an outside world. It was as though the sun had burned away troublesome thoughts and burdens. And the journey's end had seen the beginning of life. The birth of a baby was always an amazing thing to Bob, no matter how many times he saw it.

The front door stuck a little because of the cold. He had to force it, rattling the glass and curtain rod. A rush of warmth greeted him, and with it the scintillating aroma of bread baking, and of turkey basting, and the sharp scent of pine from the Christmas tree. Jake was up in an instant from where he had been sleeping in front of the fireplace, limping toward Bob, smiling, wagging his tail so rigorously his whole bottom shook.

Jake was the only one who noticed he was home. His-brother-in-law, Ed, was asleep on the sofa. The children were nowhere in sight.

Bob gave Jake's head a good rub, took off his cap and scarf and coat, and headed into the kitchen, still unnoticed. Dott was stirring something bubbly in a big pot on the stove top. Along the counter sat seven pumpkin pies.

"How's the prettiest girl in the forty-eight states of America?"

She jumped and burned her hand on the pot, dropping the wooden spoon inside. "—you scared me half to death," she said, shaking and sucking her finger, then threw her arms around him. "You made it back for the dance. Did everything go OK?"

"Everything went just fine, other than a set-to with a cougar up on Galena Summit. Where are the kids?"

Dott looked about. "Glenn was here a moment ago. Jean's down for a nap. Glennnnnn?" She unhooked her blue apron from her long white dress and threw it aside. "Glennnn?"

Jean was not down for a nap, it turned out. Turned out she was up to her eyeballs in mischief, with Glenn as the chief orchestrator. They were found at the trail's end of a powerful scent, in Bob and Dott's bedroom. Their eighteen-month-old daughter had doused herself in perfume and was standing in front of a floor length mirror with lipstick smeared all over her face and clothes, and all over the floor, the dressing table, the walls. Glenn was running a brush through her hair, light brown hair with burnishes of red that gleamed golden whenever the sun fell on it in the right way, just like her mother's. She looked up and squinted through one eye, a band of freckles dotting her nose. Glenn, who could have been Jean's twin, same freckles, same red hair, said, "I'm making her pretty like you, Mother."

After that day, Jean's favorite form of tomfoolery was to dash in when no one was looking and drench herself in perfume. Sometimes the odor would be strong enough to make the eyes water. "Shawant," was her first word, uttered while pointing to one of the jewel encased vials. "She wants."

Glenn had been inseparable from Jean since the moment of her birth. He was not yet three when she was born, unable to understand what he was witnessing. Yet somehow he did understand, this immutable law of nature, that life comes from life.

No one realized little Glenn had been there in the room during the birthing, hiding behind a round mahogany table upon which Bob's instruments had been placed. The child would peek around for a look whenever the courage would surface, then quickly disappear again. Mrs. Leopold thought he was down for a nap.

Dott was the first to see him, seconds after the birth, and shrieked in surprise. Mrs. Leopold came running in at the same moment, apologizing profusely.

As Mrs. Leopold was about to scoop him up, Bob said, "No, wait—" He placed the baby in his son's arms, keeping his hands close for support.

A smile slowly formed on Glenn's face.

"Sister," said Bob, nodding toward the newborn.

"Sister," repeated Glenn.

And a bond was sealed.

Glenn and Jean traveling in style.

It was typical of Glenn to sneak Jean out of her bed early in the morning, before the sun broke and the cock crowed. Once they spread flour all over the kitchen floor and mixed it up with water. "Makin' cement," Glenn told Dott, right before he got his licking. He'd been fascinated the previous fall by the pouring of cement sidewalks to replace the old boardwalks.

In the evenings, Bob would retire to the drawing room with a good cigar and the paper. Seconds was all it would take for Glenn to come rushing in to jump up on his lap. "Uh oh," Bob would say. "Here comes trouble."

Then together they'd read the paper, with Bob reading aloud the things that captured headlines. "…and son, they're making pennies with a picture of Lincoln on them. Here's a shiny new one for you, fresh off the press. Here, you can smell the mint on it."

Sometimes Jean would come tottering in from the bedroom, having been put down for the night. The entire floor would shake with her thumps. She'd claw her way up onto Bob's other knee and lay her head against his chest, finger in her mouth.

And a warmth would sit in Bob's chest, a calmness that bonded them, that burned like fire.

Soon Dott would appear in the doorway tapping her foot and shaking her head. "Off to bed with you, young lady. And you too, little man."

Jean would turn away and bury her head in Bob's shoulder, giving a squeal of protest.

Then Bob would rise and gesture to Dott, like an actor in a Shakespearean drama. "Maestro, if you please."

He'd place Jean on the floor, her face aglow, and bow to her, and Dott would sit at the piano and unfold a Straus waltz.

And Bob would pick little Jean up and dance her dramatically off to her bedroom while Glenn would sit beside his mother and help her play.

When Bob tucked her in he'd rub her back and "fix her dreams," put good thoughts in her head for the night, "…before the sandman comes."

The thirty-one-year-old physician's life, personally and professionally, was incredibly complete. He'd seen some radical changes over the course of the past four years, changes in medicine, in technology, in society, in his own life. There were now forty-eight stars on the flag, Arizona being

The Wright family, 1912.

the latest. Eight simultaneous messages could be sent through a single telegraph wire. Taft had only served one term. A Democrat was now president, a man named Woodrow Wilson, whose picture hung framed on Bob's office wall, a man who promised an end to bad times.

And Bob had a new hat to replace his bowler, a white Stetson with a black band, its narrow brim bent down over the forehead, a refined look to match the maturity that experience had written into his face.

The world of medicine was seeing one discovery after another. Every month it seemed there was something new, advancements so astounding and so many that last summer he had to go back east again for more study. Osler and McCrae had just published *The Seventh Volume of Modern Medicine, its Theory and Practice*, which was helpful, but to be there at the Mayo Clinic where it was all happening, that was a thing that had no substitute. Many of the old country docs refused education, and let the knowledge sweep past them. Ironically, those were the ones the people had the most faith in.

In his personal life, most significant, was the fact that he finally gave in to Dott's wishes and went into practice on his own. They had two thousand dollars saved, all they had in the world. They used it to buy the Watt bank building at an estate auction, the building that used to house the McCormick Bank on Main. It was a frightening move. It was the abandonment of all their security—for a dream, in a time when most patients could barely afford to buy food, let alone pay their doctor. But it was working. They were making it. Growing food in the backyard, hunting for wild game in the summer, storing it for the winter. They were making it.

And he made a purchase of a thing he at one time maintained had absolutely no practical value other than to inflate a rich man's ego: an automobile. He went out and bought himself an EMF Studebaker. The only car in town. They still didn't have indoor plumbing or a water closet, but he went out and bought himself a car for seven hundred and twenty-nine dollars. It had high-perched open air seats, a drop windshield, carbide flame jet lamps for night driving—it was a handsome machine indeed. It was useless in winter, but in the summer months it more than proved itself, if the streets weren't too muddy from the rains and sewers. He could motor to the bedside of a patient at forty miles an hour or better, purring and puttering well beyond the speed of a team.

The Studebaker.

This Christmas was special. Dott's sister Holly and her husband Ed were up from Ogden for the holidays and the big dance. Ed was still asleep on the couch and Holly was at Fuld's Cash Store getting some buttons for her gown. The Christmas Eve dance was the biggest event of the year, a fancified affair. The men all dressed in Sunday suits and the women in gowns they'd been making since summer. And everyone brought food.

There was two-and-a-half feet of snow on the ground, most of it new fallen, and the sun was bright. Everywhere outside there gleamed a world of white. The snow had been pushed and shoveled from the buildings to the middle of the street, turning Main into two streets, one on either side of a huge unblemished barrier, so cleanly sliced it could have been done with a knife. Here and there pathways were cut so folks could cross over. People were moving about briskly with their overshoes and scarves, nodding and smiling to one another. The signs of the various businesses loomed over them, and seemed in their snow capped and sun drenched brilliance to insist that everyone be especially pleasant to one another on that particular day. Alturas Saddlery. The Hailey National Bank. The Elite Ice Cream and Confectionary. S. J. Benson—One Price Clothier. John C. Baugh, Druggist. A metal fish with the word "TACKLE," hung on one building. One sign read,

C.T.'s Restaurant
Regular meals 25 cents
Sunday Dinner 35 cents
All White Help.

The last comment was most likely a reference to the Chinese people in town, those who worked in the mines and the restaurants. The comment was strange, because C.T.'s was a Chinese restaurant. The vacant lot next to Bob's new office building had been turned into a skating rink and was ringed with hanging electric light globes. In the middle of the rink was an igloo, perfectly constructed from evenly hewn chunks of snow.

Bob's exhaustion was evident. He should have napped before the dance. He should have accepted Dott's offer to fix him something hot. Instead he insisted on taking everyone to Fat's for dinner "…but only if you two promise to never get into Mother's perfume again," he said, kneeling in front of the children. Little Jean nodded, as if agreeing, but of course she'd be into it again, once she found the opportunity. Glenn too nodded his head in agreement, looking apologetic, his face still wet from the tears of his scolding. Semi-scolding, would be more accurate. When Dott had seen his little body begin to shake and his mouth shudder from the shock of his disappointment, because his efforts to please her had failed, she opened her arms and said, "Come here, you," and held him while he sobbed into her shoulder.

Fat's Place was down on the south end of River Street, in Chinatown about ten blocks away. There was a bell above the door that jingled when someone opened it. Inside was a second entrance, shrouded in hanging bead curtains and smoky curls of Oriental incense. Bob parted them. Fat was there to greet them. He bowed.

Bob bowed back and said, "Nee-how. How-pong-yo."

Fat said, "Doctor Wright honors me by speaking my language." Fat looked like he was in his fifties, though some folks said he was closer to seventy. He wore a long robe made of ornamented tapestry cloth with wide sleeves. He was clean shaven except for a narrow white beard that covered only the point of his chin. "Doctor Wright's family is welcome in my humble establishment."

On the mornings of the all-nighters, when Bob would stop in to have Fat fix him up some breakfast, they'd have long talks and share stories of vastly different cultures. The friendship enriched them both.

Fat led them to a center table. Blue and white checkered tablecloths seemed out of place among the life size Foo Dogs, the replicas of the steep roofed Chinese monasteries that surrounded the doorways, and the detailed ink brushings that hung on the walls. The room was dark, except for one single wide beam of sunshine that came in from a west window to rest a foot and a half away. No one else was there except for four middle-aged Chinese women at a table in a corner playing Mahjong.

"Fat, bring us a huge platter of Ma Poh Tofu," said Bob, "and your finest tea. That green stuff. The kind with all those leaves in the bottom."

Fat, his smile ever present, bowed and retreated to the kitchen.

"Sir, how come some people don't like Fat?" Glenn asked Bob.

"Shhhhh, lower your voice," said Dott, looking over at the women playing Mahjong, who were taking no notice of anything other than their game.

Bob asked, "Who doesn't like Fat?"

"Oh, just kids. Some of them throw rocks at him. They call him names. What's a chink?"

Bob folded his hands on the table and leaned forward. "Son, there are those in this world who don't like people simply because they're different. For no other reason. Do you think that's right?"

Glenn shook his head.

"I don't either, and neither does your mother, nor do Aunt Holly and Uncle Ed. The measure of a man is the way he lives his life, not the shape of his eyes or the language he speaks."

"Yes, sir."

"You didn't throw any rocks, did you?" Bob moved his hat onto the post of his chair from where it was on the table, and leaned further forward.

Glenn shook his head no. "No, sir."

Affirmed Bob with a nod, "Good."

"They wanted me to, but I didn't."

"I never want to hear of you doing anything like that. I'm proud of you, son."

"What if I say no and then they start throwing rocks at me?"

Bob put his hand on top of Glenn's hand. "Son, let me ask you. Do you think throwing rocks at someone just because they're different is the right thing to do?'

"No, sir."

"If you go through life walking on the right side of what you think is right, I'll always be proud of you, even if you get rocks thrown at you for it, and you can be proud of yourself."

Fat returned with the tea, a porcelain pot and five tiny cups, one each for Bob, Dott, Glenn, Holly, and Ed. Jean was seated on a pile of books and tied to the back of the chair, and was pounding the table and squealing in delight. One never knows what will amuse a baby. Perhaps it was Fat's infectious smile.

"Why is your name Fat?" asked Glenn. "Are you fat?"

Fat grinned. "It was a name given me in this country. I know not why. Maybe I have a fat head. Hmmmm?" It was hard to tell what was underneath that huge Chinese robe, but judging from the portliness of his round cheeks, Fat probably was fat.

Ten minutes later Fat returned with two large platters that steamed with the smell of Oriental spices and herbs, something delicious that Glenn had never tasted before. His eyes watered and his nose stung each time he put a fork full in his mouth.

Then came the fortune cookies. "Which one shall I choose, Daddy?" asked Glenn.

"Whichever one you want," answered Bob.

"Daddy, I want you to choose for me."

"All right, son. Eenie meenie miny moe… This one. Right here."

"Open it for me."

"Let's see. It says, 'You will be blessed with wisdom and a long life.'"

After that day, every Sunday after church they'd make it a ritual to go to Fat's Place for "Sum-Sum." That's what Glenn called it. Sum-Sum. Because Bob had allowed him first to taste some from his own fork, to see how he fared with the spices. "You want some?" he had asked.

"I want some."

A common question from Glenn would be, "Can we go to Fat's Place for some Sum?" Sum-Sum.

And that day before Christmas in 1912 proved once again that crises never came one at a time. When they got home, before Bob was able to crawl in bed for a brief nap before the party, he got a call to perform an appendectomy on a little girl. Dr. Bernard had made the diagnosis and had requested Bob do the surgery. Bernard would assist.

The child was clearly in serious pain. When Bob arrived she was on her mother's lap in a rocking chair, twisting her body and moving her head from side to side. She was five, Glenn's age. Bob drew blood, poked, prodded, listened, tapped…and prescribed pears.

The pears worked. The girl kept her appendix until the day she died, seventy-one years later.

It had been a busy afternoon. While Bob had been consulting with Dr. Bernard, Dott had gone into the office to attend to Bob Galloway. The old fool had nearly cut his leg off last week chopping wood and needed the dressing changed before the dance. Everyone came to the Christmas Eve dance, even Bob Galloway on crutches.

The Odd Fellow's Hall was decorated for the affair with hanging rows of incandescent lights, their bulbs painted brightly in colors of red, green, and yellow. Pine bows and wreaths hung on the walls and above the windows. In the right hand corner was a huge Christmas tree, twenty feet tall, scraping the ceiling. Next to the tree, upon a stage, was an odd mix of a band—a piano, a violin, a bass fiddle, a banjo, a mandolin, and a trombone. It filled the high-ceilinged building with music traditional and modern. Christmas carols. Waltzes. As well as the new dances sweeping the East Coast—the Crab Step and the Fox Trot. And a new song by a young writer named Irving Berlin, "Alexander's Ragtime Band."

The evening had barely begun when Bob was summoned to the Kilpatrick ranch where a couple of sheepherders had cut themselves up in a knife fight. Jack Gutchess ran in yelling for Doc Wright. "Word is one of 'em is hurt pretty bad. Kin 'a Joe Uberuaga."

Dott looked up at Bob in her white gown, trimmed in pink and light blue lace, her strawberry blond hair done up in Gibson girl fashion, except for that stubborn strand that always wanted to fall loose on the right side, sometimes laying over her face in a way to give her a look of reckless authority, and stormed, "I absolutely won't have it!"

Bob was surprised, stunned in fact—speechless for a few moments. He hadn't expected that reaction. "Dott, you know I have to go. I don't have a choice."

"I'm not saying you can't go. I'm only saying you can't go without me. Bob, it's Christmas."

Dott's sister Holly insisted on coming too. Holly looked a lot like Dott. A little heavier. And with spectacles.

"Yes," echoed Ed. "We'll come. You could use the help on a night like this."

Indeed he could. The sky was such that the whole Picabo and Gannet valley would soon be fogged in. He could tell by the haze of the moon.

"Well, all right then," he agreed. "The livery is readying a team. It will be set up in twenty minutes. I want all of you changed and ready. With warm clothes."

It was cold. The crystals of the snow sparkled before the shine of the moon and squeaked beneath the runners of the sleigh. Dott and Holly sat in back on the floor behind the driver's seat to shelter themselves. The sleigh was in reality a buckboard with the wheels replaced by runners. The four horses that pulled it made good time, blowing puffs of chilled air that floated like steam behind them, following along the railroad tracks at almost a prance pace, pounding out a path through the stiff and chunky snow. Occasionally the fleeting shadow of a snowshoe rabbit or a coyote whiffed by. Harsh winters drew the wildlife down to the farmlands, particularly at night.

The depth of the snow gradually diminished the further south they drove. It was down to a foot at the Gannet-Picabo cutoff, so that the fence posts of the roads and sheep trails were clearly defined. At the cutoff they hooked onto the main sheep trail that ran all the way down from Ketchum, fenced on either side. Ketchum was a major sheep and wool shipping outlet for the mountain west. Most time the herders used the roads anyway. In summer it was common to have to negotiate a horse and buggy, or in Bob's case an automobile, through a myriad of tightly packed sheep and clattering bells. It was that way all the way up into the 1950s. Amazing to Bob was the way a small and scraggly sheepdog could keep a herd in line, scampering back and forth yapping and nipping. One good dog could drive a thousand head through a five-foot-wide gate on a single whistle command.

A blanket of fog appeared across the flatlands, a fallen cloud. The sheep trail, outlined by the shine of the moon, dead-ended into it. A giant black wall. It was as if the fog was alive and beckoning to them, inviting them into a world unseen.

They were like ghosts disappearing into a mile-high barricade, so thick and abrupt was the fog bank. Even the guideposts of the fences were lost. Bob couldn't see the very horses he was driving. It was a wet and cold fog, minute ice crystals floating in the air. But the horses kept pressing foreword, steady and sure, like they could see just fine. Sure enough, a road was there. Dott and Holly could tell, because every once in a while they'd get a glimpse of the telegraph lines running alongside.

Bob knew where to turn; how was a mystery to Dott. He pulled the team to a stop. "I think it's right about here," he said.

Ed jumped to the snowy ground and wandered up the road a ways—the road was frozen into ruts and powdered with ice dust—and shouted back, "Here it is. They've hung a lantern on the fence."

The entrance was through a gateway of tall pine poles, beneath a sign etched with the name "Kilpatrick." The main ranch house was only a quarter of a mile in, and another quarter-mile beyond that would see the end of an agonizing wait for a young fifteen-year-old boy who was slowly choking to death on his own blood, his throat sliced open. Each moment was bringing the terror of suffocation. Each breath was drawing sputters of blood into his lungs. He was afraid to breathe, afraid not to breathe. He wanted to run from himself, outside of himself, but of course he couldn't, and that made his desperation all the worse.

In the days before turn-of-the-century medicine this young teen would have had to wait for hours, days maybe, before death would have rescued him. Bob was taken to him immediately. Holly and Ed were made comfortable in the house. Dott came with him to assist, knowing him as well as he knew himself, silently watching, anticipating his movements and his needs, handing him instruments when needed, cleansing them, soaking up blood.

The boy was sitting on the edge of his wall-mounted bed in the families' tiny canvas-covered sheep wagon, bending forward, staring at the floor, because that was the only position that would allow him breath and survival. His mother was standing next to him, stroking his head, helpless except to give useless comfort. His father was kneeling, his hand on his son's arm.

A coal oil lantern sat atop a fold-down table. Water was boiling on a small pot bellied stove at the other end of the wagon. Bob knelt and examined the wound, and talked to the lad, while Dott laid out his pre-sterilized instruments—scissors, clamps, retractors, pliers, scalpel, sutures—she placed them all out, not knowing yet which would be needed, being careful to touch only the handles.

The family was Basque. The foreman who brought Bob to the wagon was acting as an interpreter. He spoke in a heavy accent. "She say her son is dying. She pleads to you. She say you must do something quickly. She say her son drowns in his own blood."

Dott said, "Bob?...I don't think blood is the problem." She reached out with her slim fingers and spread the skin around the wound. "I think there's a torn piece of cartilage obstructing the airway."

Bob took the lantern and brought it in close, swabbing and soaking up blood with gauze, talking as if to himself. "Yep, that's our culprit. Sure enough. It's not allowing enough air through. And the air that is getting through is mixing with the blood."

"Yup, sure enough," he repeated. "The blood flow itself has slowed, it appears. That's good." Dott handed him the scissors. They were long handled and bent at the blades at a forty-five degree angle. "I want you to explain to the boy what I'm going to be doing," he told the interpreter. "I have to cut that cartilage loose. I'm going to try to reach it by going in through the hole in his neck."

The boy nodded, his eyes begging for help. Each bubbled breath conveyed the depth of his desperation.

"His name is Miguel," said the interpreter. "He is understand and speak English. His momma and pappa not so good. But Miguel, he is understand."

Bob took a critical second in the midst of the boy's terror and touched his wrist. "I'm going to help you, Miguel. All right?"

The boy nodded again.

"It's going to be uncomfortable. I can't anesthetize. There's not enough time."

The foreman explained to the parents what Bob was saying, and the boy, hearing it a second time in his native tongue, gripped the sides of the bed, prepared. Meantime Ed had come in with two more lanterns.

Bob went in, forcing the scissors into the opening, into the airway, trying to find the piece of cartilage, hoping to grasp it and cut it loose. But it was a blind probe, and the boy flailed in fear as he choked on the instrument. One of his hands caught Dott hard on the side of the cheek.

Bob withdrew the instrument.

The boy shook in convulsions and gasped for air. Dott took one of her hands and brushed at her teared-up eyes.

"We're going to try one more time," said Bob.

The boy let him, but again thrashed and pushed.

Again Bob withdrew the scissors.

The boy was blue and suddenly unresponsive. His eyes were bulging, and the gasps were less desperate. No longer was there the strength to try to breathe.

"We're losing him," murmured Bob. "All right—we're going to do something different here." He reached for his scalpel and cut a section out of his stethoscope and doused it with carbolic acid, then poured some on the scalpel, then, in a matter of seconds, cut an opening in the windpipe below the obstruction, below the larynx, where the breastbones come together, and inserted the hose and taped it in tight. And prayed the rubber was firm enough to keep from collapsing.

There followed a beautiful sound. The boy's chest filled with air, again and again, over and over. And the blue was replaced with flush red, the fear with relief, the desperation with peace.

Now Bob had the time to work. He re-inserted the instrument.

He was able to reach the impediment and was able to widen the scissors enough to get the blades around it...but he hesitated, almost squeezing. He withdrew.

The offending piece was large enough that he feared he might not be able to extricate it, or that he would loose his grip on it and it would end up further lodged within the trachea, perhaps below the breathing line.

"All right, son—" said Bob. "I'm going to give you some morphine." He drew it into a syringe, squeezed out the air, flicked off the drops and plunged it into Miguel's arm, and waited for it to act. "I'm going to do a little minor surgery here. You shouldn't feel much more than some pressure on your throat. There's no reason for you to be afraid, because I'll be doing it above your airway. You'll still be able to breath. At the most you'll feel some stinging. Grab your momma's arm if you have to, but I want you to hold real still. OK?"

The boy nodded in the affirmative.

"Dear, I want you to steady his head for me." Dott reached out her two comforting hands and placed them on Miguel's cheeks, not as the grip of a vice, but as the gentle touch of a woman. "I have to take my time and do it right," Bob said. "It needs to be a clean cut. I don't want to tear into a blood vessel."

There were times when the miracles of an old country doctor were due as much to creativity and ingenuity as they were to the advancement of medicine. Sometimes a country doctor invented procedures before they'd been developed by the profession. Bob's skillful hands opened the throat in a large half triangle, which he folded down to expose the obstructing cartilage. He cut it free and sutured and bandaged the wound. "Let him sleep," he instructed to the interpreter. "Then first thing tomorrow, at first light, I want you to bring him up to Hailey where I can keep a close eye on him. There's a Basque family there. Usebio Arriaga. Do you know the Arriagas?"

Bob waited for the translation.

They did.

"Good. I'll make arrangements for him to stay there, with Usebio. It will be all right. The Arriagas have done this before for me, with other Basque patients. Just get up there as soon as you are able, as soon as the fog lifts and it's safe to travel. They'll be expecting you. I'll see to that. Don't give him any food. Soak a rag with water and let him suck on it when he's thirsty. Tomorrow we'll start him on some broth. And above all, you've got to keep that bandage on and clean. If his throat gets infected it will swell, and that won't be good."

Miguel apologized copiously for what he had done to Dott. "Pshaww," was all she said, and patted his hand. "You just get better now, hear? That's how you can make it up to me."

"Now let's take a look at that shiner," stated the doctor to his wife. Doctors do that; they state instead of ask. But Dott would have none of it. "I'm fine," she said, and reminded him there still was another patient to be attended to. Bob grumbled—after all, who was the doctor here?—but acquiesced, and quickly, systematically, packed his bags and on they went to the other injured man, in another part of the camp, in another wagon. He was older, also Basque, in his mid-thirties. He had several cuts, less severe, a shoulder laceration, a cut on the back of one hand and a deep puncture under the left ribcage that somehow missed all vital organs. The patch-up job was time consuming but simple. Basic disinfection and suturing. Then Bob attended to his wife, never mind her protests. Indeed she was fine, strong of body and will.

They never knew what the fight was about. They never asked. The Basque were generally a non-violent people. They had a strong sense of ethics and family unity. They carried with them a troubled history of prejudice and persecution, beginning hundreds of years earlier during their brutal conversion to Christianity under the heavy hand of Pope Gregory and his Inquisition. In the process, a folklore symbol was born, in a twist of irony. Notable of history is the fact that when one society conquers another, the conquering society takes the conquered societies' image of God as their devil. Curiously, the simple goat herders of the Spanish hillsides envisioned God to look like a goat, with horns and cloven hooves.

Before leaving Bob checked on the young man. He was doing fine, sleeping. "Be sure you get him up to Usebio's tomorrow, first thing, so I can keep him under observation."

The boy's mother handed Bob a gunny sack full of potatoes and said something in the Basque tongue, her cheeks wet from weeping. Bob didn't know the words, but he understood. She also offered a hot meal and a steaming cup of coffee.

Bob considered the bill paid in full.

It was 5 a.m. when they arrived back home. Christmas morning. The clatter woke Mrs. Leopold and the children. Glenn thought the noise was Santa and came out gingerly, creeping, afraid to look, because he knew what the jolly old elf had for him, the business end of a switch and a lump of coal. When he saw otherwise, when he saw presents, he was beside himself with glee, especially when he found the toy bugle.

The presents were all opened by 5:30. And by 5:35 Bob was asleep in the overstuffed wing back chair, with two children crawling up on him every few minutes, jerking him awake. Dott tried to get him off to bed, but he chose the chair, to be with everybody. After all, it was Christmas.

At 8:30 the phone rang.

He was still in the chair, still heavily clad in his outdoor clothes. He twitched at the sound. Dott was fearful to answer it, but did.

It was Joe Fuld. "Merry Christmas, all," he said. "—and may God grant Peace on Earth."

Bob stood and stretched. "Let's go eat," he said. That's what he always said after a job well done.

Chapter 11

A One-Way Ticket

San Antonio, Texas

1952

I DON'T REMEMBER EXACTLY HOW OLD I was when I went to see my Texas grandparents, four, five maybe. However old, it wasn't old enough to recognize the complications of adult existence, to know that these two giants of perfection I called Mom and Dad weren't exactly perfect. I wasn't old enough to realize that I was being tricked, that this trip to Texas had a one-way ticket. There were four things I had always wanted to do: go to the jungle, see Queen Elizabeth, ride in an airplane, and visit my Texas grandparents and Uncle Tommy. This was two down at once. "Dad, when we come back, can me and you go to the jungle?" I asked him.

I remember there being a strange look in his face. "We'll see," he said.

Had I not known better I would have thought he was about ready to cry. But men don't cry. Especially not men like Dad.

"Why don't you stay here with me?" he said.

And miss a chance for an airplane ride? An abrupt "No!" roared from my mouth.

The day we left Dad asked me again, at the airport, "Why not stay here with me. We'll go look for wood in the morning." Scrounging riverbeds for driftwood was one of my favorite activities.

"Yes," said O'You. "Stay here. Stay here with us."

"Don't you want to stay with us?" reiterated Nanna. "And go find some wood? Maybe we can see some beavers."

But I looked over at the Beech Staggerwing hugging the tarmac, its candy apple red cowling hiding 450 horsepower of Pratt & Whitney radial muscle, shining in the midnight darkness, and grabbed tighter onto Mom's hand. No way was I going to lose out on this opportunity. Just the smell of the thing was intoxicating—a unique blend of grease, motor oil, and aviation fuel—a rugged scent. I've never smelled it since, even though I'm a pilot.

Lawrence Johnson put Mom's two suitcases in the baggage compartment in the tail section, a somber look on his face. I didn't know why we were leaving at night—perhaps to meet the connecting flight in Twin Falls—and darkness made the mystery of my airplane ride all the more intriguing.

Lawrence lifted me into the back seat and buckled my seat belt. He set Fuzz and Buzz, my two teddy bears, in beside me. Dad had named them. "What Fuzz does, Buzz does, and what Buzz does, Fuzz does."

I told Lawrence that Fuzz and Buzz needed seat belts, too.

So he fastened them under the belt as well.

Then he helped Mom step up and into the high front seat. And without saying a word Lawrence fastened his own seat belt and pushed some buttons and wrenched on some levers and clicked some switches. The massive eight cylinder engine popped and sputtered and the propeller began to roll, shaking the entire airframe. Lawrence Johnson removed his long billed cap just long enough to scratch his head, as though in bewilderment, then opened the door and threw out the stub of his cigar, then closed it up and eased in the throttle and taxied out onto the runway. In his grease-covered coveralls he looked more like a mechanic than a pilot, but he was one of the best. He regularly flew backpackers into the rugged Middle Fork region, swooping down into canyons to find narrow cliff-hewn landing strips. Pistol Creek. Wilson Bar. Mile High. Often he flew fishermen and hunters up into the Alaskan wilderness.

I waved at Dad and Nanna and O'You. I could still see them as the plane lifted off and began to float. It was the oddest feeling—the shaking and the sensation of speed was suddenly gone.

Dad was waving, still waving, as he and Nanna and O'You turned to tiny specks and disappeared, faded into darkness. The entire ground disappeared into a carpet of black—houses, trees, everything.

And as we flew on into the night, into the distance, floating, with Lawrence now and then reaching up and making adjustments to the controls, I was clueless that this trip might be anything other than an adventure. I was thinking I was the one in control, that I could have stayed in Hailey had I wanted to. All I wanted was an airplane ride. And a visit with my Texas grandparents.

Lawrence flew us to Twin Falls where more excitement awaited, a ride on a United Airlines DC-4—four engines, propellers bigger than cars, stewardesses waiting on us, meals, bathrooms. The Staggerwing was tiny in comparison. I even got to look in the cockpit. It made me want to do what they did, those men called pilots.

Dallas was the biggest place I had ever seen, and the hottest. The exhaust in the air upset my stomach and made me feel like throwing up. Uncle Tommy, star of Mom's childhood stories, picked us up in his convertible to drive us to San Antonio.

My Texas grandmother was sick. That's why we were there. Or so I thought. That was part of it, I'm sure. Our first stop was at the hospital. I don't remember much about it, except that the halls were long and gray and that my grandmother was very nice. But then Dad had already assured me that "she's a wonderfully special woman."

Across the street from the house in San Antonio was a park, expansive with lawn and trees. I was allowed to play there if I obeyed the rules— always look both ways before crossing the street, never go near water, never play with water moccasins, never speak to strangers…and never, never play with little boys with black skin. One was pointed out to me. "They carry knives," I was told.

Time is a thing immeasurable to a child that young. Its passage brought a dulling to my memories. The visage of my Idaho home was becoming a thing relegated to a place at the back of my mind, a thing among cobwebs. At night I found myself fending off sleep so I could think, so I could keep those memories alive. In my mind I would trace the image of Dad's face, the way he'd look sitting at his desk in the apartment, over by the bare brick wall. In front of him was a typewriter. Beside the typewriter was a cup filled with sharpened yellow pencils. Beside the cup was a can of Lucky Lager beer, its stiff masculine aroma drifting upward from two triangular openings. On the wall was a polished redwood cigarette pack holder he had made in the shop. It could hold an entire carton—pull out a pack, another falls into place. I'd run up and pounce on his lap and start pounding on the typewriter keys, clogging them all up in the middle. Dad would put his strong arm around me and say, "Hi guy—how's your copperosity sagaciating? " And then he'd unbunch the keys and take a drink of his Lucky Lager.

The apartment in Hailey was my jungle, my 2,000-square-foot make-believe jungle. It had three enormous rooms, a kitchen, a bedroom, and a bathroom. My bed was partitioned off from Mom and Dad's with curtains and a divider. Better than a separate bedroom, because I always knew they were there. I could hear them talking and laughing. I could hear them breathing if I was quiet enough. In the kitchen was a wood-burning cookstove encircled by a screen. I was never to touch it. That was the big rule there. Mom would cook on it and I'd sit in front of it and watch her.

I missed Petey, too—Lord Petey Ottertwitch II, with his regal feline walk, like he owned the place. I guess he did, kind of, between the boundaries of Carbonate and Bullion streets. Petey was king of all that walked, crawled, or slithered within those borders. Legally the records showed O'You as the owner of the whole block. But his house and manicured lawn sat on a small piece of it only. The rest was choked up with blackberries and aspens, and ruled over by a long haired tangled cat with broken off whiskers everyone knew belonged to the doctor. Or the doctor belonged to the cat, more appropriately.

And I missed driving Gertrude. I missed sitting on Dad's lap weaving all over the road. Gertrude was our pickup, me and Dad's. Named after Gertrude Stein. "A rose is a rose is a rose." I couldn't quite imagine anyone looking like Gertrude, especially a lady—bubble nosed hood with louvered sides that folded up, headlights that poked out like eyes, running boards, bright red all over.

Sometimes at night I would dream that Dad had come down to San Antonio and was sitting on my bed, just like he'd do at home—and my eyes would pop open, heart pounding, but he wouldn't be there. Nothing would be there, except the smell of unfamiliar furniture, of unfamiliar clothes, of stiff sheets and neatly pressed bedding—lonely, distant smells. When I'd play in the park I would imagine that I could hear him whistle for me. He had this way of whistling with two fingers that could be heard a mile away.

And then one day—there he was. Standing in front of me. Right there in the house. I was playing in the living room and turned around and there he was. Like magic. I was so stunned I didn't react. He probably thought I wasn't excited to see him. He was dressed strangely, like what he'd wear in church, the light brown tweed suit with the red bow tie.

I was sent across the street to the park to play. Memory is vague from that long ago, but I think I heard angry shouts as I walked away, people in the house arguing.

Time that morning passed VERY slowly. All I did was sit in the lawn of the park and pick at things, making sure—of course—that no water moccasins were there in between the blades of grass. No one ever bothered to tell me how big water moccasins were, or what they looked like. The warning was just, "Watch out for water moccasins—they can kill you." I even looked under the bed at night, and shook out the covers just to be safe.

I was hoping Dad had driven Gertrude down. We had good times in Gertrude, me and Dad, bouncing over bumps, hauling wood, driving up Greenhorn to look for agates, me sitting on his lap gripping that big black steering wheel. We were closest then, in Gertrude, because that was a time when I could ask him things. I could ask him anything. He always had the answer.

"Mmmm…Dad?"

Dad would bend his head forward.

"How tall is the tallest man in the world?"

"'Bout eight feet, I'd guess."

"Mmmm…Dad?"

"Yeah?"

"What's the biggest thing in the world?"

"The pyramids in Egypt."

"What's a pyramid?"

"A very large tombstone, to mark the grave of a great king."

"Mmm…Dad?"

"Yeah?"

"Who's the fastest man in the world?"

"Chuck Yaeger."

"Who's the slowest man in the world?"

"Del Panning—when he's working on Gertrude."

I never asked him who the smartest man in the world was—I figured that was Dad.

Suddenly there he was again. Walking toward me. The sight of the familiar walk—the straight back, the brisk strides—dissolved my melancholy mood.

Thrust through with joy, I leapt up to run to him, but hesitated when I saw him rumple the hair of a young colored boy and smile down at him.

And the colored boy started following him! Skipping after him!

"Dad!" I yelled. "Watch out. He gots a knife."

Dad ignored the warning and kept on walking. "Hi guy," he said, and scooped me up with one sweep of his giant arm, broad smile on his square jawed face. "—how's Little Workshop doing?" The world always seemed different when I was up high like that, a much safer place.

"Dad—," I insisted. "He gots a knife."

Dad put me down and kneeled in front of the colored boy. "That true, son?"

The boy acknowledged with a wide-eyed nod of his head.

"Can I see it?"

The boy pulled out a pocket knife. "I make things with it."

"Can you show me?"

The boy took from his hip pocket a hand carved whistle.

"Can you play it?"

The boy affirmed that he could.

"Let me see you. Play something for me."

The boy put it to his mouth and blew some simple tones, and tapped his foot to the rhythm.

"Good job. You keep that up son, pretty soon you'll be on stage alongside Furry Lewis." He gave him a quarter. "Go buy yourself some sweets."

"Thanks, mister!" said the boy. And off he loped.

All Dad said about it was, "You see that you always mind your mother and grandparents while you're down here. Hear?"

I assured him I would.

And soon we were home. All three of us. Home in Idaho. Where the sun comes over the mountain in a way that no other part of the world knows.

After that there were no more Lucky Lager cans, only empty cardboard cases in the basement by the coal bins.

Chapter 12

The Rocky Mountain Spotted Fever Epidemic

Squaw Tit Mountain

1914

I WAS ONE OF THOSE LITTLE KIDS that had to climb into bed with a running leap to avoid the reach of the monsters under the bed. It didn't get a whole lot better as I got older. The monsters just got smarter and found better places to hide, like in the corners of O'You's office basement where the light wouldn't reach, where they knew I had to venture at night to fill up those buckets of coal for O'You's furnace. Rickety wood stairs led down to the coal bins. An old circular light switch without a cover was mounted on the wall just inside the door, and it had to be turned carefully to avoid a shock. I'd always forget. I was always in such a hurry because of those unearthly things lurking behind me that I'd slam my hand on it and get zapped, though I never told a soul. A sixteen-year-old afraid of monsters? That was my secret!

I finally did confess to O'You one day, when I was old enough to find humor in it.

"Monsters do exist," he told me.

In 1914 the mountains and plains of Idaho were full of monsters. And they killed. If you brushed up against a piece of sagebrush one would be on your clothes. Barely bigger than the head of a pin, it would crawl around unnoticed for hours, first on clothing, then on bare skin, searching for a place to bore its head, preferably in the warmth of a body cavity. Then, when gorged and puffed with blood, it would drop off to lay eggs, and leave behind an evil, the Rocky Mountain Spotted Fever microbe.

There had been little measurable rain that spring, and the air was hot enough to breed ticks at an alarming rate. Spotted fever was epidemic among the sheepherders of the lower valley. Once proud and strong, able to snag a hawk out of midair with their long bolos, they now lay bedridden, herds wandering unattended. It was the most unusual April Bob had ever seen—hot, dry, and wet all at the same time. The snow melt was turning the roads into rivers and mud holes. He couldn't risk taking the Studebaker, or even a buggy. A single horse was the only way to ensure arrival.

He was holding his mount at a slow gallop, sitting loose in the saddle, yet with a firm grip, rolling with the rhythm of the horse so it wouldn't have to work as hard. Still, sweat was heavy upon the hair of its neck. Splotches of mud flew up to spatter Bob's new blue suit, one hitting him in the face.

He was coming up on Squaw Tit Mountain. It was more of a hill than a mountain, a brown bump peppered with the deadly bluish green of the sagebrush. It was used as a reference point, a lookout where someone would meet the doctor and give directions to the camps of the sick. First Bob had to cross a road washout, an overflow from a nearby creek. Water and mud were knee high to the horse.

A man was waiting on the other side, in a turnout in the road. He sat atop a buckskin mare, its tail flipping away flies, and leaned forward on the saddle horn to peer into the hot sun at the rider crossing the washout, wondering if it could be Dr. Wright. The man had expected to see an automobile, and had expected to hear the power of an internal combustion engine. Bob's last trip was in the Studebaker, but he bogged in up to the axles and Joe Uberuaga had to pull him out with a team.

The man on the buckskin mare was of rugged stature. He wore a heavy shirt open in front that was stuffed into a pair of denims held up by suspenders. A red beret with a stem on top was cocked to one side. At first the man thought the rider coming toward him couldn't be Dr. Wright. The rider was too good, too smooth. Then he noticed the white hat. No one but Dr. Wright had a hat like that, and he thought he saw a little yellow flower in the rider's lapel, and black medical bags bouncing on the back of the saddle.

"Aaaahhhlo Doctor Wright, Mister," yelled the man, arcing a wide wave. The man's handsome European face, stubbled with two days of a beard, turned a smile, and there seemed to be hope in his deep and thoughtful eyes. He vaulted off the saddle and ran toward Bob, a large knife riding heavy upon his hip. He would have seemed threatening, had Bob not known who he was. He was Father Bernardo Arregui, a Basque priest sent from Spain by the Bishop of Vittoria at the request of the Boise Diocese to minister to the isolated and lonely herders. The intimidating knife was only for cutting firewood and draining snakebites.

Bob dismounted and greeted Father Arregui with a loud voice, and shook his hand and slapped his shoulder. "Own-gee e-tor-ee," Bob said. "Se-lawn saw-ghos." That was about the extent of Bob's command of the Basque language. It meant, "Hello, how are you."

Father Arregui, though he struggled, was able to converse in English, unlike his Basque counterparts. The vast majority of the herders spoke only their native language, and, ironically, had never herded sheep before their arrival in America. In the early history of their ancestry raising sheep and goats was common, during the fifteenth and sixteenth century, as it was for many of the Europeans, particularly in the mountains of Spain, France, and Austria. But at the time of their migration to America their livelihood came from far different efforts. Most were coastal fishermen. They wound up as sheepherders in America because those were the only jobs available where language presented no barrier. In Spain they were very social people. Their lives were filled with celebrations and dancing. Then, in the early 1800s, upon fleeing the hated Spanish oppression and the revival of the Inquisition, they suddenly found themselves in the isolated Idaho and Nevada mountains doing something completely unfamiliar to them, in the midst of unfamiliar people whose only response to their attempts at socialization was to make fun of them as they tripped over words and phrases. One poor fellow, determined to learn English, came in out of the mountains and began to eat at a particular restaurant, figuring he could pick up at least enough words to learn the basics with which to carry on a conversation. He gave up after several weeks, hopelessly confused. He learned later he was eating at a Chinese restaurant.

At first the men came to America by themselves, young men mostly, sending for wives and sweethearts later after saving enough money. They worked hard and learned the craft well. They were frugal and resourceful. One herder brought twenty-five hundred head through the winter on only fifty dollars, all of them fat and healthy. He'd grazed them at night on the grassy lands of the Idaho State Penitentiary.

Father Arregui said, "—she's not so good. Very hot. Very hot." He was referring to the two-year-old Erquiaga girl, on the other side of the mountain, where the family was camped by the spring.

"All right, Father. We'll go there first. Are there any others?"

"I am yes, afraid so. The two Echevarria brothers, also by the spring. They feel not so good also. Felipe Arriola, down-a-ways by Shoshone. He either."

Spotted Fever begins with lethargy, a lack of energy. At first the victim feels like something psychological is happening, like one is being overcome by laziness. There is at first no corresponding physical symptom, only the draining of energy, very disturbing to a man such as a Basque, a man steeped in the pride of the work ethic. Soon it becomes obvious that something real is happening, something frightening. The victim is struck with a sudden and severe headache, then chills, then muscle aches and high fever. An unproductive, harassing cough develops. On about the fourth day of the fever a rash appears, spotted and raised, first on the wrists and ankles, then spreading rapidly to the rest of the body. At first the rash is pink. Later the spots become darkened and ulcerated, sometimes running together. The fever escalates, rising to as high as 104 degrees, sometimes higher. There are spells of delirium, as the microbe migrates deeper into brain tissue. Right before death the victim seems to make a turnaround. Hope is given, just before the loved one is taken, for some cruel reason. As with scarlet fever and diphtheria, hope is given, just before death.

Bob traveled the valley almost daily in the tick-ripe summer seasons, sponging Spotted Fever patients, giving cool baths of alcohol compresses, building their bodies with whiskey treatments, building their attitudes with reassuring conversation. Sometimes he wondered if he did any good at all. The disease progressed and there was no cure, only the comfort of his presence until it either killed or passed on its own. He had medicines to relieve the pain, he had ointments to sooth the itch. Maybe the spongings and the whiskey treatments did some good. He needed to believe that. Common medical belief was that the whiskey, augmented with a strong diet, would stimulate the body to function more effectively, thereby creating its own battleground to fight the invaders. And maybe the belief the patient had in Bob's ability to heal, the confidence he brought, maybe that helped as well.

Bob and Father Arregui watered the horses in the creek and mounted up for the ride around the mountain, being careful to stay within the roads and trails, avoiding contact with the sagebrush, until the mountainside transformed. Dusty sagebrush turned into cottonwoods and tall grass. Sheltered within this oasis of green was a crystal clear spring the size of a small lake.

On one side of the spring was a narrow canvas-covered wagon with a stove pipe sticking out. Four black horses grazed in the grass, strong animals, obviously well cared for. Inside the living quarters, crowded but neat, was a wooden crib against one wall, carved in loving detail by the child's father, who sat in a chair ten feet away, exhausted, relieved. The mother stood before the crib with the child in her arms. A smile of joy was transfixed on her face and her cheeks were wet with happiness, for her 20-month-old baby, only moments ago near death, was giggling.

The mother was hugging the child, then looking at her, hugging her again, tipping her upside down to hear her laugh.

She spoke something in Basque to Bob and Father Arregui.

"She say it is a miracle," translated Father Arregui. "She say God has answered her prayers." He crossed his heart in thanks. "I must be going."

Bob reached out and grabbed his arm. "No. Father. Don't. Stay." He had seen something that only he understood. The lesions were open and bleeding. And they were purple. Usually it happens in the morning, the sudden upturn, right after the spots turn purple, then the patient dies. It happened a week ago with a baby down by Shoshone, a two-month-old infant, just old enough to smile.

An agonizing dilemma. It was a thing he troubled over every time he faced it. Should he allow the parents the cruelty of their hope? Or should he be truthful? He chose the lie, the lie that is spoken without speaking. He did not have the courage to handle it in any other way.

He asked Father Arregui to do something for him. "Go send word to Doctor Fox. Tell him to come to the Squaw Tit turnout. Meet him there, and direct him to the other cases." That way Bob could keep vigil on the child. "Then I need for you to return here. It's quite important. And pray, Father. Pray for the child."

The confused priest left, and when he re-entered the wagon two hours later he walked into a different situation. Instead of laughing and giggling, the child was lying in the crib crying, covered with sweat. It was a weak cry, coming between short gasps for breath. Within each bleeding sore was the pain of a deep itch, one that goes far below the skin. Every once in a while the child would gather the strength to respond to it and kick and roll and thrash about. What was going on within the innocence of her little mind one can only suppose. Sometimes she'd sleep a little, but even that wasn't much relief. It probably was a sleep threaded with dreams of nonsensical shapes and images mirroring her agony. Bob was sponging her with the coolness of alcohol, and feeding her with spoonfuls of soup. The mother would also take the child to her breast for feeding. The mother was still full with milk, even twenty months after giving birth. But the helpless father, all he could do was sit in the chair and stare ahead at nothing at all.

"I want you to speak to the child," said Bob to Father Arregui. "I want you to translate everything I say, as I say it."

"Yes," agreed Father Arregui, nodding.

"What is her name?"

"Her name is Juanita."

Bob spoke softly, tenderly. "Hello, Juanita. I'm the doctor. Sweet child. Do you know what a doctor is? A doctor is a man who is going to make you better, make the hurting go away."

Bob stopped and let Father Arregui translate.

"I'm going to stay here with you, as long as it takes. All right?"

After the translation the child nodded her head yes.

Bob was surprised, and pleased, that a child so young and in so much pain could understand. He took her temperature again. 105 degrees. He sponged some more. "Yes, my sweet thing. Yes. That feels good. I'm going to stay here until you feel well again, as long as it takes. And you've got to help me. You've got to want to feel better. Do you understand?"

Again the child nodded, after the translation.

Then he fed her a few more spoonfuls of soup, mutton soup, then a slight dab of whiskey sweetened with honey, to stimulate the expended organs, and handed her again to her mother, who took her willingly, with no fear of the open sores, cherishing her to her breast as though the child was melting into her. "Good, sweetie, real good," spoke Bob softly. "You keep eating. That's good. Build your body. Keep the fever down and build your body. Let the strength of your body be the cure."

The ordeal continued into the night. About midnight convulsions began, horrible twitchings of the face and limbs, with the eyelids half open and the eyeballs rolled back to show only the whites. Still he continued talking, and Father Arregui continued translating. The child's face was an awful color, a type of bluish white.

After a couple of minutes the twitching stopped, and hope came to everyone, including Bob. "You've got to want to feel better. You've got to keep hearing me. You've got to keep wanting to stay with me. OK?"

Again the child nodded after the translation. He gave more soup.

But the violent muscular contractions began again, worse than before, and continued longer than before.

Again and again the convulsions came and went. Then—diarrhea set in, and with no way to absorb nourishment, the child visibly withered before his eyes, in a matter of hours.

Still Bob talked to her, gently, exhausted though he was.

By mid afternoon of the next day the convulsions had lessened, but her breathing was in labored gasps, head turned to the side into her pillow, eyes unfixed, and at 106 her temperature was nearing the top of the thermometer. She should have been burning up, but her limbs were suddenly cold.

Her little arms and legs quivered, then stiffened out as if hit by a tiny jolt of electricity, then relaxed.

Circulatory failure, just like last week with the infant down by Shoshone.

Bob closed his eyes bitterly, trying to pinch off the tears that escaped just the same and ran silently down his cheeks.

The mother was shrieking, babbling unintelligible words.

It was an unusual reaction. Typically, by the time death came, the mother had accepted the fate destiny had pronounced, and watched the passing in silence.

Bob opened his eyes and saw a medical impossibility. The child was sleeping.

The mother's shrieks were ones of joy.

"It is a miracle," Father Arregui was saying over and over, first in Basque, then in English.

Indeed it was.

The cooling of the limbs had not been the rush of death. It had been the breaking of the fever.

The diarrhea had eased. Nourishment could now be retained.

"Take her to your breast; let her feed as she sleeps," said Bob.

He walked outside, away from the wagon in slow unsteady strides, and stopped, hands in his pockets, jacket slung between his arm and side, shirt disheveled and open halfway down his chest, and stood awhile, then tipped his hat back and looked over his shoulder at the wagon wherein a dream had been reborn. That simple wagon with its wheels made of wood discs and its black stovepipe sticking out of stretched canvas roofing was once again an image of hope, comfort, security to a young family. By the laws of everything physical, all that was logical, it should not have been so.

He should be feeling victory. At the very least he should be feeling relief. Instead, Bob was wondering if he would ever again be able to endure such an ordeal, or if he would be able to even see a patient again, or take another step. Funny how the beauty of a day can sometimes torment a man. The green grass of the meadow, the wagon in its midst, the horses grazing and the honeybees buzzing about, the deep blue skies, the butterflies, the glass-clear pools of the spring, the smell of nourished ground—it simply deepened his emptiness. And he didn't know why. Maybe it was because it reminded him of how precariously our lives are lived, of how close we all are to disaster by the very nature of existence. Or maybe because of the Onederra baby. Where was the miracle there? Why here, and not there?

He had no way of knowing at the time, but the tragedy of the Onederra baby would, in a sense, be transformed as well. Six months after the child's death, sometime in October, the Onederras traveled into town for a portrait sitting. When they returned to pick up the photographs, the photographer apologized and told them the pictures would have to be retaken. Smudges had shown up on the negatives. So a new appointment was made and the photos were shot again, successfully this time. The photographer, instead of destroying the flawed negatives, developed them all. "No charge for the bad ones," he said. On closer look, one of the smudges was not a smudge at all. It was the face of the dead child. A bit cloudy. Somewhat translucent. But unmistakable. The other smudges were also faces, faces of loved ones who had passed on earlier. Lula Fuld was so affected by the story and the photo that she asked that a copy be made for her. She kept it long after the Onederras moved away and showed it to everyone who came to visit. She kept it until the day she died half a century later.

"Bobbbbb—" came a shout from the road in back of him, though Bob didn't hear. It was Dr. Fox on horseback, white shirt soaked in sweat and sleeves rolled two turns to the middle of his forearms. He had on suspenders and wore a black cowboy hat, looking half like a bank teller, half like a highwayman.

"Bobbbbbbbbb—" came the shout again. Dr. Fox and his horse were ten feet away, and still Bob didn't hear, so lost was he in his thoughts.

Dr. Fox whistled to get his attention.

Bob spun around, startled. "Earl. How are you? Thanks for coming." Bob nodded toward the wagon. "The Erquiaga child pulled through." He didn't have the strength to explain further.

Dr. Fox dismounted and strode toward Bob, trailing his horse behind him. "I was just over the way there attending to the Echevarrias." A curl of smoke was spiraling up from a grove of trees on the other side of the spring. "I think they're going to make it. Felipe Arriola, though, down by Shoshone, I'm not so sure about him. He's in a bad way. I had to take him up to Hailey to stay with Usebio."

"Water and rest your animal," said Bob. "Take a breather. Then we'll have a final look around, check on the Echevarria brothers, see how some of the other folks are doing. Dott must be worried. I need to get word to her."

"No need to," said Dr. Fox. "I passed Joe Uberuaga on the way over. He told me he telephoned her. He told her you were still down here." Neighbors were that way. They'd see him passing by, or notice his car or horse somewhere and they'd ring up Dott to tell her. Sometimes she would have messages to pass on to him, emergency calls, thereby saving him precious time.

The water in the spring was so clear you could count the spots on the fish lazily angling back and forth. "Should have brought my pole," commented Bob, sitting back against a thick clump of aspen seedlings. He was sitting with both hands down at his sides on the ground, hat in his lap, in a way that seemed to show both exhaustion and victory.

"Mmmm," echoed Dr. Fox mindlessly, like he was experiencing the same exhaustion.

"It's been a difficult few days, Earl."

"Go home and get some rest," said Dr. Fox. "I'll take care of things down here."

"You know, Earl, you'd think they'd be able to come up with a cure. Some kind of a vaccine. Lord knows, they're inventing and discovering everything else under the sun. They've even done successful heart surgery. On a dog. Operated on the damn thing as the heart was beating in its chest.

"Hadn't heard that one," said Fox. Fox was suddenly half asleep, leaning also against the seedlings.

"And nobody cares about a bunch of sheepherders in Idaho who don't speak English," continued Bob. "Everybody is too worried about killing each other a half a world away. They're calling it war, Earl, a world war. Japan is fighting Germany. Austria is fighting Serbia. England and France are fighting Germany. Earl, I tell you, the world is nuts. Thank God for Wilson. He's maintaining neutrality. He'll keep us out of it. Hope he does anyway. We gotta stay outa that war. People killing people, as if nature doesn't do a good enough job. With all that's goin' on in the world, nobody gives a damn about a few hundred sheepherders."

Fox was twirling a long piece of grass in his mouth, his hat tipped over his eyes. "I've got this friend," he said. "This professor I had back at school. He's doing research on infectious diseases. What say you and I gather up some of these ticks and ship them back to him."

The ticks were sent, along with impassioned letters from Bob and Dr. Fox describing the scenes of the epidemic. The professor was responsive. He wrote back saying that these were the most poisonous ticks he'd ever put under a microscope. He promised his best efforts in the matter. A Spotted Fever vaccine was developed, three years later in 1917.

At about the same time, in April 1917, President Wilson declared war on Germany in a special session of Congress, after the sinking of the *Lusitania*. And Dr. Fox would enlist in the army to be sent overseas.

Bob would be named a medical examiner by the federal government, with duties including giving physicals to the boys entering the service.

But that was the future. For now, in the purity and the timelessness of the moment, no problems existed. The emptiness had changed itself from a thing of misery to a thing of nothing at all. There existed only the warmth of the sun on his face and chest. A dragonfly was flickering here and there over the surface of the water. Darning Needles, Old John Hailey used to call them, back when Bob was a boy. Tell a lie and they'll sew your mouth shut. Bob's only thoughts were lazy and pleasant ones, memories of the simple things that make life so special. Like the time he came home after a long trip to Muldoon and found Dott in a tizzy over the behavior of "*Your son*." Glenn was always "*Your son*" when getting himself into mischief. "Would you like to know what *your son* has been up to?" she asked, arms folded, foot tapping. Bob even remembered what she was wearing, a long white dress and a floor length white apron, because the color contrasted so perfectly with the red in her face and hair. "He off and paid a visit to Dot Allen's Place."

Bob's reaction was to bite his lip and choke off laughter. That angered Dott all the more. Glenn and his pal Art Ensign had indeed visited the famed Madam, on a dare from some of the older boys.

After hiding in the bushes nearby, Glenn finally worked up the courage to approach the door. He put his little fist up, hesitated, then gave a rap.

Within seconds Dot Allen opened the door. "Well Heaven's sake," she said, placing her hands on her knees and bending over. "And what is your name, child?"

"Glenn Wright," responded the red-haired freckled-faced youngster, in complete innocence.

Dot Allen's girlish smile widened the full width of her face. "Doctor Wright's little boy?"

"Yes, ma'am," said Glenn, blushing.

She looked at Art. "And who might this fella be?"

"Arthur Ensign, ma'am."

"Well, Arthur Ensign. To what do I owe the pleasure of your visit this fine day?"

Art shrugged.

Dot Allen looked at Glenn. "Hmmmmm?"

Glenn shrugged.

"Tell you what. You children go around back. I've got some cookies coming out of the oven."

Dot Allen closed the door slowly, with both hands, smiling through the opening as her face disappeared behind it, looking more like a mother than a prostitute, except for the dark silken dress and the big blue and white bow tied into her jet black hair, like she had just let her hair down for the evening, in a two-hundred-dollar nightgown.

The cookies were moist and delicious. Gingersnaps and drop cakes. Along with fresh, cold milk.

Imagine the surprise of the older boys as they peered through the kitchen window of southern Idaho's most famous bordello to see Glenn and Art munching cookies in its sun-washed kitchen at a table looking just like mom's, next to a cast iron range looking exactly like the one in mom's kitchen, and being waited on by a woman acting just like mom.

Next thing Dot Allen knew, she was answering the back door to a dozen more boys, sitting them all down to milk and gingersnaps. Even though the houses of the prostitutes were isolated among themselves, somehow the news spread, whisper by whisper, like a raging fire. Soon telephones were ringing and mothers were running to gather up and paddle their wayward children.

Bob brought Glenn into the drawing room and sat him on his lap, thinking of what he should say, of how exactly he should admonish his son. Nothing was coming to mind. Finally he said, "—no more cookies at Dot Allen's. OK?"

"But why, Dad?"

"For two reasons. It's not a safe place. Men get into fights down there. Sometimes they get into really bad fights. The other reason is one that you can't be expected to fully understand until you're much older. But suffice it to say that some men tend to spend time with the ladies there when they should be home with their families…"

"Like they should be having their cookies at home?"

"Something like that, son. Something like that."

Bob smiled wide at the memory, almost laughed aloud. He was drifting closer to sleep, with the warmth of the sun of his neck and chest. The muttering of the dragonfly was the only sound, and the only other movement was the gentle wind in the grass and a robin redbreast poking about. A yellow crocus was budding next to him, a tiny petal no bigger than a thimble. He plucked it up and tucked it into the lapel buttonhole of his suit jacket, which, though rumpled with dirt and sweat, he had carefully folded and placed beside him. Yep, springtime. You could always tell it was spring, folks said, because of the crocus in Doc Wright's lapel. He took the old flower, weathered and brown, dead, and set it on a fallen leaf, carefully, with respect. It was gone when he awoke. Probably the robin redbreast had taken it for its nest.

He slept for two and a half hours, a good sleep, and awoke vitalized. Amazing, that a simple afternoon nap can fill one with so much energy. No ticks on that side of the mountain, thankfully. Just the same he'd have Dott check him over carefully that night.

It was deep twilight when he got home. The sun was gone, remaining only as a purple glow ringing the ridges of Della and Carbonate. All else was black, save for the light of a few dozen stars. Soon there would be so many stars the sky would be a hazy mist.

Jean was asleep on the couch. She was covered by a pink and yellow hand-made quilt that draped far beyond the length of her body. She jerked with the sound of his entrance but didn't wake up. The air was still warm. An open window channeled its gentleness to brush up against her freckled cheek. Ol' Jake was curled up on the sofa's other end; he opened one eye and flopped his tail.

Jake, with Doc and Glenn, about 1915.

"She insisted on waiting up for you," said Dott. "When we got word you were on your way she said she wouldn't go to sleep until her Daddy danced her off to bed."

Bob handed his hat to Dott and went over and dropped to one knee by the sofa, and stroked Jean's hair, that beautiful blondish-red hair. "Hey, little Princess—"

Jean smacked her lips like she was dreaming and rolled to her other side, and drew up the quilt tight under her chin, and stuck her finger in her mouth. Always her right forefinger, never her thumb.

"Hey, sweet pretty Princess, I need my dancing partner."

Jean knew he was there, though her eyes didn't open. She murmured her satisfaction. "mmhh-HUH." It came with finality in her voice, like she knew all along he'd come.

"Shall we dance to bed?"

"mm-HUH."

"If you please, Maestro—"

Dott played it out softly, "Tales of Vienna Woods," and Bob twirled with his pretty princess asleep on his shoulder, asleep but aware, contentment on her face, finger in her mouth, quilt tucked around her.

She knew he'd come.

He always did.

He always would.

Chapter 13

Indians

Hailey, Idaho

1956

T HE SUN HAD JUST COME OVER THE MOUNTAIN, and the chilled air was beginning to fill with heat. Rich with overnight dew, the air continued to hold the smell of pollen, of minty grass and leaves, of moist soil. But the sun's heat would grow, and the blistering odor of sagebrush would soon overtake the day. And the hummingbirds would begin whirring about in Nanna's flower garden. But there was no time to help Nanna with her weeding. I was doing stuff with Dad. We were planting grass.

O'You had subdivided his land and had quit claimed the piece across the alley to us. We now had a house right next to O'You's. When finished it would be a landscape pictorial that would take up three entire pages in *Better Homes and Gardens*, having about it the same smoothed-out ruggedness that gave the Workshop its appeal. People from as far away as Twin Falls and Pocatello would drive by and admire our creations: the thatched log fences encircling the sandstone walkways, the oil drums converted into barbeque barrels, the bamboo curtains that enclosed the multi-colored brick patio deck, the vividness of the flower gardens, the carpet-smooth lawn sections. I was sitting on a long wooden ladder, anchoring it while Dad pulled it over the turned up soil with a rope harnessed around his waist, like a plow mule, the sinewy muscles of his bare chest beading up in little balls of sweat. It made the bare soil so flawlessly level it looked clean, if dirt could ever look clean, like something you wanted to roll in, ready for its seed. We took a break, and Dad popped off the top of a glass bottle, put it to his lips, and let the sparkling amber liquid gurgle down his throat.

He ran the back of his wrist across his mouth and offered the bottle to me.

I hesitated.

"Go on, it's OK."

I held it in my hands. It was cold. I placed its opening to my lips and tipped my head back, like Dad had done. The cold fizzed its way into my mouth, and a sharp, gripping taste ran down my throat and into my stomach, forcing it to jerk with a belch.

Dad smiled. "Pretty good, huh?

"What is it?"

"It's called Coca Cola."

"Dad—did the Indians drink Cola Cola?" Dad had just taken me to see *The Searchers*, John Wayne at his best fighting war-whooping Comanches, and Indians were on my mind.

"They probably do. Lots of people drink it."

"You mean there are Indians around today?"

"Of course. One of my best friends is an Indian."

He never told me that before. "Can we go see him?" I was stunned. And fascinated. And a little scared.

"It's a ways away. He lives down in Pocatello at Fort Hall. We can't do it today. Work to do today."

I pleaded, and Dad wiped the sweat off his brow and went inside and made a long distance phone call to Pocatello and some man named Edward. Dad didn't say much to Edward. He never did talk much when it was long distance. Too expensive. But after he hung up he looked at me with that square-jawed smile of his, a look he'd get whenever he was about to say something that would please me, and said, "We'll go down next weekend. On Saturday. They're having a Pow Wow down on the reservation on Saturday. And you and I are invited." He took another big drink of his Coca Cola, but left the last of it for me.

I barely slept for the next four nights. I asked every day if it was Saturday yet. When it finally rolled around I was up early, right alongside Dad. Dad always got up before the sun. He fixed us eggs and flapjacks, and coffee for him and hot chocolate for me, and we were off. A solitary thrush sang to us as we eased Gertrude out onto the road, windows rolled down so we could feel the morning air whipping in at us. Gertrude was as bright and as spiffy as ever. I'd polished her oval Ford emblem myself. "A rose is a rose is a rose."

Dad pointed to a sign after we'd been driving for a couple of hours. "Bannock-Shoshone Indian Reservation," it said. I was confused. Nothing was different. All I saw was a gas station and some houses, same as in Hailey, and a trailer park, and stores, the same kinds of stores as in Hailey. No teepees. No Indians. We pulled up in front of a building that looked like it was a part of a school. Dozens of cars were in the parking lot. Cars? No horses? Dad walked up to a man and heartily shook his hand, the way Dad and his friends always shook hands, like it was some kind of a contest to see who could shake the hardest. "Shake Mr. Edmo's hand, son," he said to me. "And remember to look him in the eye when you do it."

"Hello young man," said Edward Edmo, as I held my hand out for the big man to grab. He enclosed it completely within his huge paw. "Your granddaddy gave me my first spanking." Apparently half the people born in southern Idaho got their first spanking at birth from O'You.

This man didn't look anything like an Indian. I'd been duped. Mr. Edmo's skin wasn't red, like the Indians in the movies. A browner shade, maybe, but not red. He didn't look any different than Dad. If anything, it was Dad's skin that was red; he had a sunburn. And the dancers in the gymnasium lined up and waiting to perform had wrist watches and pants underneath their costumes, and regular shoes. Like they were playing dress up.

Then something happened that defined these people in a way that went beyond the clothes they wore or the houses in which they lived. When we went to take our seats we accidentally sat in a space in front where there was a sign we didn't notice. *Reserved for Elders.* When Dad saw it, he read it to me and explained that we had to move, that the Indians had these seats set aside for elders.

"What are elders?" I asked him.

"Indians have this enormous respect for old people," he told me. "They call them elders. Instead of making fun of old people," he said, "and making jokes about them, and mimicking the way they talk and drawing cartoon caricatures of them, Indians revere them."

"What does revere mean?" I asked.

"Well, put it this way. The elderly have paved the way for us. They've loved us, and they've protected us, and made the world a better and safer place for us, and for that they deserve to be treated a whole lot better than they are. They deserve to be treated like the Indians treat them, with honor and respect. They deserve to be revered."

And as if to underscore the explanation, after we found our new seats up in the bleachers, the young man at the microphone announced that one of the elders would be speaking, and walked down to where she was sitting in her wheelchair, and with loving patience rolled her up onto the stage, and unscrewed the microphone and lowered it to her level. She was fragile, but was smiling with the power of an inward strength, and though her voice was cracked, and though the lips that formed the words she spoke were misshapen by the advance of time, the people were listening. Not just out of polite boredom, but truly listening. Instead of letting the image qualify the substance, the people in the audience were allowing the substance to form the image. Even the children up in the bleachers were quiet. You could have heard a feather fall.

And as she spoke Lawnmower Moe came unwelcome into my mind, probably because of that thing Dad had said about old people—Lawn-mower Moe was old—and probably because of something the old lady in the wheelchair said, quoting a famous Indian woman, something about how if you make fun of people you become lower than they are. We always made fun of Lawnmower Moe. Dumbo, Fatso, Retard, any name we could think of we would sling at him. And the aging simple-ton, with forearms as big as railroad ties, would come running after us in flat-footed thumps of thunder that we would easily outrun. It was like a dog swimming after ducks on the wing. I often wondered what he would have done if he had caught any of us. Sometimes I wondered what Moe did for fun, especially at night, with no TV, and with no one to talk to—he couldn't read, most likely—he just lived this lonely and tormented life, dragging that clattering rusty push mower from job to job. A couple of days earlier we hid up on a hill, out of sight, on a gigantic mound of gravel at an excavation site overlooking Lawnmower Moe's place and threw rocks down on his house. This time it was even more fun. This time Moe didn't get mad; he got scared. He couldn't see us. He came out and looked around, and looked up, and ducked as the rocks flew by, and pleaded with whoever it was to stop. It was like he thought it was some kind of wrath from heaven. Truth of it, none of the rocks were thrown by me, but neither did I do anything to stop it. And I laughed right along with them.

I never told Dad about it. He would have taken me over to apologize to Moe, and make me mow *his* lawn. Worse, he would have been ashamed of me, because he thought of me as better than that. I was ashamed of myself. I'm ashamed still, fifty years later. I'd go back today and fix it, if I could. But of course Moe is gone now, passed on into what surely must be a better place.

And so it was that I learned a little bit about Indians, and about myself.

I also found out that O'You delivered half the Native American population of Idaho—well, maybe not half, but a good share of them. "Your granddaddy has an attic full of Indian artifacts," Dad told me on the way home, "from back when he used to tend to their medical needs."

Chapter 14

Rosie Tincup

Hailey, Idaho

1916

THE SEASONS OF SOUTHERN IDAHO ARE DISTINCT. Come the first of September the leaves begin to turn and blow in the air. Golds and reds and purples whirl and spin like tiny treasures. One day it's summer, the next day it's fall. It's that dramatic, like the opening of a door. The sun in fall is just as bright as it is in the summertime. It just doesn't bring the heat anymore. And there is a different smell to things, as the earth is about the process of cleansing itself.

It's a time when the Indians migrate, traveling with all their belongings to the inter-tribal Pow-Wows of Montana. It's a time when the salmon are returning to their birthplaces. It's a time when the great V's of the Canadian Geese can be seen overhead.

As Bob and Dott approached their home, the door was ajar. "Didn't you shut it?" asked Dott.

"I did," said Bob. "I absolutely did." Bob opened it the rest of the way and peered his head inside. It didn't seem logical that a thief would have entered. It was two in the afternoon, in the midst of a day's business activity, and their house was on Main Street. Besides, there was no way Ol' Jake would let anybody in.

An odd sound came from within—whump, whump, whump—something they'd never heard before.

"Wait here," Bob said. Dott gathered Glenn and Jean away from the door.

Moments later she heard Bob's loud voice greeting someone, then many voices. Dott walked inside, cautiously moving forward with the children behind her, and saw nothing.

The boisterous voices grew louder. They were coming from the kitchen.

She pushed open the swinging kitchen door and saw four Indians sitting cross-legged on the floor, laughing and smiling and pointing to Rosie Tincup. Rosie was eating sugar cubes and Bob was kneeling beside her listening to her bulging stomach with his stethoscope.

"You've got a healthy baby in there, Rosie," Bob said.

Rosie would munch three or four sugar cubes then give a slight grimace of pain with a contraction. At first the expressions were imperceptible, she hid them so well. Or maybe she wasn't hiding them; maybe the birth process just came easy to her. This would be her seventh. She and her husband Red Crow were hoping for a boy. Red Crow was sitting beside her smoking a pipe, calmly, proudly. He looked as much like a local farmer as he did an Indian. Trousers and riding boots, beaded breastplate. Flat brimmed black hat, braided black hair. Halfway between two worlds, halfway between two cultures.

Sitting beside Red Crow was Ol' Jake, whopping his tail on the floor—whump, whump, whump—every time Red Crow would pat him on the head.

The European custom of knocking was one with which the Indians were unfamiliar. For an Indian to wait outside a friend's door would be much the same as a wife waiting for an invitation from her husband to enter. It would be silly. Sometimes Indians would walk in on Dott while she was in the kitchen baking. She would give them a loaf of bread, or a pie, and they would give something to her. Over the years she and Bob collected boxes full of mementos: beaded moccasins, polished stones, jewelry, belts, blankets.

Rosie Tincup had on a long blue and red pullover, of a heavy weave from sheep's wool. Underneath it was a long, ankle-length skirt. Her neck was draped with multitudes of beads, long hoops of them. Banded around her forehead was a dark blue cloth, nearly the color of the coal black hair that washed down her back and the sides of her neck. Her thickly featured face was pleasant to look at. Pretty, some might say.

She gave birth right there on the kitchen floor. Her contractions were so advanced that Dott barely had time to boil water. Bob and Dott were but observers in the process, so smooth was the baby's emergence. Rosie squatted on the floor holding the hands of an older woman kneeling in front of her, one Bob guessed was her grandmother, and with a single tiny squeal at the final and heaviest contraction, brought forth her baby boy.

Glenn and Jean were kept occupied in a corner of the kitchen by a young woman who told them tales of Indian life and adventure. She had the most gentle smile, and was dressed in soft deerskin with trimmings of turquoise and tassels of white.

Dott was grateful. "What is your name?" she asked.

The young woman looked shyly to the floor, then lifted her eyes and said, "Jenny-with-the-Beautiful-Voice."

Red Crow paid for the delivery with an exquisite pair of handmade deerskin gloves and the head of a war club, chiseled from stone and carved with a ring of stars and crescent moons.

And the new life, innocent, pure, went off with his family into a polarized world of extremes, a world of brilliance, a world of madness. A world struggling to save itself, a world struggling to destroy itself.

It was a world where new discoveries continued to astonish the medical community. The mystery of heredity was being uncovered. Heparin had been discovered, an anticoagulant produced by the liver. And a process for storing blood had been introduced, spawning an idea for blood banks.

Yet it was a world upside down. The whole of Europe was aflame. Hundreds of thousands of soldiers lost their lives on one battlefield alone, at the Somme, where the scarred land held seven thousand corpses to the square mile. Both sides lost an entire generation. Neither side gained a thing militarily. Soon the United States would be involved. It was inevitable. President Wilson had as much as said so. He had given Germany an ultimatum: stop sinking unarmed ships or face consequences.

Henry Ford produced his one millionth automobile. And a physicist named Albert Einstein laid claim to a theory more fantastic than logic, that time and energy are related to the speed of light.

A world of brilliance. A world of madness. Advancing on both fronts.

Chapter 15

The Seagull
Hailey, Idaho
1958

CHUCK ENSIGN AND I FOUND an injured seagull once and took it to O'You. O'You could fix anything, like when he sat me down in a kitchen chair and stitched up my upper lip after I'd split it playing baseball. I barely have a scar. The bird's right leg had been severed and was dangling by a piece of skin. O'You went inside and came back out with his bag and a pair of cuticle scissors. "The only thing that can be done is to cut it off," he explained, and carefully snipped it away and covered it with disinfectant. "He may not live. The shock to his system may be too great. You should know, too, that birds use their feet like airplane rudders, to steer and turn with. Even if he does survive, chances are he won't ever fly again."

I sensed a distant tone to O'You's words. "You mad at me?" I asked. I was thinking he might have been annoyed at the silliness of me worrying about a seagull.

"No—son—" said the tall and stately old man who looked more dignified than he did old. His hair was still black, but ringed with a crest of silver. "I'm just reminded of something that happened a long time ago."

"What?"

"I'll tell you about it sometime."

"Like when?"

"Maybe tonight. Remind me."

But *Rawhide* was on. About the heroes of the Old West. I forgot all about it.

And the bird? It adapted. For weeks it flopped along on the ground while I fed and cared for it. Once it made it ten feet in the air before tumbling. Then—one day—I lifted it up and held it high—and off it flew. It circled once, twice, then vanished into the blue distance.

One evening about a month later I went into O'You's room as the sun was setting. He was propped up in bed reading the paper, as he always did at night, reading and listing to KFI, its 50,000 watts of power threading its way from Los Angeles in and around the mountains with barely a hint of distant static. He was stroking Petey, Lord Petey Ottertwitch II. Petey was more like a dog than a cat, following O'You around everywhere, hoping for a fish. O'You always threw him the first of the catch when he'd come home from a day on the river.

Suddenly Petey took a notion to spring up and jump onto the window sill, tail switching. I looked outside to see what he was looking at. Perched on one of the backyard fence posts, steady as the post itself, was a seagull with one leg. I started to run outside to feed him, but O'You cautioned against it. "You don't want to make him dependent on us," he said. "He's got to learn to make it on his own, if he's going to live a life of freedom. He's made it so far. He'll be OK. Everyone needs some help now and again. But there comes a time when we have to make it on our own. It's his time."

"But why did he come back?'

"I don't know."

"Did he come to say thank you?"

"Maybe," said O'You. "Sure could be."

"You were going to tell me something, a story about what the seagull reminded you of."

And so he did. He told me about a time when he had to cut off a man's right arm. Tom Jay's arm. "In those days a man without a right arm was a man useless, a man better off dead. But let me tell you something, son." O'You was looking at me with eyes as solemn and serious as I'd ever seen. "The seagull made it, Tom Jay made it, and you will make it, when life cuts something off of you. As long as you keep trying to fly. A time will come when life will hit you pretty hard. It may not happen tomorrow. It may not happen for many years. It may or may not be something physical. It may be that it will be a wound to your heart. But mark my word, it will happen. Happens to everybody."

"Did it happen to you?"

He didn't answer me, not directly anyway. He just said, "Happens to everybody," and went on to tell me about Tom Jay.

Chapter 16

The North Star Mine Tragedy

Hailey, Idaho

1917

DOTT WAS IN PICABO when she began to get the news. She was on board the midnight train to Ogden, taking her mother to live with Holly and Ed for a time, for health reasons. Her mother hadn't been well ever since her father died a few years earlier. The slow-moving train, double-headed with its snowplow-engine, toiling its way through two and a half feet of newly fallen snow, at times at speeds no more than the pace of a man on foot, had stopped in Picabo to take on water and pick up mail. Instead of a sleeping town, Dott saw the bobbing lights of lanterns and people running and shouting. She thought she heard one voice say, "Doc Wright wants all able bodied men up there pronto."

Came another distant voice, muffled by the hissing idle of the train and the cushion of the falling snow, "…heard it said that most are dead. The others are buried alive."

Someone shouted, "—up at the North Star." Then she knew. There had been an avalanche at the North Star Mine. She sat helpless and frozen. If there had been a train going back the other way she would have taken it.

Bob had been awakened within an hour of having crawled in bed. It felt like he'd just closed his eyes, just begun to feel the freshness of sleep wash over him. The clatter of the telephone jarred him awake. He pulled the chain on his bedside lamp. Several times. It wasn't working. He left it swinging and tinkling in the dark and stumbled across the room for the wall switch. It turned heavily. And brought no light. He tripped and bumped his way toward the phone. Usually Dott would retrieve the call or answer the door. She would answer questions, pleasantly pacify the hypochondriacs, and, if need be, rouse Bob. Even then a good majority of the time he would arrive at a destination only to find the patient having undergone a miraculous medical transformation.

On the phone was Superintendent Rising of the Hailey Electric Light Works. A slide had come down at East Fork, a big one, at the North Star Mine. "I don't know how bad it is," Rising said. "But I think it's bad. It took out all the utility poles and pumps. There's no water, no electricity, no phones. Tyler James called me on the company line." The Federal Mining and Smelting Company, owners of the North Star, maintained a private line to Rising. It was the only one left intact by the storm. "He asked me to call you. Doc—like I say, it's bad. Real bad. The road's blocked. The East Fork River is all dammed up. The power is gone. No water. The buildings are all gone. Buried. The men inside the mine on the night shift were the only ones spared. The rest are gone. All of them. We need to get as many men and as many doctors as we can up there."

Bob could see out the window, the big snowflakes falling, floating. Such quiet. Such beauty. Such devastation.

He called Doctors Kleinman, Raaf, and Plumer of Hailey first, quickly, not wasting words, while the local lines were still serviceable. "Meet me in twenty minutes at the Livery," he said. "Bring blankets, quilts, flashlights, and buckets of water, lots of water. Cap 'em off so they don't spill. There's no power or water up there. The slide has completely blocked the river."

The phone lines to Bellevue were still up. He called Doctors Byrd and Dutton down there. "You'll have to meet us up at the mine," he told them. "We'll be gone by the time you're able to get to Hailey. Bring blankets, flashlights, water. Food, if you can, something that doesn't have to be cooked."

Mrs. Leopold came shuffling out. She was there to help care for Glenn and Jean while Dott was away. Bob turned to her as he was throwing on his horsehide coat, speaking as his long strides were taking him toward the door. "Get on the telephone and spread the word. We need men and wagons up there." The coat still bore the stain of Mary Stewart's blood, a faint outline only, a badge of honor only Bob could see, good luck, a superstition he kept to himself. Something nobody else would understand. Funny, it didn't seem like it had been that long ago, the night of the midnight blizzard, the Placenta Previa case, as Bob and Dott had come to call it, but the baby boy whose life Bob had saved that night was now eleven years old, "a lad stout and strong, and smart as a whip," as John Stewart would proudly remark. "And call the railroad. See if you can get a train through to Gimlet, up to the East Fork junction. We're going to need it to transport the injured." His bags were waiting by the door. He always kept them there.

The shouting and the commotion woke Glenn and Jean. They could hear from their bedroom. They felt humbled, frightened, proud. They felt small amongst a powerful and threatening world, protected from it, yet vulnerable to it. Each sound, each thump, each footstep caused them to jump. It sounded distant, a world away, because their door was shut, yet they could hear it all. And they heard the tremble in Mrs. Leopold's voice as she said goodbye. "You be careful, Doctor. Those slides are like-as-not still coming down. You be careful—" The rest of what she said became muffled to the children, probably because she was following him out the door.

When she peeked in and saw that the children were awake she got them up and they all prayed, on their knees, for the safety of everyone, rescuers and miners alike. Many of the people up there were friends and neighbors. Sam LaBarge, foreman on the night-shift at the mine, lived right across the street with his wife and family.

By the time Bob got to the Livery several men were already waiting, volunteers, and more began to arrive as the bob-sleigh was being harnessed. Others were on their way up to the mine. Word was spreading. The flickering lights of candles and lanterns were appearing in windows. Neighbors were going door to door. The electricity was out all over town; a slide had also come off the steep cliffs of Carbonate and had blocked the river and buried the power station there.

They took the big bob-sleigh, a full buckboard with seating for twelve, modified for winter hauling by thick wooden runners in place of wheels, and pulled by a four-horse team.

The trip to the East Fork junction went quickly. They followed the newly-plowed railroad tracks. The snow was hard packed between the ties, easy for the horses. After the turnoff at Gimlet, where the East Fork of the Big Wood goes up the canyon, four single riders had to go ahead of the wagons to break down the snow. The snow's weight was so heavy that the horses could do little more than a walk. The rescuers could tell the slide had blocked the river further on up because the water flow had been reduced to a trickle and falling snow had all but covered the riverbed, leaving only an indentation to mark its former course.

The men were silent in anticipation of what lay ahead, of what they might soon be seeing. The men on horseback guided their mounts without speaking, looking down and over their shoulders, watching as the hooves beat down the snow. The doctors and the volunteers in the sled sat hunched over and listened to the sounds of the sled runners on the snow and the breathing of the horses, thunderous sounds it seemed. Bob had the reins, but there wasn't much to do. The team more or less guided itself. He slapped the reins now and again, urging the horses along with measured, gentle force, asking, not demanding, knowing they were doing what they could. A mile behind them was another wagon full of a dozen more volunteers.

The men couldn't see the canyon sides, but they could feel them, narrowing, rising, hovering above them with their loads of deadly snow. Had the night sky allowed they would have been able to see the avalanche trails, twisting like bizarre roads plowed to bare ground.

The remnants of one such slide blocked their way. Icy chunks the size of boulders lay across the road, smoothed over by new-fallen snow. Gone from sight, sanitized by its softness, were the imbedded pockets of dirt and rocks, twigs and leaves. A squirrel's tail was visible from beneath the snow-cover. At first it looked like it was wiggling, but it was only the rising wind flopping it back and forth. The further up the canyon they went, the more forceful it became.

With picks and shovels the men and the doctors bored their way through, striking enough of a path for the horses and sleds to totter their way over.

Word of the tragedy, in those early hours, spread even to Pocatello, reaching there ahead of the train. When Dott and her mother were having breakfast during a stopover they overheard a group of old men talking. Gathered around a stove, smoking, chewing, sipping coffee, they were speaking their minds, unaware of Dott's anxiety. One said, "Here tell nary a man survived. Two hundred men gone, swept away in the middle of the night in their sleep. Hear tell search crews are on their way. Might as well not even bother. It'll be spring before they find 'em." Said another, "A sane man wouldn't go in there."

"I 'spect not."

"Them fellers goin' in there, them search crews, they're mad as hatters. Be a bone yard for them too."

"I seen one back in '89 up in the Yukon. Came down a mountain, crossed a mile-wide valley. Kilt a feller standin' on the mountain on the other side." The man speaking opened the stove and spat a wad into the fire and listened to it pop. "I seen it with my own eyes."

"The nice thing about folks is, ever time a body lands on the wrong side 'a danger, there's always some fool willin' to walk in after him. Just the way the Good Lord put us together, I s'pose."

"I s'pose."

Once back on the train Dott closed her eyes and laid back on the head rest cushion. Her mother wondered how she could sleep at a time like this. But she wasn't sleeping; she was coping. She was remembering the precious moments of a few hours earlier, the simple things, the things that will never make the newspapers or the history books, like how pretty she felt in her long white dress and equally long white apron, and how warm she felt in her cheeks as she walked from the hot kitchen with a steaming platter of lamb chops, and the children's voices at the dinner table, and how Bob and the children made a game out of washing the dishes while she relaxed with her crotchet basket out in the living room in front of the fireplace. Outside snowflakes the size of silver dollars floated.

"A wet snow," Bob had commented. "Slide weather."

Up and down Main Street and all over town people were putting out their lights and turning in for the night, earlier than usual, as if trying to hide from something ominous. And the snow continued to fall, six inches to the hour. Dott had a funny feeling about her trip to Ogden with her mother—maybe this wasn't the best time to take a trip. She should have paid a mind to her "inner voice." But the train was up in Ketchum taking on water and coal, ready to roll. The next opportunity to get her mother to Ogden may not come for a while. The line had been closed for days. Finally the rotary plow was brought in. Driven by its own engine, it had been able to clear the tracks by nightfall, a yard at a time, chewing through five to eight foot drifts.

The doctors had agreed to put Bob in charge of the rescue effort. It was decided that Dr. Plumer would stay behind to organize things locally. "Get hold of Ralph Harris," Bob had told him. Ralph was the undertaker. "See if we can use his place for a combination morgue and hospital. Could be, with what we're going to be bringing down that mountain, that that place of his will be the only space big enough to handle it all."

By the time Dott and her mother were crossing into Utah at 5:00 a.m., Bob and the men were at their destination. There were no lights. Everything was black. The wind was blasting furiously against their faces and foreheads. It was a cold wind—they could feel the ice of it—and that was good. Cold weather meant stable snow.

They could hear sounds from beyond the wind's moaning, if they strained. Shouts. Screams. Once in a while a light would flash, then be gone. The Federal Mining and Smelting operation spanned several hundred yards of mountainside and included numerous buildings. It was a small city. They were at the base of it. To the left up on the hill should be the mine entrance and the pump house. On the other side, to the right, on a hilltop knoll, should be where the bunkhouse was located. But it wasn't there. Nothing of what should have been there was there. The beams of their flashlights could access only chunks of snow in front of them. All else was blackness.

They left Felipe Ariola to wait for the others and tend to the horses. With flashlights as beacons they struck out on foot, yelling, picking their path over boulders of snow splintered with shards of smashed timber, and over uprooted trunks of trees shaved clean of limbs, following the sounds of the voices that beckoned them. Then suddenly, without the whisper of a

The remains of the Bunkhouse, North Star Mine.
Idaho State Historical Society.

warning, one of the rescuers dropped from sight—Jack Lane, a newcomer, a sheep man. The snow bed beneath him had turned to instant slush, icy quicksand, from what cause no one ever knew. Maybe it was from the clogged river being soaked up into the snow, as if by a sponge, or maybe from a broken water pipe or sluice line. It swallowed him so fast it left only his head visible, and before the shock of the cold would allow him to scream he was gone completely.

Flashlight beams marked where Jack's head had gone under. Bob jumped spread-eagle onto the very same spot. "Grab my ankles," he screamed. If he'd have taken the time to think, he wouldn't have done it. That kind of courage comes as an automatic reaction. He jabbed the full length of his arm in and felt nothing. He brought it up. "Hold me," he yelled and dove his entire upper body in. The quickmire of the cement-like slush gripped him, sucked in around him like glue. The cold was unbelievably painful, and he was terrified beyond anything he'd ever felt in his life. He couldn't breathe, he couldn't see, he couldn't move backwards to free himself. He felt something! His hand touched something hard. He snatched hold of what he thought was hair, but lost his grip when the men pulled him up. His lungs, panic stricken, grabbed at the air. At first they wouldn't work. His diaphragm had been so traumatized it simply wouldn't respond. And when it did he used it to rasp the words, "*Give me a rope—tie it off in a loop. Slip knot.*"

"When I kick my feet pull me up." Again he dove. Sometimes human beings perform impossible feats when the lives of others are threatened, like when a mother lifts the front end of an automobile off a child, or when someone runs into a burning building and returns through the flames with a rescued victim. Such is the only explanation for how Bob was able to hook that loop underneath Jack's arms, against the gripping weight of the slush hole. Or—there seemed to have been a downward flow, like watery snow being sucked into something—perhaps that's how it occurred. Maybe Bob's hands were sucked into just the right position. Maybe it was nothing more than that. An accident.

Whatever it was, Jack lived to see another day, and to rescue three trapped miners. He was blue when he came out, as blue as a mid-morning sky. Dr. Raaf worked to revive him while Klineman tended to Bob. Raff used the Schaeffer method, pushed on Jack's back so hard it seemed his ribs would break. Indeed there was a cracking sound, but with it fluid ran out of Jack's lifeless mouth. Then Raaf pumped his arms and pushed again. Then a third time. And Jack coughed and began to shiver. Both men were shivering, so violently, so uncontrollably that they could barely breathe. They were stripped and covered with coats given up by the other men and helped back down to where the horses were. By then the second group of rescuers had arrived.

The men all joked about it. Odd that hearty men seem to have a need to follow near-tragedy with laughter. "He warn't savin' you, Jack," said one. "He was just worried about them sheep 'a yourn."

"It wasn't that," came another. "The doc just realized you hadn't paid your bill."

"At least it washed that sheep stink off'n you," guffawed another.

And hearty men they both were. Within minutes Jack and Bob were outfitted in dry clothes—no man ventures into an Idaho storm without several changes of clothing—and were back searching again, joints swollen, fingers stiff and numb, lungs burning with an ice cold pain, convulsing with an urge to cough. But it was a strange pain—refreshing? Like each breath was a cleansing thing that smelled sweet, and that washed through the limbs and arteries of the soul.

Dott swears she felt something at that exact time, a hammering twist in her chest. She thought at the time that she was having a heart attack.

The men picked a higher trail this time, walking hurriedly but carefully, poking at the snow ahead of them.

There had been sixty-five men up at the North Star that night. Half had been on shift inside the mine and were uninjured, and were now scurrying about on the surface with their carbide helmet lamps and flashlights, looking, digging for bodies, answering calls for help. Their relief when they saw Bob and the other doctors was overwhelming. Bob thought he saw tears in the eyes of one of the burly men.

The rescuers were led to the compressor shed. It was the only building left reasonably intact and was being used as a temporary shelter for the injured. Its vague outline looked something like a half-collapsed rectangular box with one end shoved into the snow. Teasing flickers of light could be seen through the windows. A veterinary surgeon was inside giving first aid. He happened to have been at the mine tending to some horses when the slide came.

Bob told Klineman to help the veterinarian, then directed that another shelter be set up in the mine's mouth, assigning two men to the task. Then he gathered together the rest of the men. There were fifty of them. With long probes, galvanized sections of threaded pipe, they began their search, walking shoulder to shoulder, driving twenty, thirty, forty feet into the snow. Instructed Bob, "Whenever you hit something, I want two men to break off and start digging. Go careful when you get to the hard spot. It could be a body. The rest of you continue to probe."

Sometimes it would be a rock they'd find, or a piece of timber, sometimes it would be a body.

By the first slice of dawn seventy-five men were lined up probing the snow. By 9:00 a.m. there were a hundred.

And, as if the Good Lord had mercy, the storm began to die, and smoky bands of sunshine began to thread through the clouds.

Emmett Russell's body was found in the bunkhouse area twelve feet down. There was not a mark on his body, not even a bruise.

Frank Mangino was found only five feet down, underneath the timekeeper's shed. The shed had been smashed into kindling wood. Frank's internal organs had been shoved up into his chest cavity with such force that they actually burst through his neck. His teeth had pierced his upper lip just underneath his nose, giving him a horrific look.

Andy Smith was heard calling for help from beneath the snow. At first the rescuers didn't know where the muffled sound was coming from. Then they realized it was coming from directly under them! He was trapped a few feet down underneath a tree trunk, still alive. The massive tree had come tumbling end-over-end at the head of the avalanche's first wave, rolling down right on top of him, breaking both his legs and one arm and in the process saving his life, cradling him from suffocation.

John Lillquist had flailed his arms as the snow hit. It had created a pocket around his head, now a tomb of ice. He was only six inches below the surface, but was unable to move, unable to breath. The last of his air was gone. Strangely, so was the claustrophobic panic. And gone also was the awful pain of the cold. The cold was there, but it was suddenly pleasant to feel. It penetrated every inch of his body, but it felt good, euphoric even. The tapping of the rescuers on his ice cocoon seemed a nuisance. John had gotten up in the middle of the night to take a trip to the outhouse, a short ten-foot walk, but it was just enough to put him on the slide's outer fringe. He hadn't even buttoned his coat, thinking he wouldn't be away that long. The avalanche had come down in an S, traversing the mountainside several times before striking, as though the thing had intelligence, as though it was picking its spot. John had heard it coming. His hand had been on the outhouse door, ready to open it and step inside. He was a biblically inclined man, and as he looked up toward the mountain into the blackness he was convinced that the approaching thunder was the sound of the Four Horsemen of the Apocalypse. And as he prayed for his soul the footing beneath him turned to powder. He was swept from his feet like the pulling of a rug. Next he knew he was opening his eyes. He thought at first he was in his bed in the bunkhouse, waking because he was chilled. Awfully chilled. He tried to reach for his blanket. He could not. He could not so much as move a finger. Nor could he see. And there was something the size of a locomotive on his chest, making each icy breath a supreme effort. Then there came to John Lillquist a panic the likes of which a human being should not have to experience.

Six hours later he was free, and alive, uninjured save for frostbitten extremities, thanks to a hundred brave men.

The body of Israel Peterlin was unrecognizable when they brought him up. They knew it was him; he had a tattoo of his wife's name on his arm. They found him under thirty feet of snow. His head looked like it had exploded from the inside. He had no face, only frozen skin and tissue, two extremely large holes for eyes, and a hole in the middle of his head where his nose should have been. The warm body was steaming on the snow, or so it seemed anyway, to the emotionally worn and bleary-eyed rescuers. One of them reached out and touched it. To make sure he was dead? Who knows. Obviously Israel was dead. Maybe there is something about a horrific scene that makes one mistrust the senses. The snow packed inside his skull actually bulged through the empty eye and nose cavities. One of the men laughed at the bizarre sight.

When they dug up Bert Judd they found him alive inside a cavern, unconscious but alive, in an ice hole of sorts, like the bulb around John Lillquist's head, only larger, large enough for a person to sit up and move about in. The only thing they could figure is that the avalanching snow must have formed a whirling vortex and trapped him inside, tumbling him like an ant in a bottle.

Sam LaBarge was one of the last to be found. Some of the survivors said they thought he was in his office in the pump house when the slide hit. The pump house wreckage was strewn and buried over several hundred yards of slope. The large center beam that had supported the roof had been broken to bits. When they found Sam there was not a mark on him. They found him ten feet down still sitting in his rocking chair, snow packed around him so tight they had to use picks and shovels to extract him. "It was the damndest thing," Bob said later, "the way he was sitting there, he was like a statue, like someone had painstakingly packed and preserved him. He didn't even look dead. You half expected him to get up and start telling one of those crazy jokes of his."

By then Dott was back in Hailey. She had taken the next available train from Ogden. The sun was out and the air was warm, but inside she was cold. No one had any word. The only news was that the injured would be coming in by rail, the dead by wagon.

Eventually a distant train whistle sounded. The townsfolk hurried to the depot through the deep-cut paths and street walkways, most on foot, some on horseback, some in bobsleighs.

Dott's anxiety lifted when she saw Bob, but returned when she saw in his face the agony of what he'd been through. His clothes were disheveled and wet. His face was shadowed in whiskers. He was helping Tom Jay off the train. Tom was limping. His arm was gone, severed below the elbow, its stub wrapped in bloody bandages.

Some of the folks didn't find what they were looking for. Their questions wouldn't be answered for another forty-five minutes, until the big hay wagon with the sled runners came into town. Dott saw the look on Mary LaBarge's face when she couldn't find Sam—and decided to wait there with her for the hay wagon, instead of going with Bob.

Tom Jay had been the final survivor found. His cry for help had been so feeble the rescuers almost missed him. It came from past the mill house wreckage, from over a bluff on the other side of the road, about a quarter of the way down a steep slope that fell off into a slag pool. He appeared to be trapped beneath a piece of machinery that had been torn from the mill house and had lodged on a ledge about twenty feet down. There was so much snow that it was impossible to tell what had been the hillside and what was the avalanche. There were gargantuan fragments

of the avalanche piled all the way down to the river, all smoothed over
by the fresh snow. At first no one could see him. The fresh snow had
entirely covered him up, all but his face, which he kept clear by continually brushing it away with his free hand. The other hand was trapped
by the machinery. For eight hours he had brushed the falling snow off
his face. It had finally stopped, but so much of it had fallen that a cone
of it surrounded him, the sides of which kept flaking off and tumbling
down onto his face. Each time he cleared it off, the chunk of metal on
top of him would slip a little, and tiny round balls of snow would roll on
down to the slag pool, fingering out with dotted tracer tracks. He knew
there were people up there looking down at him. He could hear them,
but couldn't see them because he was looking up straight into the sun.

"Move away, men," Tom could hear someone shout. "That slope is
unstable."

At the bottom, another forty feet down, was the slag pool, clogged
with avalanche chunks and swollen with water from the dammed up
river, higher and deeper than it had ever been. "We have to get him out
of there now," came a voice.

Tom didn't know who was talking. All he knew was that a rescue
party was there.

"Can we come at him from below?"

"No, you could never climb in that snow. We have to go down from
the top."

"Get a couple 'a men to anchor a rope and lower me down."

"No. It needs to be me." That was Bob's voice, though Tom didn't
recognize it. Sometimes it seemed like chaos, there were so many voices
talking.

"We can't go down from the top either. She'll give way right on top
of him."

"We'll lower two men, one on both sides of him. Then they can walk
over to him."

"Can't risk two men on that slope. She'll never stand up to it."

"All right, one man then. We'll lower the doc, from up yonder, on
the north side there."

Tom could hear Bob coming, could hear the snow crumbling and
falling. Bob was suspended by the rope, parallel to Tom, about ten feet

away, clawing his way over. When he got to him the hunk of machinery started to give way completely. Bob reached out and stopped it with one hand, two tons of metal. That's how precariously the thing was balanced. A push either way could move it. It was a section of the mine's conveyor. "Done got my hand caught in the dad-blamed fool thing," said Tom apologetically.

Tom had been feeding ore into the crusher when his hand became caught, at almost the exact moment the slide came down. Tom would have been drawn into it, but for the slide. He would have been killed, smashed in seconds between carbon steel drums, a device that pops rocks like sacks of flour. The irony—the avalanche saved his life. The devastation that claimed twenty lives saved his. In that instant when his arm was disappearing in splatters of his own blood the building blew apart, the whole world it seemed like, and he found himself spinning in circles upon the bed of the conveyor, riding the crest of the avalanche.

"We're going to get you outa here," Bob told him.

Tom said, "The only way you'll be gettin' me outa here is by cutting my arm off."

"You let me be the judge of that."

"Just do it, doc, and get me the hell outa here. My arm's gone anyway." Tom was angry, speaking as if ordering a child. "It got trapped by the crusher. It's inside the fool thing."

"I'm going to get this snow off from around you before I do anything."

Bob had a hand shovel and a snow axe strapped to his back, along with his medical bags. He leaned back against the rope and reached for the shovel and dug it in…and made an alarming discovery. The weight of the snow was holding the conveyer piece in place, balancing it. The conveyor started to tilt and slide.

He put the shovel-full of snow back on the pile. The tilt stopped.

Bob suddenly noticed something else, a crack in the snow, a wedge-shaped fissure surrounding them. As he watched, it grew, rapidly widening, first an inch, then six inches, then two feet.

Tom saw it too, though not directly. He saw it in Bob's eyes, a startled look, like one might have upon noticing a mountain lion above one's head in a mid-air leap, or upon seeing a revolver pointed at one's head. Bob snatched the ice-hatchet from off his back and swung it at Tom's arm.

The East Fork Valley rebounded with the echoes of Tom's surprise, and of the deep sound of the gigantic snowfield fracturing.

Bob dropped the hatchet and grabbed for Tom. And held on to him. How, he didn't know. He wouldn't remember much of those moments, only that chunks of ice and snow were buffeting him, and that he had to close his mouth to keep from swallowing the spray.

The men topside were doing their job, pulling, anchoring, holding them secure. Joe Fuld, short but stout and strong, was the end man, rope secured in back of his waist and entwined around his thick arm. If Bob went, so would Joe.

Bob and Tom must have looked like toys on a string, the way they were being batted around. Bob remembered looking down and seeing the snow slab and the conveyor slide into depths of ice and water, dirty green water. The slab was as big as a house, and disappeared almost completely into the pool, the displaced water rushing up at its victims with a bubbling vengeance. But they were safe; they were being pulled out of harm's way, by the brave souls topside. Tom's screams sounded more like shouts of victory than of pain, and in fact they were, because in Tom's mind he had beaten the devil. Blood was pumping out of the stub and Bob was tying on a tourniquet even as the rescuers were reaching their hands down to pull them to safety.

Elsewhere other dramas were being played out. Kleinman and Raaf were performing surgery on the floor of the broken up compressor house on a man whose abdomen had been riddled with wood splinters. It was as serious as any gunshot wound. And Byrd was treating a man for severe frostbite, fighting to save his legs, while Dutton was stitching up the gashed side of a man's throat.

Though Tom never said so, Bob often wondered if he ever resented the loss of his arm, the way it happened. Many a man in those days would rather die than be forced to live without the use of a right arm. People adapt though, like the seagull. Tom moved back east where someone said he got into politics.

Chapter 17

The Switch Engine Case and the Ghost of Black Jack Ketchum

Hailey, Idaho

1918

D AD HAD A BIT OF A TEMPER. Once he lost his temper with Johnny Odegard, a rancher from down at the Base Line. Johnny had been boasting how his dogs treed a "cat" and how he had picked the animal off with one easy shot. I thought they were going to come to blows, Dad was so angry. Cougars were a menace to livestock, especially during rough winters when natural food stock was low. The whole town must have thought Dad was crazy, defending a predator like that. One day Dad told me a story, and I understood why…

"Father, when I'm big will you still dance with me?"

"Of course." Bob drew the two heavy quilts around Jean's neck, and placed her doll in close. He always took the time to tuck her in, even when he was in a hurry, even if it consisted of no more than a kiss on the cheek. "You're getting so tall. I don't have to bend way over or carry you anymore when we dance. We can do a real waltz together."

Jean looked past him, like she was looking inward, silent in the sanctuary of her thoughts, secure in the clouds of approaching sleep. "Father—do you think I'm pretty?"

"Princess—you're the prettiest thing I've ever seen." Bob had on his heavy coat. Soon he'd be out in the freezing night. His bags were sitting ready by the door. "You've been into your mother's perfume again, haven't you?"

"Yesssssss," she confessed, with trouble in her eyes and a smile that charmed it all away.

"You've got to learn to mind your mother. You know that? It might seem like a little thing, but the point is, it's something your mother doesn't want you to do."

"She lets me sometimes."

"Well, you just make sure you have her permission."

"Even with my freckles, do you think I'm pretty?"

"They're not freckles, Princess, they're stars. God took some of the stars from the sky and put them right there on your cheeks."

"I had my first knitting lesson today."

"Do you like to knit?"

"Yeaahhh—but I like climbin' trees with Glenn better."

"I tell you what then. You close your eyes and dream about climbing those trees. The sand man's a comin' and Jack Frost is at the window. Time for all little girls to be asleep."

"Father?"

"Yes, sweetheart?"

"Can I be a doctor when I grow up?"

"You sure can."

"Why don't I see any lady doctors anywhere?"

"There were three women in my graduating class at American."

"Father—why do you have to go to Ketchum tonight? Why can't you go tomorrow?"

"There are some very sick people up there. If you were bad sick, wouldn't you want me to come tonight?"

"Why are they sick?"

"They have severe colds."

"Why do you have to take the train?"

"There are no roads on account of the deep snow. The railroad sent the snowplow. Burrowed its way clean through. Took them all day. The crew is planning to bed down in Ketchum for the night, so the engineer and the fireman are going to run the engine back down to pick me up."

"Father?"

"Mmmmmm?"

"Am I a bumpkin?"

"A what?"

"There's this new girl at school—she's visiting from Boston—she says people from Idaho are backwoods bumpkins."

"That so. Tell you what. You ask her if her mother can vote."

"Why, Father?"

"Women from Boston can't vote."

"Why?"

"In Massachusetts, which is where Boston is, it's against the law for women to vote. Idaho, it just so happens, is one of the most progressive states in the Union. Women in Idaho were given the vote way back in 1896. That's one of the reasons your mother and I moved here from Missouri. Backwoods bumpkins. Hmmmmppff."

"Why is it against the law?"

"In most states back east women can't vote."

"But why, Father?"

"I don't know, Princess. I've never understood that one myself."

"Know what I would do? If I were magic? I would wish that women everywhere could vote."

"That would be a good wish—I'm afraid, though, that it will take more than wishes to bring that about."

"Well—I'm going to wish it anyway—just in case I am magic."

"OK, Princess. That's a really good wish."

"Jack Frost is sure here all right," said Jean, looking over at the window. It was caked in a frame of ice. On the inside! Next to the window was a mahogany dresser with a circular mirror casting its reflections through opaque circles of fog forming on the glass from the contrast of cold and heat, cold from the window, heat from the fireplace out in the other room. "Ghosts," she said, pointing to the patterns on the mirror.

"No such thing as ghosts," reminded Bob, the response Jean was hoping for.

"Yes-Huh!" she said with wide-eyed insistence. "Glenn says."

"*What* does he say?"

"If mirrors look funny, means you have a ghost."

"Nonsense. Your brother is just trying to frighten you. I guess I'm going to have to have a little talk with him."

"Well what about the picture Mrs. Fuld has? Of the little baby what died? What about that?"

Bob thought for a bit. "I suspect that was a special case where God let the baby come down from Heaven to visit with his mama for awhile."

Jean snuggled further in under the big quilts. "That was nice of God. If I ever die I'm going to ask him if I can come visit you. We can dance."

Bob brushed his hand slowly through her long hair and kissed her on the forehead. "You're not doing to die, Princess. Not for a long, long time."

Jean's eyes were closed. She was nearly asleep. "Am I pretty even with my eyeglasses?"

"So that's what this is all about. Yes, of course you're pretty, especially with your eyeglasses."

"There's this kid at school what calls me four eyes."

"You just never mind him. Your father says you're pretty and that's all there is to it."

"Mmmm," she murmured.

"Your mother has started wearing eyeglasses. Don't you think she's pretty?"

Jean's head nodded twice.

"Well there you go."

"Did I have to get glasses 'cause of the weasles?"

"Measles, Princess. Measles."

"Oh."

"I love you, Princess."

"Me too."

Jean Wright, 1918.

She was asleep, adrift in mountains of feathers and quilts, safe within the castle walls of her knobbed brass bed. She was growing into a little girl.

Bob crept quietly over to Glenn's side of the room. Dott was there sitting on his bed. "Nighty-night," she said, and kissed him and patted his arm. "You're my little man. You know that?"

"Uh-huh," responded Glenn. "Can I have some cake?" Through their door, adjacent to the kitchen, there traveled the hot smell of a cake baking, and of fresh wood burning in the range. Spice cake. Made from an 1894 recipe of his grandmother's, with cinnamon, cloves, allspice, nutmeg, and mace.

"Tomorrow," said Dott. "Promise. Right after breakfast."

"OK," said Glenn reluctantly.

"You get some sleep now. Mrs. Leopold will be over in the morning. You have to be rested if you want to help us make breakfast."

Dott turned to Bob before leaving. "I'll make you some coffee for your trip."

"Dad—"

Bob sat and heartily shook his son's leg. "My boy. How's your copperosity sagaciating?"

Jake was curled up on the foot of the bed. He raised his head and thumped his tail twice. He was starting to show his age. His face was graying and arthritis in his bad hip had slowed him to a permanent limp.

"Fine. Dad? Are you going to ride in the switch engine?"

Contract with the Oregon Short Line Railroad.

"Yes, son, looks like I am."

"Are you going to ride up with the engineer and the fireman?"

"Yes, son."

"Can I come? Please?"

"Not this time. Another time maybe."

"Are you the doctor for the railroad?"

"Yes, son, I sure am. The official Union Pacific Doctor."

"I thought the railroad was called the Oregon Short Line."

"The Oregon Short Line and the Union Pacific are pretty much the same thing. They're the same family. Like me and you. We're different but a part of the same family."

"Do you get to doctor the people from the railroad? The engineers and the firemen and the brakemen and the conductors?"

"Yes, indeed. That's what it means. I fix them all. For a contract price of ten dollars a month."

"Do the people up in Ketchum all have colds?"

"Many folks do. That's why I have to go"

"Is this that one cold? That bad one? The one that's killing everybody?"

"I'll have to wait until I get there to find that out." An influenza epidemic was traveling westward from the east coast, having first arrived from Europe on the steamers. Eventually it would consume forty-six states before its end in 1920, claiming more lives worldwide in a single year than died in battle in World War I, World War II, the Korean War, and Vietnam combined.

"How come you don't catch things? Like colds and things?"

"I'm careful. I don't let people cough on me. I always wash my hands thoroughly and sterilize instruments before and after procedures." Still he felt apprehension about walking into a household full of something which has no cure—colds, influenza, scarlet fever, measles, whooping cough—something that can reach within you simply because you breathe. But as Dott always said, "The Good Lord surely watches out for our doctors." This one was a puzzler though, this particular influenza strain. He quite frankly had never seen anything like it. It made no sense. The symptoms were those of influenza, except that it attacked twenty and thirty year olds with as much ferocity as it did the young and the old, and the speed with which it consumed its prey was triple the norm. A headache and muscle weakness in the morning, dead by nightfall, in some cases. And the coughing—it almost seemed that the victims actually drowned in the phlegm they were hacking up. He knew of an autopsy that was done by one doctor back east. The lungs had been reduced to lumps of sodden bloody flesh.

"Dad—is it snowing outside?"

"Too cold to snow."

Bob was wrong. Snow started falling as soon as he got to the rendezvous point, the second crossing north of the depot. Little balled-up flakes, corn snow. The flakes were so heavy they pattered as they fell. It was a purring sound, like the rustling of tissue paper. Pretty soon the chug and puff of the engine came to be heard. Things sound different when it snows, softer, like there is no echo, like the snow absorbs the sound.

The engine started to slow. Bob was on the track waving his flashlight. It was the only place he could be seen, smack in the middle of the tracks, in a canyon cut clean by the whirling blades of the plow. The banks were six feet up. Horse drawn wagons with bob-sleigh runners had broken through at the crossing, leaving a knee high barrier across the tracks. The seventy ton engine turned it to powder as it slid through it to its stop, like a bomb made of snow. Bob had stepped ten feet to the side and still it sprayed him, so hard it stung his face.

"Evenin' Doc," yelled Sam Doolittle from high up in the cab window. "You lookin' for a ride?" The cab had stopped right where Bob had stood. "Damn, I'm good. I could stop this thing on a pencil mark." Below Sam's window was stenciled the number 9435.

Bob uncovered his bags from the snow and threw them up to Sam and climbed on in. Riding in the switch engine was always a thrill—the immense size of the thing, the smell of the coal in the tender, the smell of the oil, the sound of the fire in the box.

"Doc, meet Joe Briggs," said Sam, introducing him to his fireman.

"It's hot in here," said Bob.

Sam released the brake and threw foreword the throttle. Steam roared and the switch engine jerked backward to begin its reverse trip to Ketchum. "You can always walk," he joked.

"I intend to pay my fare." Bob opened one of his bags. "You see, I've got some medicine for you two fellas." He brought out hot coffee and spice cake, still warm from the oven.

The snow had stopped by the time Dott and the children and Mrs. Leopold were having breakfast. The sun was out. By then Bob had seen seven families. Sid Venables of the Ketchum Livery had readied a team and had it waiting at the Ketchum train yard with two horses and a light sleigh. Bob drove from house to house, sleeping in the sleigh between visits for ten, twenty minutes at a time. One patient died, sadly, the Widow Jenkins. She used to bake the most incredible upside down cake. He surely would miss that cake!

He thought for awhile he was going to lose one of the Brass girls. She was terribly sick. A high fever, chills, delirium. He worked for hours to keep fluids in her, and kept talking to her, telling her she was going to get well, making her believe it, making her body believe it. He borrowed a treatment from Dr. Durham, the old snake oil salesman—and sweetened a cup of hot water with a drop of whiskey. "Now you're going to be fine," he said, as she slowly sipped down the magical brew. The Brass girl recovered fully, though at some expense to Bob's own well being. The trip out to the Brass Ranch, a mile east of Ketchum just below Trail Creek, was made against the rising morning sun and left his eyes painfully sunburned. The ranch was in the middle of a ring of rolling hills and mountains. It was its own valley, and in the wintertime was a vortex of reflected sunshine. On his way back he stopped off to tend to Jack Lane. Jack was having a tough time of it, too.

For some, for those not ill, it was a beautiful day. White was everywhere, sparkling and brilliant. The morning after a snowstorm always seemed to refresh, seemed to bring out the pleasantness in folks. People rose a bit earlier, had bigger breakfasts, were kinder to one another, greeted and helped one another, shoveled walks and roofs, widened paths, pushed out automobiles, and brought wood and groceries to the elderly.

For the children in school, with the snow beckoning through the school house windows, the hours until afternoon dismissal passed torturously, driving many to mischief. Glenn was one such child, busying himself placing the end of one of Susan Dearborn's long blond braids into his inkwell. He was skillful, wrinkling his freckled face as he squinted one eye, holding his tongue to the side of his mouth, carefully guiding the braid so Susan wouldn't feel a tug. It was something he had to do. He couldn't help himself. The braid was hanging there by the inkwell, right in front of him, asking for it, begging for it. A string dangling before a kitten.

"Master Wright, step forward if you please," sounded Mistress Lela Montgomery's sudden voice. "Make your manners first, if you please."

She was standing beside him, slapping her long wooden pointer on her palm. It was like she had appeared from nowhere. He'd get it now for sure. Then when he got home he'd get twice as many.

He swallowed against the lump in his throat and got to his feet, and put one hand behind his back, the other in front, and bowed. "Yes, Mistress Montgomery." The boys made their manners by bowing, the girls by curtsying.

"Please walk to the front of the class and read from the paper aloud. It may be an article of your own choosing."

Thank you, God! The misdeed had gone unnoticed.

The fear in his face turned to a grin. He put his little cap on his head, atop his buzzed-off, inch-high hair, and walked with satisfaction to the front of the class, delighting in the glory of the snickers of the other children. He looked too proper to be a mischief maker—suit coat tied in at the waist, white shirt, necktie, short pants tucked under at the knee, brown leggings. Soon he would have his first pair of long pants, this Sunday for church.

He picked up the newspaper from the teacher's desk.

"Oh—Master Wright—one thing," said Mistress Montgomery, arms folded,

Glenn Wright.

holding the pointer. "Before you begin would you be so kind as to grab your ankles? So that you may learn that we must ask permission from little girls before we change their hair color?" Now the smile of satisfaction was on Mistress Montgomery's face, and she made her way to the front, slowly, swishing her feet across the floor in deliberate steps. A bug was scurrying by. She paused and stepped on it, just to show her power, calmly raising her floor length skirt enough to scoot out her lace-up ankle boot and crush it.

Glenn took the swats with a smile—a matter of pride—though his face turned vermillion. Mistress Montgomery quit when the front end of the pointer went flying off across the room.

"You may read," she said, taking a breath to compose herself.

"Yes, Mistress Montgomery," Glenn said in a voice seemingly unaffected by the thrashing. He was honor bound, a code among the boys, not to show pain after a whipping. He picked up the newspaper and read a recent account of the British entering Jerusalem in December 1917, a part of the global war that U.S. forces had only recently joined. Glenn was only ten, but he could read at a high school level.

At lunchtime the devil came back. Glenn and Art Ensign busied

themselves inside the fire escape laying plans for an afternoon of adventure—an adventure that did not include school. The "fire escape" was an enclosed metal tube that protruded from the top floor of the three story brick schoolhouse. The children needed no fire as an excuse to use it. It was steep and slippery— only the most athletic of the boys were able to climb to the top and carve their names into the outside of the wooden exit doors. One girl's name was there—Jean Eleanor Wright. Glenn's sister was as agile as a spider on a wall—a cute, freckled tomboy with flowered dresses and big bows who could climb almost anything.

Art finally agreed to let Jean come along, primarily because that was the only condition under which Glenn would go. Glenn looked

Jean Wright and her doll.

straight into Jean's eyes, and made her hold up her right hand. "Swear, swear on Mother's Bible that you won't tell," he ordered.

Jean raised her hand. "I swear."

It would be an easy get away. For the remainder of the afternoon, the children were supposed to practice for the Valentine's Day spelling bee. Everyone would be gathering in one classroom. It would be so crowded no one would notice their absence.

Two Chinese boys saw them leave. They were Fat's nephews, six and seven, Jean's age. Fat had them sent over from China for schooling. They were sitting by themselves in a corner of the playground behind a tall bank of piled up snow when Glenn and Jean and Art walked by.

"Don't worry," said Glenn. "They won't tell." Glenn once had defended them against some of the older boys who had been teasing and bullying them. Glenn sported a black eye for two weeks as a result of the incident. He felt a certain kinship with the boys, ever since the night they came looking for the doctor because Fat was sick with asthma. The boys had been terrified. They thought Fat was going to die. Glenn knew how he would have felt had it been his parents that were dying, or his sister, or his Uncle John.

Glenn and Art and Jean trudged through the snow, on down past Main, past River Street, and parted the curtains of reality to walk into their world of adventure. They were headed west toward the caves of Carbonate. The mountain loomed upward from directly across the river. Its slope, so steep it approached vertical in spots, was ornamented with cliffs and rocky crags, and splotches of loose shale. In the winter its white hillsides were blemished with avalanche trails. It was no place for children. But it was the perfect place for a desperado to hide half a million in gold. Forty years earlier Black Jack Ketchum robbed the Wells Fargo Line down south—according to legend—and hid it somewhere in the Idaho hills. "We're going to make ourselves rich," said Glenn. They were at the base of a cable car tower that had been used for transportation across the river in the days before the bridge. They had to climb to the platform, about thirty feet up, then get in the car, a box about three by five, and pull themselves across to the other side. They could have crossed at the bridge four hundred yards down, but then it wouldn't be an adventure. And anyway—when Black Jack Ketchum hid the gold there wouldn't have been a bridge. He would have taken this very car. The gold is probably right on the other side, in a cave right over there, said Glenn. Jean sat in the middle and gripped the sides with her mittens as the car swung back and forth, as Art and Glenn pulled it along by the lower cable. From a distance they looked a bit like two gentlemen and a lady out for the evening, Jean sitting properly in the middle, long coat, silver broached black hat, Glenn and Art on either end.

Forty-five feet below were icy rapids. Beautiful. Deadly. The air above steamed and swirled and rolled up to the car, like demonic fingers. It was probably what frightened the children, and caused them to loose their grip.

The car rolled backwards, jerking, swaying.

Art and Glenn stumbled and fell to one side, tipping the car nearly perpendicular and spilling Jean over the edge.

She was able grab the side and hang on, but only for seconds. Her weight tipped the car further and her mittened hands began to slip. She spun the air with her dangling feet and looked at Glenn, eyes pleading, her face too terrified to scream.

Glenn reached but missed. She let out a squeal as his hand swept past her. The car swung more and one of her hands came loose. Now she was only anchored by the fingers of the other one. A few seconds more and she would be falling. The thought struck Glenn with such horror that he released his own grip and lunged forward with both his hands. He couldn't have reached his sister in any other way, and of course the decision made no sense, because now he was falling, too. There is no rational process at work in the split second of such a decision. There is only reaction, reflex.

Then came an extraordinary coincidence. Glenn's bulky upper pant leg caught on the end of a large protruding bolt, suspending them both just by the strength of that fabric. Glenn was holding Jean by her coat, the fabric of his pant leg was holding them both.

There was silence as they looked at each other. Then there was the sound of fabric ripping. They dropped another inch.

Glenn gripped tighter. The realization that they'd never be able to get back up into the car didn't come. Nor did he think about the fact that his pant leg could only hold the weight for seconds more. "I've got you sis, I've got you, it's OK," is what he said instead. "It's OK. Now what I want you to do is, I want you to climb up me, just like I was a tree."

Jean looked at him with vacant confusion.

"Hey now. Relax. Forget about everything and pretend you're only hanging two feet off the ground. Then you wouldn't have any problem with it. You'd be climbing me like I was that old maple down the street. You've got to do it. And you've got to do it now. Go on now. Do it. Right now."

But Jean was frozen in immobility, save for the dangling of her legs. The pant leg ripped again and dropped them still more.

"Now, sis. Right now. Hell's bells, you're the best climber in school. Better than any boy."

Jean's lips quivered. She was gathering courage.

Then she did it.

"That's it. Just like I was a tree. 'At's a girl."

She pulled and gripped and scraped—the pant leg ripped more—and she was up, in seconds.

"Good job, sis! Now go back onto the other side of the car and balance us. Good girl."

The car began to right itself.

"Good. Good. Now stay there."

Art had been holding Glenn by the legs as best he could, with one hand. He needed the other hand to keep himself from falling until Jean's weight repositioned the car.

Glenn was strong and limber. With the car right-side up, and with Art's help, he was easily able to reach back and roll himself up.

They sat in the car perfectly still as it swung back and forth on the cable, as the cable swayed and bounced. They were afraid to move, afraid to speak, afraid to breathe. Glenn noticed something wet and cold on his leg. Blood? He had to take a moment to figure out why. It must have happened when his pant leg ripped. Funny, how the mind can be so focused it even blots out pain. Even now there was only a little pain, not much, just a stinging in rhythm to his still racing heart. He wrapped it tight with Jean's scarf, just like he'd been taught to do by his dad.

Eventually everything was still, then they noticed something else. "We have another problem," whispered Art, the first to speak. He pointed upward. "The pulleys have jumped the track." Both wheels guiding the car had dislodged and were wedged to the side of the cable.

They thought about waiting for someone to come. But no one used the cable crossing anymore, and they were nearly a half a mile from the bridge. Nobody would come. There would be no reason for anyone to come. And shouting would be useless. They were too far away from anybody or anything to be heard.

"We're going to have to climb the cable," said Glenn.

"I'm cold," whimpered Jean. "I don't want to. I want to be home."

"I'm not doin' that either," said Art. "Uh-uh. No."

Glenn ignored their reluctance. "We're only a little ways away. Look." They were at the low point of the cable's sag, within ten to fifteen feet of the snow shrouded bank on the mountain side. "We grab hold of the cable and go hand over hand. Just like climbin' another tree."

Stress was ripping at him. It balled up like a fist in his stomach. In those crucial moments Glenn learned something about himself. He was at his best in a crisis. In those moments life had its greatest meaning. His thoughts were clearest, his decisions most effective. In moments like that he gave himself totally to a situation, and therein lay the fulfillment.

There was an old length of rope soaked through with dirty oil in the car, used apparently to secure loads. With it he tied Jean to the cable, around her waist and around the cable, and guided her on her way. She started off gingerly, inch by painful inch, upside down, hand over hand, feet hooked over the cable, backing along like a sloth on a limb. Below was the Big Wood's current at its angriest, slamming into an ice flow lodged up against the rock wall of the shore, then rolling over the top of it into a slow turning froth of deep green. Her hands were shaking. Twice her bulky mittens missed their grip. Each time she caught herself with her other hand, never having to test the security of the rope.

Confidence came when she saw the shore beneath her. From then on it was like she was on the playground. She was at the tower in a matter of seconds. She threw the rope back. Then it was Art's turn. He tied the rope around himself and, like Jean, climbed hand over hand to shore. But when Art tried to toss the rope back, it spiraled into the rapids and the ice flows.

So—Glenn had to do without its protection. He forced himself, and he did it, without hesitating, without slipping.

By then so much energy had been expended, so much effort put forth, that the simple task of climbing down from the platform was the most difficult of all. The tower was built out of tall stands of timber and painted a dirty white, bark still in place. Lumber as thick as railroad ties anchored the stands together into a tall, narrow pyramid. A ladder of two-by-fours ran from the platform to the ground and was sculpted in eerie patterns of stiff wind-blown snow. They picked their way down as if the soft snow beneath them was boiling acid.

The adventure was gone. All they wanted now was home. "It's probably time for my piano lesson," spoke Jean, shaking, nearly in tears. "Mother promised to teach me some Jelly Roll Morton songs."

The sun had dropped behind the mountain's crest and its gleam on the snow had been dulled into shadows. It was indeed time to go home.

Damndest thing though—right in front of them, carved into the side of Carbonate's cliffs, was a cave. A long narrow slit of snow and ice. They hadn't seen it at first, because it looked like it was only part of the terracing snow formations.

But they were going home.

Except—

A noise? From within the cave?

Rustling sounds. Digging noises, it sounded like.

A ghost? Legend had it—in fireside tales—that Black Jack Ketchum never could relocate that stash of his and spent the remainder of his life searching for it. His spirit prowls the hills still, digging, looking for that gold.

They stood steadfast, all three of them. They had all heard the noise. It had come from the cave, from within its triangular hole of drifted snow bisected by a long single icicle.

"It *is* his ghost!" said Art. "Don't anyone go in there."

For Jean, such a warning was simply bait. She never had been able to resist the temptation of a curiosity, frightening or otherwise.

"Jean—" barked Glenn. "Wait—don't—"

She was already waist deep in snow, clawing her way toward the opening.

"Jean—don't—the snow might come down on you."

Wise caution. But truth was, Glenn was more worried about the ghost than anything of physical substance. Glenn was as frightened of ghost stories as Jean was fascinated.

She stood outside the hole, peering inside, into the dark, trying to see.

The icicle came loose and sliced into the snow, as if to offer an invitation, and Jean scrunched around it and stepped inside. It caused Glenn to go limp with fear. He waded over to the opening. He saw nothing but black.

But he heard breathing. And it wasn't from Jean. Something *was* in there.

He stepped inside.

The opening turned cavernous, large enough for him to stand. Still he couldn't see Jean. He couldn't see anything. There was only the blackness.

And the breathing.

And a stench so strong it brought him to nausea.

He felt urine run down his legs, then a stinging as it turned cold and seeped into his wound.

Art's voice blasted from outside. "What's in there?" It brought a snarl from the darkness.

Glenn's insides jerked; he didn't move. As his eyes adjusted he began to distinguish the outline of something that up until now he had only seen in pictures and drawings. A mountain lion. It was lying there as if half asleep, not poised to attack, just lying there.

Then Glenn saw Jean. She was rigid, too terrified to speak, very nearly close enough for it to reach her.

The big cat snarled again and took a swipe at the air.

Glenn jumped in front of his sister, then closed his eyes and waited for the slam of the beast into his chest.

It didn't come.

When Glenn opened his eyes again the animal was still there, same position, curled up the way a house cat sits—like it was tired, or injured, or simply lacked the will to move, other than to swipe at the air again, two quick swipes, like a boxer double punching. They were half hearted swipes. As more light sifted into their eyes the children saw that there was a vulnerable look on its face. And it was so thin that its bones were practically ripping through its skin.

"I think he's hurt," whispered Glenn.

"He's hungry," said Jean.

They backed toward the opening. The big animal's muscles twitched as if to trigger movement, though none came.

They climbed out and swore Art to secrecy. "We can't even tell our folks," Glenn said. "If people find out they'll come up and kill it, sure as I'm standin' here."

Now they had a new mission. A new adventure.

They returned with scraps of meat from Sam Dorsey, the butcher. They told Sam it was for Jake. They brought it wrapped in paper and opened it and pushed it toward the cat with a pole. He sniffed it, then looked up helplessly.

"I don't think he has any teeth," said Jean.

The mountain lion was old. The children could see that now, even in the dim light of the nearly set sun. His skin was wrinkled and grey, and his whiskers were gone. And he was lying in his own waste.

This time he didn't snarl. He sniffed and licked at the meat, over and over, then looked up at the children again. An expression on an animal can speak more than words sometimes. He had a face on him like Ol' Jake would sometimes get when smelling something from the kitchen he knew he would never be able to have.

The children arrived home after dark. Dott was half out of her mind with worry, then furious once she found out they were safe. Glenn took the switching for it, saying that playing hooky was his idea. When he was being hauled off to the woodshed by the ear he flashed a look at Jean. "Don't you dare tell about the cougar," it said.

Bob was still in Ketchum, thankfully. It was always easier to get the licking from his mother. Glenn fashioned a story that he and Jean had taken a notion to walk to Bullion.

Dott exclaimed, "What ever possessed you to do such a thing? It's over seven miles to Bullion. You could have frozen to death along the way. Or caught your death of a cold. Land alive, you're smart as the dickens in school, but sometimes I think you haven't the common sense the Good Lord gave a fence post."

Eventually she noticed the makeshift bandage and the ripped pant leg and dried blood. "What in Heaven's name?—"

"Oh," he said. "Uh, we climbed on some boxes and boards and stuff. Must 'a happened then."

It was a huge gash, baring skin and muscle half an inch down. Dott called Dr. Kleinman, not knowing when Bob would be home, fearing it needed to be looked at right away. Dr. Kleinman boiled a curved needle in a pot on the stove and sat Glenn down on the edge of the kitchen table, legs dangling. "Now," he said. "I know I won't have to worry about you hollerin'. Your pappy tells me that you're pert' near a man now. I hear tell you'll be getting your long pants soon. So I guess I won't have to worry about you hollerin'."

Glenn was sitting with a pack of ice on his leg. The cold would numb the pain of the needle, Dr. Kleinman said.

And funny, there really wasn't much pain, it just smarted a bit when the sutures were pulled through. Jean seemed to be the one in pain. She was watching from a corner of the kitchen, legs pulled up, gripping her knees, pulling them tighter every time the needle went in and each time it came out, dragging the skin outward with it.

That night Jean and Glenn both dreamed of the mountain lion. The next day neither thought of anything else. After school they went straight away with a bucket to Fat's restaurant, asking for table scraps, anything soft an animal without any teeth could eat. "They're for poor ol' Jake," Glenn said. "He's getting on in years, you know. Can't chew like he used to." They told Fat he probably shouldn't oughta say anything to their mother and father. "Because they think Jake should be on a diet."

Then they went the wrong direction, out toward Carbonate, instead of back toward home.

They took the long stick and slid the bucket over to the mountain lion.

At first they thought he was dead, because he didn't move when they entered the cave, and the meat scraps from the day before were untouched. But the cougar lifted his head with a weary effort when he caught the odor of diced pork. He eventually put his head in the bucket, but then withdrew it without eating and laid it back down between his paws.

Jean reached in her large coat pocket and brought out a pint milk bottle and popped off the lid…and crept on all fours over to where she could have touched the lion if she'd have had a mind to…slowly, slowly…and poured the milk out onto the frozen ground. Its flow reached the animal's nostrils and he shook his head and sneezed, and began lapping it up.

Then the cougar put his head in the bucket and ate. At first he ate with only little dips of his tongue—and sneezed again several times—then began swallowing it with huge slobbering gulps.

The children left quickly. The entire trip took less than forty-five minutes. Carbonate was close, skirting the edge of town. They were home within the time expected of them.

This they did every day for the remainder of the winter and into the coming of spring. Most of the time Art went too. One of them went every day. And no one was the wiser, though Dott and Bob should have guessed something was awry, the way Ol' Jake would bark and carry on when they'd get home, the way he'd smell their clothes up and down.

The cougar grew fatter and even began to move around, and to cleanse himself with his tongue and paws. And he began to scratch about and bury his droppings. Once when they went he wasn't even in the cave.

The children were always cautious, always a little frightened when entering the cave. They never had the courage to touch the animal, even though the huge cat would purr with the sound of an automobile and rub his head up against them when they'd get close enough. They were surprised at the way his fur felt, wiry, instead of soft like it looked. Once he licked milk off of the back of Jean's hand. It was then that they saw he had only one fang and it was black and useless.

They saved their own table scraps, stews and soup remnants, and with money earned from shoveling walks they bought milk. And Fat was always accommodating with his leftovers. One day he smiled and said, "A child who shows kindness is the greatest of all living creatures. So says Lao Tsu." Fat knew.

Then one day, in early spring—the old cougar didn't raise his head, not even for the milk.

"I think he's dead," Glenn said, in a voice barely to be heard.

Jean shook her head in denial, with tears moistening her freckled cheeks. "He can't die. He just can't."

"Let's go," said Glenn. "There ain't nothin' we can do."

Jean reached out and placed her hand on the animal's head. The cougar was lying with his head between his paws, like when he slept.

There was no movement. She moved her hand back and forth, stroking his fur. Nothing. She shook the huge head. Nothing. And his sides were motionless. "We've got to get Father," she cried.

"Are you crazy, girl? He'll give us the licking of our lives, coming out here day after day like this."

"Father can fix him. Father can fix anything. We just have to."

Glenn saw the hurt. "…all right." He knew the animal was dead, that no doctor in the world could fix him, that all they were headed for was trouble, but—"All right," he said. "Let's go get Dad."

Bob was in his office at his desk when Glenn and Jean came clamoring in. Jean ran in first, clomping across the waiting room floor in leaps. "Father, Father, Father." She was running so fast she rammed into the side of the big leather-top table in the middle of the waiting room and nearly tripped over the big black leather sofa.

His inner office door was open. He was on the telephone. At first Bob was angry at the interruption.

"Father, Father, come quick. He's dying. You've got to save him." She and Glenn had run almost the entire way, down to the road, across the bridge up to Main, close to a mile. Their faces were flushed red and Jean was breathing so hard she could barely speak. "Come Father. Come quick."

"All right, Princess, all right, hold on." He spoke then into the phone mouthpiece, telling whoever it was he had to attend to an emergency.

"Father, please!" Jean was stamping her feet and clenching her fists.

Bob placed the receiver on the hook and took up his bag. "All right children, what's this all about?"

"Just hurry."

He tucked his bag under his arm and rolled down his desk. His desk was the only piece of furniture in the inner office that wasn't painted white. Everything else, all four walls, fluoroscope, metal examining table, glass case full of various sorts of instruments, was white. There was a half-sized door to a little anteroom, also white, where the oddest things could be found, like the jar of formaldehyde with the tape worm floating inside, and the jar half-full of liquid mercury that was so heavy Glenn needed both hands to lift it.

The adjacent waiting room was just the opposite, full of masculine browns and dark greens—bold green wallpaper, a stuffed bald eagle mounted above the front door, its wings spread in flight, a glass case full of medical volumes, a rustic grandfather's clock that chimed the time of day at the top of the hour and once on the half hour.

Bob locked the outer door, then knelt and spoke gently. "Children. Calm down. Now what is it? You're going to have to tell me. Is it Mother? Has something happened to Mother?"

"No—he's down by the river—come, hurry," hastened Jean.

Bob put the children in the car, a new 1918 two door Studebaker with an electric starter and a water bag hung on the front. "Son, how about you tell me what's going on, calmly now. I'm not going to be able to help unless I know where I'm going and what I'm going to be doing."

"Yes, sir," Glenn said softly, fearfully.

"Well?"

"It's an animal, sir. We've been caring for an animal."

"You two know better than to handle sick animals."

"Yes, sir."

Bob asked no more questions. He negotiated the Studebaker through the muddy springtime washes, right up to the base of Carbonate Mountain. It wasn't until he poked his head into the cave's opening, now much larger in the absence of snow, that he realized it was a mountain lion. "Well saw my legs off and call me Shorty," he said. He removed his hat and crawled in on his hands and knees.

"Please, Father," pleaded Jean. "Fix him. You can fix him. I know you can."

"Stay back, children," he ordered. "Way back."

Came Glenn's voice, "He's dead, Dad."

Jean burst out, "He's not, he's not, he's not. You can fix him, Father."

The animal's limbs appeared to be stiff with rigor. Bob thought for a moment. Not even a fool would approach a sleeping or injured mountain lion. He returned to the car with the children and brought back a canvas tarp and laid it over the animal. Then, with the tarp as protection, he cut a slit and slipped the opening over its head. And at that point he was sure. Its neck and ears were hardened, its jaw locked shut.

He lifted away the tarp and began an examination—for Jean's benefit—checking for a heartbeat, looking into its eyes, pretending to try to open its mouth. "Did he bite or scratch either of you?"

"No, Father," came Jean's voiced from outside of the cave where she and Glenn had been ordered to stay. "Is he going to be all right?"

"Glenn, what about that gash you got a spell back, the one Kleinman stitched up? You get that from this animal?"

"No, sir."

"Is he going to be all right Father?" Jean asked again.

Bob closed up his bag. "Come here, Princess. You too, son."

Still on his knees, Bob put his arms out for his beloved children, and sheltered them, one under each arm, and looked down at the cougar. Then Jean knew, too.

"I'm glad he had you two for his last days."

"Is he in Heaven?" asked Jean quietly.

"I suspect so."

They made their way outside and Bob pointed out across the river to the rolling water's edge, high from spring melt. "See that over there? One of my favorite fishing spots. They jump right out into my pockets."

Jean sniffled and smiled. "Nuh uh."

"It's best a little later on in the season, when the water level drops a bit, when it just kind 'a trickles over the sand and the pebbles. I wade in and cast into that hole over there." He hugged them with the grip of his hands on their shoulders. "Let's all go eat, what do you say. We'll go get your mother and make a night of it at the Hiawatha. Finest hotel between Denver and the Pacific Ocean. What do you say?"

"Can we go to Fat's instead, for some Sum?" asked Glenn.

"Another night. Tonight it's the Hiawatha."

"Dad—are we going to get whippins'?" he asked.

"Do you deserve a whipping?"

"Yes, sir, I guess I do. Not Jean though. It was me that led her down here."

"I don't ever want you down by the river again. Ever. Either one of you. Understood?"

"Yes, sir."

"Let's just leave it at that then. Deal?"

"Deal."

They made their way back to the car. The ground beneath their feet was matted by thousands and thousands of last fall's leaves, damp and composted with six months of snow and sheltered under the newly budding leaves of the towering cottonwoods.

"Will you whistle me up some mushrooms?" asked Jean.

"Ohhh, I don't know," Bob said. "My whistler is awful dry. Not sure I can."

"Pleeeease."

Pretty soon he saw the tip of one poking up through the mulch bed, one of the rare morels that Idahoans so cherish. He gave a whistle.

Jean's face came bursting alive with glee.

Bob winked at Glenn and bent over and plucked it up.

Chapter 18

At Aunt Lillie's House

Bellevue, Idaho

1956

Uncle John and Aunt Lillie, who lived in Bellevue, were one of the first to have a TV. On Friday nights we would go down to "watch the fights"—sponsored by Gillette—from Madison Square Garden. It was the most boring night of the week. Those guys on TV, they didn't know how to fight, poking at each other and dancing around. Put John Wayne in there, then there'd be a show. The night Floyd Patterson KO'd Archie Moore was one to remember, because that was the night I had the big stomachache, right after Aunt Lillie served apple pie and ice cream.

"He probably ate the ice cream too fast; it's awfully cold," figured Nanna.

"Maybe I have an ulcer too," I said. Dad had one the size of a silver dollar, something that had plagued him ever since the war. Sometimes it caused him to walk half doubled over. O'You had him on a special liquid protein diet, a powdery mixture called Sustagen. Worry is what caused it, said O'You. Dad was a constant worrier.

O'You cleared a spot and hoisted me up onto the dining room table. "Let's have a look at you," he said. "Lay back now and lift up your shirt." He took two fingers and thumped on my stomach, and pushed and felt and prodded. "Show me exactly where it hurts."

I pointed low on my right side—and O'You became very still. It was sort of like he was holding his breath. He pressed on the spot.

I remember jerking when he did it.

O'You, without speaking, pulled his lower lip in tight and stood up and walked to the kitchen.

"I want Moritz on the phone," I could hear him say.

O'You's voice was always booming loud, but it was particularly loud that night. "Yes, Central, connect me with Doctor Moritz in Sun Valley. Thank you."

183

While O'You was talking to Dr. Moritz, and while Mom and Dad and Nanna were buzzing around in whispers, George Merrick tried to keep me distracted. George was my cousin, an adult who was more like a kid, and was one of the dozen or so relatives that congregated at Aunt Lillie's on Friday nights. I liked George a lot. He was funny and big and boisterous, but never threatening, never overpowering. "What's that you got in your pocket?" George asked.

I reached in and pried out a black lump.

"A rock? You keep rocks in your pockets? What's that for? To keep you from blowing away in a windstorm?"

"It's ore from up Triumph Mine."

"How'd you come by that?"

"Gary Miller's dad gave it to me. He works there." Triumph Mine, the old North Star renamed, was the last of the mines to still produce. It was all that remained of the old days. There were no more gold mines, there was no more Chinatown, no more Red Light District, all of it gone, except in the colorful stories Nanna would tell. Had it not been for Sun Valley, the whole place would by now be no more than a collection of ghost towns.

George played with me and kept me occupied, kept my mind off the things being said, though it wasn't necessary. I had confidence. And the confidence grew, even as we were riding up to Sun Valley.

Even as the nurses were examining me and drawing blood, and speaking words like peritonitis and white count, I had confidence.

"Am I going to have to have my appendix out?" I asked.

"Maybe," said Dad, in a soft voice and with a smile. "We're not sure just yet." He was sitting on my bedside, the same way he would when he'd put me to bed, his hand on my knee.

My life was filled with love. I was well taken care of as a child, so well that the thought of anything happening to me while under the protection of these larger than life guardians was unthinkable. From as early as I could remember it had been that way. If I fell and scraped myself, O'You would fix it. If I got a stomach ache, O'You would fix it. At night, with Mom and Dad asleep on the other side of the wall, if I was thirsty or if I had a sore throat all I had to do was knock on that wall and Dad would come.

To me, the trip to the hospital was just another adventure. "Is O'You going to do the operation?"

"Doctor Moritz will be doing the surgery," Dad said.

I protested. "I want O'You to do it." I guess I was feeling slighted.

"He'll be there. In the room with you."

"Where is he now? Gettin' ready?"

"Yep. He's talking to Doctor Moritz. They're figuring things out."

"How come he's not here?"

"He's got to help Doctor Moritz get ready. He wouldn't very well be able to do that if he was in here with you, now would he?"

That was probably true. He was probably prepping for surgery. But it would have helped if he would have come in, and like Dad, patted me on the knee and said everything would be OK, like he always did whenever else I was sick. I had no way of knowing that there might have been a reason—superstition, because of another time he stood beside a child and made promises. It never occurred to me, in hearing all the stories about Jean, to ask where she was, why there wasn't an adult Aunt Jean somewhere. Nor did it occur to me to question the oddity of Nanna's and O'You's "upstairs." One side was a vast storage area where I loved to play, where treasures could be found, like old books, and Dad's army clothes, and the Indian artifacts Nanna and O'You had been given over the years. The other half consisted of two neatly kept bedrooms side by side with a half bath between them, guest bedrooms. One had been Dad's when he was a kid like me, the other Jean's. The beds were made and dressers were kept clean and dusted. Dad's closet was empty; Jean's was full of children's clothes, frilly dresses of a style forty years gone, as if one would expect her to come walking in at any moment. I never questioned it because it seemed normal. It was just the way things were. And there was something else. Every Sunday afternoon after church we'd all go to the cemetery and trim a spot next to a lilac bush, and put flowers beneath a headstone. Like the closet full of clothes, it was something I never questioned, because it was normal. We did it every Sunday. I'd run and play, jump off the headstones, do somersaults, play trucks in the dirt, watch the airplanes on approach to the airport across the highway, what any child would do to cope with the monotony of perplexing adult rituals—and then we'd go home, until next Sunday. One day I decided to read the headstone. *JEAN ELEANOR WRIGHT, Born - June 25, 1911, Died - August 4, 1919*

Nanna was there with me, in the hospital room in a chair in the corner, knitting on a sweater, making me feel good with simply her presence, with her pearly white hair and sweet smile. "How did Jean die?" I asked her, because suddenly I thought of her. Nanna had a way of dodging questions, of answering them without really answering them. I can't remember what she said exactly, just that the answer satisfied me, and that the curiosity was gone, even though I still didn't know. And she smiled and stroked my forehead, with a healing hand. If there was the pain of a memory beneath that smile she gave no indication of it.

Mom was there too, sitting at the foot of the bed.

I didn't see O'You's face until I was in the operating room, and then I only saw his eyes above the mask. I could tell it was him by how tall and straight he stood, and because of the thin black hair streaked with gray, combed straight back. But I wished I could see behind the mask, see O'You's mouth, the way it was always set firm with confidence. Because now I was starting to get scared. Just a little.

"All right, Bobby," came Dr. Moritz' monotone voice. "I'm going to place this over your mouth and nose. Nothing to be afraid of. I want you to count backwards from a hundred. Can you do that? When you get to one you'll be back in your room. That's how simple it's going to be. All right. Let's begin...go ahead..."

"One hundred...ninety-nine..." I felt something heavy on my arm. I looked over. Attached to it was a long brown board, tied on with white tape, stretching my arm stiff, and a needle was dripping something into it through a tube. I tensed and began thrashing it up and down, banging the board against the bed rail, not really knowing why.

Mom's and Nanna's face calmed me. Nanna was softly stroking my head. "It's OK," she was saying. Her face was right above me, the sweet smile and the crystal white hair. "It's OK. You're going to be fine." I thought I even saw tears in her eyes.

Dr. Moritz appeared and pulled the needle out of my arm and untaped the board. "How are you feeling?" he asked.

"When are you going to operate?"

Dr. Moritz's mouth, normally frozen in seriousness, broke into a smile. "We did. You're done. You came through it fine, minus one appendix."

"I feel like throwing up."

"You just go ahead if you have to." Dr. Moritz put a curved bowl up by my head. "The nausea is caused by the anesthesia. It won't last long."

It was as though a magician had snapped his fingers, or blinked an eye. One instant I was in the operating room, the next I was in the recovery room. It had been exactly that dramatic. I had no memory of anything in between. No dreams. No mystical experiences. Nothing. Not even blackness. Nothing.

"Where's O'You?" I asked.

Said Nanna, emotions overwhelming her eyes, "He had some things to do. He'll be along shortly." She was busying herself as she talked, straightening covers, fluffing my pillow, moving glasses and things about.

On Mom's face was the steadfast look of serenity, like she knew all along everything was going to be fine—her Christian Science upbringing.

Then Dad burst in with an arm load of comic books. *The Adventures of Uncle Scrooge. Donald Duck.* Classic Comics editions of *Moby Dick* and *The Count of Monte Christo*. But no *Superman* or *Black Hawk* comics. Garbage, Dad maintained. Holding no literary value whatsoever. Dad was a voracious reader. Sometimes he would read a book a day. He once looked at me with fire in his eyes and said, "You want adventure? Here—" He tossed me an H. Rider Haggard novel. And I became Allan Quatermain with pistol and bullwhip, battling African sorcerers and house-sized crabs in search of the legendary fortune of King Solomon. "You want scary? Here—" And he handed me Edgar Allen Poe. "Now that right there, that is literature." Well, needless to say, after *The Pit and the Pendulum* and *The Tell-Tale Heart*, I had to sleep with the light on—until George Merrick explained to me that electricity was the medium by which ghosts could enter the physical world. Thanks, George.

O'You came later that afternoon, mouth set firm in that usual way, yet turned up a little at the left hand corner, like he was about ready to tell a joke, yellow flower in his lapel. "How's your copperosity sagaciating?"

"All right."

"You're going to be fine. Just fine."

I recovered at Nanna's and O'You's house. I stayed there for two weeks, in Nanna's room, flat on my back. O'You wanted me close, wanted to "keep a good eye on me." Had it not been for *The Hound of the Baskervilles* I probably would have been so consumed in boredom I would have died from that alone as an affliction. It was hard reading for an eight year old. I had to take it word by word and sentence by sentence. I had no choice—there was nothing else to do. Pretty soon the story obsessed me, and I had no choice but to wade through the long sentences and the big words, dictionary in hand, if I wanted to find out who the bearded stranger was, or the lonely figure on the moor. That's absolutely what got me through those two weeks, *The Hound of the Baskervilles*, that and the picture on the wall, which was another mystery. It was on the opposite wall—every time I'd look up from the book I'd see it—a large, elegantly framed portrait photograph of a girl with a shy yet consuming smile. It was placed in such a way that it was the single most observed item from any point in the room. It was Nanna's *Mona Lisa*, where the eyes followed you wherever you went. The girl had blond hair, blond enough that it could have been white, and large mysterious eyes that seemed to want to speak of something. It had always been there. I couldn't remember a time it wasn't. It was so normal hanging there, so much a part of the house, that like the bedroom upstairs, I never thought to question it, never thought to ask about it. I sometimes wondered if it was Jean. Probably not. Jean's photo was on the opposite wall, a long thin frame containing a series of poses in a turn-of-the-century dress with a large bow on the top of her head, taken when she was probably four or five. This photograph was of an older girl, nine or ten. And the facial features were different. Just a picture, something hanging on the wall simply because it was supposed to be there. I did end up asking Nanna about it, during the recuperation, because I was always looking at it. Like with the question about Jean, she dodged it artfully, in such a way that I was left believing that nobody knew, that it was just a piece of art that Nanna liked to look at. It never occurred to me that everybody else knew and that I was the only one who didn't.

Sometimes when I'd close my eyes at night I would imagine the pictures would come alive, and that little Jean and the girl with the mysterious eyes would play with me. Right there in the room. Sometimes I could make my imagination so vivid I could hear their laughter. Once I even thought I could smell them, like they had been playing in Nanna's perfume, a scent so strong I felt it in my lungs.

The picture of the baby in the crib on O'You's desk at the office was yet another mystery. Like the picture on the wall, it seemed normal, so much a part of things, like it belonged there, that I never gave it much thought. Except once. Once I did ask about it, while Dad and I were carrying buckets of coal to O'You's furnace. "Who's that?" I asked, thinking Dad would answer like Nanna, with a reply that wasn't really a lie, but wasn't the truth either, so that I'd be left knowing no more than when I asked.

"That's my daughter," he said simply. Dad was incapable of telling a lie. That was his nature.

I looked at him like I'd been shot in the chest with a cannon.

"I was married before, before I met your mother. We had a little girl."

My voice, I suspect, carried a hollowness, an emptiness, like the way someone sounds who is very, very alone. Because I was hardly able to stand. "Where is she now?"

"I don't know."

The answer was inconceivable. It made no sense to the rationality of my young mind. "How old is she?"

Dad answered without having to think about it. "She would be twenty…"

"Is that the picture on Nanna's wall? Is that her?"

"Yes."

"What's her name?"

"Patricia. You must never tell your mother that I told you this."

I never did. Something about the way it was said, the seriousness in his voice. In fact, I never spoke of it again.

But each time I'd fill the stove and pass O'You's desk I'd think about my sister, wonder about her, where she was, what she was doing, what she looked like, why I was never allowed to know her. And the unshakable confidence I had in the adults who loved me, who protected me, weakened a bit.

Chapter 19

Our Darling

Hailey, Idaho

1919

"**L**OOK DOWN THERE," Glenn said. He and Jean were on top of Buttercup, an almost perfect pyramid of a mountain directly east of town. Its treeless slopes were dotted with sagebrush, wheat grass, and wild flowers. It was the first and smallest of dozens of triangular shaped mountains and foothills that formed the Wood River Valley's wall, rising as if in protection, painted with washes of bluish greens, purples, and yellows. Almost since the day she began to speak, Jean had wanted to climb Buttercup, to go to the "very tippy top." Finally Bob and Dott said yes, now that she was eight, if Glenn went with her, and if they had their tick shots. And if they would do their best to keep clear of the sagebrush. Still, Bob and Dott let it be known it was "against our better judgment." No one really knew how effective the Spotted Fever vaccine was. Sometimes it seemed to work, sometimes it didn't.

"That's Bellevue." Glenn pointed south with his arm, so Jean could sight along it. "You can see the black spot from where the war ended." Eight months earlier, on November 18, when word came that the Armistice had been signed, the town had celebrated with a huge bonfire in the middle of Main Street. The fire had been so hot that the black spot remained, a reminder of a war that changed the face of two continents, toppled kings and queens, forever altering the way people live their lives. "And way up there—you see that? That's Baldy. Bald Mountain. And right down there below it is Ketchum." The valley was narrower at Ketchum, and the mountains taller. Baldy spired nine thousand feet and was covered with evergreens, except for that one little spot on top above the timberline. Past Ketchum the peaks turned palatial. The White Cloud range was aptly named, jagged mountains soaring so high they truly did pierce the clouds. Jean looked around in every direction, then put her lips together and tipped her head toward him triumphantly. She had made it. A white floppy hat protected her fair skin from the blistering August sun. Half her face was shaded, and the way the shadow sliced across that expression, that look of victory, it gave her an adult appearance, a momentary presence of grown-up beauty. Glenn imagined that that must be how she'd look ten or so years from now. He never forgot that look. "Do you think Father and Mother can see us?" she asked. Twin strands of pig tails, braided tight along her head and tied in back by a bow, danced on her back as she jumped up and down and waved. As was typical, Dott had put her in a dress, even though she was hiking, a cute green and blue plaid dress with black stockings and high button shoes.

"Here, let's do this." Glenn took off his bright red shirt and flew it back and forth over his head. "If Mother and Dad are watching, they'll for sure see this."

"Up here it's not a point at all," marveled Jean. "It's big and flat. Father was right."

"It looks like a point from down there because it's so far away. Faraway things always look small."

Jean ran around the perimeter, a hundred feet in a circle, then came back and started waving with Glenn. Grasshoppers clicked and fluttered in the hot and dusty air, a calming thing, a thing of beauty, in a different sort of way.

From way down in town Bob and Dott were peering through an expandable seaman's glass. "There they are," said Bob, glass telescoped out and pressed tightly to his eye.

"Let me see, let me look."

Bob handed her the glass.

"Where? I don't see anything."

Bob steered her twenty degrees to the right. "There. Right up there."

Into the shaky little circle appeared two figures, Glenn and Jean jumping up and down. Then Dott saw Jean grip her stomach and fall over out of sight behind a clump of sagebrush. Then Glenn disappeared.

Came Dott's voice in confusion, "Bob?"

"Did you lose them again?"

"Why can't I see them? Oh my. Bob? I think something has happened to Jean—"

"They probably just sat down to have their lunch. Or maybe they started back down the mountain."

"No, I saw Jean fall over. It was like something hit her in the stomach."

Bob took the glass and panned the mountain. Nothing.

"Oh, Bob. You don't suppose. A rattlesnake?"

"You sure she fell and didn't just sit?"

"Yes. She grabbed her stomach and fell."

A dry mid-day in August. It certainly could have been a rattler. With a rattlesnake strike, if it had been in the groin, if it pierced an artery, she'd be dead in a matter of hours. They took the Studebaker and in ten minutes were at the base of the mountain. They hadn't taken but two or three steps when Glenn came suddenly into view, appearing over the top of a crest carrying Jean. He was cradling her in his arms, half running, half sliding. He was only ten, eleven in two weeks, but in that moment he looked like a man. The open collar of his shirt, stained in sweat, showed the sinews of his straining muscles.

Jean was conscious. Bob took her gently. "Heeyyyy, Princess, what seems to be the trouble? What happened to my girl?"

"My tummy hurts. Really bad."

Dott stroked her forehead. "Oh precious, you had us so worried. We're going to fix you up fine. Everything will be OK."

"What happened, son?"

Glenn was breathing in heavy gasps. "I don't know Dad. She just all of a sudden hunched over and started crying."

"Could it have been a snake bite?"

"No, sir, I don't think so. There was no snake that I saw."

"Could be she has a bit of heat stroke," Bob speculated.

"Maybe she ate something that was poison," offered Glenn.

Jake was barking from the car, feet moving, body twitching, wanting to run up to them. He traveled everywhere with them. Whenever the car door was open he'd scramble in, but he never ventured beyond the car, because of his hip. He could get in, but he couldn't get out. Bob dropped one hand to give him a pat while swinging Jean up into the front seat. "Good Ol' Jake. The best damn wheel dog on the continent. All right, Princess, show me where it hurts."

The top was down on their new Big Six touring car. Again, a Studebaker. Jean was high up in the front seat, eye level to Bob as he stood outside on the ground, one foot on the running board, leaning through the open door. "It doesn't hurt as bad now," she said. "I just had a side ache from walking so fast up the mountain, is all."

"All right, Princess. But I want you to show me where. Can you do that? Point to where it hurts."

"Right there." She put her hand over her lower right side.

"Did you eat any berries?"

"No."

"Did you eat anything?"

"Just our lunch. What Mother made for us. We got hungry and ate it half-way up."

"Glenn, do you feel all right?"

"Yes, sir. I feel fine."

Bob turned back to Jean. "How long have you been having these pains?"

"It happens when I run, or when I twist real fast. Sometimes it happens at night if I have bad dreams."

"How long has this been going on? A week? Two weeks?"

She lifted her shoulders. "I don't know."

"Are they bad pains?"

"Not like this one. Father, it hurt so bad I couldn't stand up. I couldn't even hardly breathe. But it's better now."

"And this has been going on for a while?"

"Yeah, I guess so. But not as bad as now."

"Why haven't you said anything?"

"I don' know…"

Bob looked in her eyes, felt her pulse, listened to her chest, tapped on her stomach. "All right, Princess. Let's get you back to the office. I want to do up some blood work on you."

"Can I sit on your lap and drive?"

"Not this time."

"But can I set the choke and retard the spark?"

"That's your job, isn't it?"

An hour later Jean was tucked into bed in her room. And Bob and Dott were out in the hallway whispering, thinking Jean couldn't hear. "Her white count's way up," Bob was saying. "I want Fox to come down and take a look at her."

Dr. Fox concurred. It was appendicitis. "She needs immediate surgery," he told Bob.

Bob wanted to wait, just a bit, to monitor her blood and watch her abdomen. He wanted to be sure.

In the meantime Glenn came in with something he'd made for her, a block of wood upon which was carved the raised image of a flower. Jake was curled up on the foot of her bed with a worried look on his face. Glenn read to her from Dickens. He had vocabulary and reading skills far beyond his age, better than many adults. Jean loved to have him read to her.

The pain was more or less steady and seemed to be getting worse. It made concentration hard and forced her onto her side with her legs curled up. Bob was coming in and out checking on her, tapping on her stomach, looking in her eyes, listening. And he drew another syringe full of blood.

Jean and Glenn could hear people talking from the kitchen, and on the telephone, words they didn't understand, like peritoneum and vermiform. It was both comforting and frightening. Sometimes, in order to hear what was being said, Glenn would lower his voice, or stop reading altogether.

"I want to get her to Salt Lake City," came Bob's voice. They heard it distinctly because he said it with such force. "I want the operation done there. Next to Seattle, they've got the finest facilities this side of the Mississippi."

Came Dott's voice, "Bob, I want you to do the operation."

They had to strain to hear what their father said next. He'd dropped his voice considerably.

"No. Absolutely not. I will not operate on my own child. I want the best. The best surgeon. The best hospital."

"I want the best too. Bob, *you* are the best. You know anatomy better than any of them."

Bob shook his head, more like a shiver, as though he was shrinking from the mere thought of it. "I care too much…"

"But Bob, Salt Lake is three hundred miles away."

There was silence for a brief while. Then spoke Bob, "Earl, will you do the surgery?"

They recognized Dr. Fox's voice in response. "I have this friend, this friend from the war. A pilot. He flew SE-5's over Germany against the Red Baron himself. There's not a better pilot alive. He's down in Shoshone right now, flying around, putting on shows, giving people rides. Barnstorming, he calls it. I can get word to him. He'll get her to Salt Lake. He'll have her there before you can say jack-rabbit."

As they waited for the plane—it was at 3:00 a.m.—Glenn kept asking, "Will she be back for my party?" He would be eleven in two weeks. Jean had just turned eight. "Yes dear," assured Dott repeatedly. "Jean will be at your party. Promise." They were on a long stretch of road out by the cemetery, away from telephone poles. Two cars were positioned at opposite ends with headlights blazing. On either side of the road, in between the cars, were men and women with lanterns and flashlights marking the landing site.

The sky was adorned with stars, so many the heavens were awash with softness. It was as though they too loved little Jean. Soon one began to float to earth. Then came the distant purring of an engine and the shadowed outline of something that hovered and droned like a gigantic dragon fly, double winged, dropping, gliding to earth.

The plane floated for a few seconds, just above the makeshift runway, then arched back and settled down as the airspeed dropped off. The wheels touched down smoothly. Barely a blade of grass was bent. The plane seemed as though it was trying to lift and fly even as it was coming to its stop. The engine sputtered and popped, and wham, the huge propeller stood instantly still, straight up and down. The twinkling light they had all seen had been a battery driven lantern lashed between the struts of the right bi-wing. It had given the plane an off-center look as it was approaching.

The plane looked to be more than twice the size of a car, at least measured by the wing span, and eleven feet high. It was the first time either Jean or Glenn had seen one. Joseph Boudwin was the flyer's name. He brought the plane over from England on a steamer. He claimed he flew it over, but everyone knew different. Stenciled on the side was the number 19 and a bull's-eye circle, and the caricature of a little man swinging an executioner's axe, the emblem of the 25th Aero Squadron. The bi-plane's top wing was slanted slightly ahead of the bottom one, giving it a look of speed, of aggression. Exhaust vents fanned out from the engine into a long horizontal pipe that ran half the length of the fuselage. It was a two seat conversion, modified from the original with an expanded center section and a gravity tank between the spars.

Jean was dressed in a woolen coat, with scarf and mittens and a big winter hat that came down and covered her ears. Boudwin had cautioned them to dress warmly, since they would be flying at eight thousand feet above sea level, three thousand feet above the ground. "It gets a wee bit chilly up there," he had told Dr. Fox over the telephone as arrangements were being made.

He seated Bob first, then placed Jean on Bob's lap and ran a belt over both of them. "There you go missy." He had a cockney accent as thick as a British fog. "You tell your pappy if you start to get light in the head, and he'll tell me and I'll take her down a might. And I don't want you frettin' your pretty head over any of this. It's as safe as a night's ride in your own bed. I'm as good at what I do as your pappy is at what he does." He put goggles on both of them and jumped to the ground and ran out and put both hands on the propeller and gave it a pull. It chugged a quarter of a turn. Boudwin did it again and the engine started, advancing quarter turns at first then becoming a puttering blur, drawing the flying machine forward in tiny little leaps. By then Boudwin was in the cockpit, the seat behind Bob and Jean, having vaulted in as effortlessly as Bob used to mount a horse in the old days. Then the plane was taxiing into place for takeoff, its tail rudder and elevators flexing, gripping at the air. In mere seconds they were gone, leaving Glenn and Dott behind as specks on the ground, waving.

Dott involuntarily stepped toward them as they rose skyward, as if to scold them for not having said goodbye. She watched, she and Glenn, as the sky took the other half of her family into itself. She watched until the sky became once again nothing more than a sea of motionless stars.

Boudwin yelled forward to Bob. "We're loaded with four good hours of fuel. We travel at puttin' near a hunr't miles an hour. Salt Lake is about three hunr't miles. We'll make 'er."

Clasped within the strength of her father's arms, little Jean Wright felt no fear. An incredible adventure was about to be laid before her, beginning with the rich smell of spent fuel and the powerful purr of a 200-horsepower Wolseley Viper engine, and the dull scream of an eight-foot propeller, and the pitch and roll of a twenty-six-foot wingspan as the bird floated like an angel to meet the morning. The horizon quickly took shape as they rose, outlined first in shades of pink and purple, then in the brilliance of a sunrise, all within minutes.

"Is Mother coming?" she asked.

"Speak up, Princess. It's hard to hear over the wind."

"IS MOTHER COMING?"

"You bet your life she is. She and your brother will be on the noon train. They'll be there tonight, to see you and tuck you in. And by then it will be all over. Your appendix will be out and you'll be all better."

"Will it hurt when they put me to sleep?"

"Not a bit."

"What will it feel like?"

"It won't feel like anything. We'll put a mask over your nose and ask you to count backwards from ten. That's all there is to it. When you get to one it will be all over. And we'll all be right there at your bedside when you open your eyes."

She liked that, and leaned back against him. He pressed his face down into the nape of her neck and against her long braids. Her hair was cool and smooth, silky smooth, and smelled like peaches. "I love you, Princess."

"Me too, Father. Father, tell me again about the house."

He had to put his mouth close to her ear to be heard without shouting. And though her face was hot and fevered, upon it was a smile as he talked. And inside them both was the glow, the warmth, the connection.

"Well, you'll have your own room, upstairs, right next to Glenn's. Yours and Glenn's doors will only be a few feet apart. And you two will have your own private water closet."

"We won't have to go to the outhouse anymore?"

"No more outhouses. And we'll have water inside at the tap, hot water out of one side and cold water out of the other."

"We won't have to heat water on the stove anymore?"

"No more heating water. And no more pumps."

"No more pumps," she repeated.

The morning sun was on one side, the moon on the other, translucent, hardly distinguishable from the pearly luster of the sky. Jean asked, "How far is it to the moon?"

"A long ways. A long, long ways."

"Could we fly there?"

"No, Princess, 'fraid not."

"If we wanted?"

"No. I'm afraid not."

Visible from three thousand feet in the air was a sight most human beings had never seen, and Jean's pain seemed to fade before it—crashing sunlight, shaded mountain silhouettes, a carpet of black. When the sun was high enough to finally illuminate the valley floor she saw patchwork fields, perfect squares and colored rectangles. Children and farmers looked up in awe and waved at the odd looking thing in the sky, something they'd heard of only in war stories, or seen in pictures. Some had never heard of an airplane at all, and had no idea what they were seeing.

Soon they were over the Salt Flats, and Great Salt Lake. "When you swim there you don't sink," said Bob. "Because it's so full of salt. You float so high you tip over."

"When we get back can we go swimming at the Guyer Plunge?"

"Absolutely. We sure can. Know what else?"

"What."

"When we move into the new house we're going to buy a Victrola, just so you and I can dance."

By noon they were in the operating room. "Is that you, Father?"

"Yes, Princess, it's me."

"Why you have that thing on your face?"

"It's a surgical mask. It's going to help keep me from breathing germs on you during the operation."

"Are you going to take my 'pendix out?"

"Doctor Sarandon will be doing that."

"Hello Jean," said another man behind a mask.

"But Father, I want you to do it."

Bob had hold of her hand. He squeezed it and patted it. "I'll be right here the whole time."

"Promise?"

"I promise."

"The whole time?"

"The whole time."

"The whole entire time?"

"Absolutely. Holding your hand. And when we're done we'll wheel you on down to a room that's all fresh and waiting just for you. Your very own room. Room 115. Right down the hall there. We've got all your clothes there. Hair brush. Ribbons. Know what? I even brought one of mother's perfumes for you." Bob brought his finger to his mouth and whispered. "Shhhhh. Don't tell."

Jean giggled, then grimaced. The laughter had intensified the pain. "It hurts, Father."

"I know, sweetie, but not for long. Not for long. And when that old nasty appendix is out I'll still have hold of this hand. The whole time. I promise."

"It'll be fine, sweetheart," reaffirmed Dr. Sarandon. "I do these all the time. Sometimes twice a day."

"Where's Mother?"

"Hmmmmm. I would guess that right about now Mother and Glenn are in Shoshone. Aunt Holly and Uncle Ed will pick them up at the Salt Lake depot. Then they'll all come over here. Right to room 115 where the cutest little girl in the world will be. They might even be there before you wake up."

"Uncle Ed and Aunt Holly, too?"

"Uncle Ed and Aunt Holly, too."

"Glenn, too?"

"You betcha."

"I want Glenn to finish reading *Oliver Twist* to me."

"All right. He loves you very much. You know that?"

"Mmmmm Hmm."

Came the voice of the second man behind the mask, "Jean, tell me, what's your favorite nursery rhyme?"

Jean didn't know, said her expression.

"What about Jack Sprat? Do you know that one? Jack Sprat ate no fat, his wife could eat no lean. You know that one?"

Jean nodded her head, wide eyed in apprehension, but confident.

Bob squeezed her hand again, reassuring with the silent gesture.

"Good," said the second man. "I want you to recite it for me. Real slow. Do you think you can do that?"

"Father said alls I would have to do is count backwards from ten."

"All right. Backwards from ten it is. Do that for me then?"

Jean nodded.

"Good. I'm going to put this over your mouth and nose. Nothing to be afraid of. There we go. Now you can start. Backwards from ten."

Began Jean, "Ten…nine…eight…"

"Goooood."

Bob squeezed one final time. "See you when you get to one. You're my special girl. You know that? My special, special girl. Sweet Princess."

With eyes large and filled with confidence she moved her head up and down, and allowed her eyelids to fall…

Two hours later, in room 115, Bob sat on an empty bed, sheets fresh and undisturbed, except for the spot where he had been sitting. He could hear Dott and Glenn coming down the hallway, and Uncle Ed and Aunt Holly. The sounds of their footfalls and their voices were terrifying.

"Let me see now—your Daddy said room 115. Should be right over there."

"Mother, can I give Jean my present first?"

Bob's eyes had a hollow look when they met Dott's, like those of a specter from the grave, a phantom come with news of the unthinkable, that which could not be spoken…so instead he just gave a meaningless shrug of the shoulders.

Dott was confused at first. She looked around the room. Then she put both hands over her mouth and looked at Bob again, asking with her eyes, pleading. She had been carrying flowers. They fell to the floor, along with a roll of sheet music tied with a blue ribbon. Ferdinand Morton's "Jelly Roll Blues."

Bob answered by not answering.

That night at Holly and Ed's, neither Bob nor Dott slept. They just held each other all night long, living in isolated worlds, yet clinging to one another.

Jean's body was transported back to Idaho by train, free of charge by the Union Pacific.

A small two inch clip in the *Times-News-Miner* read:

JEAN WRIGHT AT REST

This afternoon little Jean Wright, the eight-year-old daughter of Dr. and Mrs. R. H. Wright was laid to rest.

Death came Saturday afternoon as the result of complications following an operation.

A profusion of flowers covered the little casket, mute evidence of the love of her playmates and friends.

The profound sympathy of the community is with the mother and father in their great bereavement and with Glenn, Jean's brother. He and his sister had been almost inseparable companions and so great a sorrow, so early in life, fortunately, comes to but few.

The funeral services were conducted from the family home on Main Street by the Rev. Nickerson of Bellevue and were under the direction of Ralph Harris.

Before interment the open casket had laid in Bob and Dott's home, in the bedroom next to their bed. Family and friends were there, and were supportive. Everyone cared, at least for two or three weeks they would care, then life would be expected to return to normal. Then everyone would forget...except for Bob, for Dott, and for Glenn.

Jean's skin was cold, like plastic, like a doll's, wrinkled and puffed at the ankles and joints. Instead of the scent of peaches, or of the perfume she wasn't supposed to have, what surrounded her was the inanimate smell of embalming fluid. In a punishing sort of way, it seemed like the smell was a good one, because it was a part of Jean, even though it really wasn't. They dressed her in the most beautiful dress, red and pink and white with lace trim. Dott buttoned it up and tied the bows while Bob watched, and they both held her and kissed her.

Then Dott took scissors and cut a length of Jean's hair. Then she cut her own hair, three feet of it, all the way to the scalp, and put both swatches in a box along with the following penned poem.

Dear Little Jean

A little ray of sunshine
Of beauteous, golden sheen
Into our hearts, direct from God
Dear little Jean.

A little soul that belonged to Him
Back to His gentle care,
Heaven does not seem so far
Since Jean is there.

A tender, lovely little flower
That blossomed on the green
Too fragile for the storms of life
Dear little Jean

How we will miss her gentle voice
Her face, we long to see
But little Jean has left with us
The sweetest mem-o-ry.

Jean's and Dott's hair saved in remembrance.

Both swatches were the same golden blond. Jean's had a touch more red, like it was dipped in the shine of a sunset.

Bob held her again, and danced with her, just like he promised. He asked that Dott play Auld Lang Syne. For the longest time he danced with her, hugging her tight, afraid to put her down, knowing that when he did it would be for the last time.

Two single roses were placed within her hands, and her doll was tucked under her arm. And the casket was closed.

Each morning for months following the funeral, before the break of dawn, Bob would rise while everyone else was sleeping and crawl into Jean's empty bed. He'd pull the sheets and the quilt up to his neck and drift off to pleasant sleep for an hour or two. The sheets were the same ones Jean slept in, untouched, unwashed, and with their touch he felt close to her. They had her smell, the smell of fresh peaches. One such morning the oddest thing happened. The scent of perfume filled the air, so strong it burned his nostrils, so strong he felt it in his lungs and tasted it at the back of his mouth. Stunned, curious, bewildered, he walked through the entire house. No one was awake, and none of Dott's perfume vials had been left open.

There was a strange euphoria attached to the scent. It calmed him, gave him a sense that everything in the world was OK, for that moment at least, everything. He wished he'd been a poet, or a composer like Brahms so he could have somehow explained it, remembered it, so that he could come back to it in his memory, in all its encompassing completeness. It was a fire in his chest. The sun itself couldn't have been any more powerful. It stilled his loneliness, muted his suffering, swallowed and destroyed all that was wrong with the world, all that was evil and separate. And he did something foolish, while bathing in its glow, something that would have been embarrassing, had anyone seen. But nobody was there to look. Nobody would ever know. He opened his arms and began waltzing, holding someone invisible, in case it was his precious daughter.

Then it was gone.

The following Sunday he asked Reverend Nickerson to baptize him.

The new Wright home.

They eventually moved into the new house, on the corner of 4th and Carbonate, with the indoor plumbing and the hot and cold running water, and the Victrola. Bob had his own bedroom and Dott had hers, like kings and queens, presidents and first ladies. Bob's room was decorated in dark woods and masculine colors, with a mahogany four-poster bed. The decor of Dott's room was befitting a fine and handsome woman such as herself—pale yellow furnishings, flowered wallpaper, a dressing table with a full-length mirror. Both bedrooms faced the rising eastern sun, as did the kitchen. Upstairs, adjoining a center bathroom, were two more rooms, Glenn's and Jean's. In Jean's room was her brass bed, polished and fitted with her sheets and quilts. Her mirrored dressing table and chest of drawers was there, and her clothes were hung in the closet, and her hope chest was at the foot of her bed on the floor. It remained so until the day the house was sold many, many years later, long after Dott and Bob had passed on.

Every Sunday after church Bob and Dott and Glenn would visit the little white marble headstone and bring flowers. Lilacs if they were in season. Jean loved lilacs. Upon its top was the carving of a lamb, and beneath it was inscribed:

JEAN ELEANOR WRIGHT
Born - June 25, 1911 Died - August 4, 1919
Daughter of Dr. and Mrs. R. H. Wright
"Our Darling"

And life went on.

In time everyone forgot. Everyone except three people. For those three, time insisted that they remember. Scenes of past memories would periodically burst into their minds. The images would intrude at the oddest times, maybe during a dinner conversation, or while playing the organ at the church, or during a stroll, or while on the front porch in the evening. For Dott, the demon of her mind was the memory of throwing a rose onto the coffin and watching as shovelfuls of fresh earth sprayed over it, breaking and spoiling the fragile petals, and of remembering how she wanted to jump in and pull Jean out before she was forever sealed. For Glenn it was the vision of the way his sister looked up on Buttercup, that grown up look, and the way she looked lying still in the open casket in her red and white dress, that same grown up look, but vacant of life, and of remembering how he wished she could have been cremated, like the Indians, high up on pillars of wood so she'd rise up in the freedom of smoke, instead of being locked in the cold, dark ground. For Bob, what happened in that sterile-white and stainless steel operating room was his demon. Jean's abdominal walls were too rigid. Something was not right. Closure seemed far too difficult. The surgeon shouldn't have had to pull and stretch like that. Bob was still holding her hand. He hadn't let go. A promise is a promise. But it was clammy, and cold. He suddenly could feel his heart thudding all the way up into his throat. He spread her fingers. The nail beds were black. He looked at her face. Her lips were blue. He felt her wrist for a pulse, searching different spots. He felt under her neck. There was none. And her chest was motionless.

A groan came rolling from his mouth, like he was throwing up, like everything inside him that animated life was tumbling out. Gutturally whispered words of, "Oh, Goddd," fell forth, softly.

Dr. Sarandon noticed it at about the same time and began respirating. He drew the arms up quickly over her head, then drove them down to her chest, then back above her head again. As the arms came slamming down there was a quiet whooshing sound, an empty sound. Over and over, the empty sound. The empty wooshing sound. For ten minutes Dr. Sarandon kept it up, then shook his head and drew a sheet over her.

After that Bob pretty much went crazy, beating on her chest to start her heart, inverting her, blowing in her mouth, anything he could think of to create movement in her lungs. Two men tried to restrain him, but he threw them off.

"Let him be," said Dr. Sarandon.

So they all quietly walked out, leaving Bob on the floor holding her, rocking back and forth with her, her partially sutured abdomen spilling its contents out onto the floor.

People occasionally have reactions to anesthesia. Sometimes it happens.

Was it anybody's fault? Probably not, except that Bob would have used a different type of anesthesia. He would have used ether instead of chloroform. Personal preference. And the course of history would have been different, with one family at least, maybe with the world, because one life touches dozens of others, hundreds, thousands, and they touch thousands more, and so on.

Bob still picked a crocus on spring mornings on his way into the office, but the face of a handsome young man was gone. And the look of cockiness was gone. He wore spectacles now. They softened his ruggedness, the strong facial lines. And his hair began to thin. His lower lip seemed more prominent, turning his mouth into a bit of a scowl, even when he was smiling. If one looked deep, past the kindness, past the good humor, one could see in his eyes that he was a man who carried a silent burden.

And Dott, she went from beautiful to stately, colorful to plain, whites to darks. Maybe it was conscious, maybe it wasn't. Maybe it was just the fashion scene that changed, from billowing hats to skull-tight caps, from flowing skirts to shapeless dresses, the whole world changing around her, the whole world being cognizant of a beautiful little flower gone forever.

And two weeks before they moved into the new house Ol' Jake died.

Sun Valley, Idaho, in the 1940s.
Idaho State Historical Society.

The Count and the Little Girl
Hailey, Idaho
1936

J EAN AND JAKE TOOK THE WHOLE WORLD with them, it seemed. In ten short years the country had plunged itself into a cavernous depression and the Wood River Valley had emptied. Bellevue was a mere ghost of itself. Ketchum and Hailey had only a few hundred people. Muldoon and Bullion existed only as empty buildings. Broadford was nothing more than a weed-centered roadway with a scattering of farm houses on either side. Most of the mines were empty holes. The mountainsides were strewn with their ulcerations and bleeding slag heaps. The North Star, renamed the Triumph Mine, still had a vein of coal in her belly, and provided work for at least some of the able townsfolk.

Then the oddest of things happened. A mysterious stranger came to town and, as though possessing an aura of magic, changed everything. It began during a snowstorm, about ten miles below Bellevue where the valley widens and flattens. There had been an automobile accident. A little girl lay in the whiteness of newly fallen snow, its purity soaking up the crimson of her blood. The child had gone through the windshield. Glass shards had nearly separated her head from her body, but in such a way that the carotid arteries were spared, barely, by millimeters. Encircling her were five men and a woman. The stranger, tall, thin, handsome, appearing from out of the snowstorm itself, it seemed, was one of them. He'd placed his coat over her. Another was kneeling. The man kneeling was Bob. He was packing the wound, bracing her neck and spine, checking for a concussion, calming her with conversation and stories.

"Let's see, you must be about eight," Bob said.

The little girl was able to nod.

"You can go ahead and talk."

The little girl shook her head no.

"Try. I want to see if you can. I think you can."

"OK," she finally said, straining it out while looking at Bob with eyes full of terror.

"Gooood. That means there's no damage to the larynx. That's what we doctors call your voice box."

The automobile had its front end wrapped around a four-foot-high tree stump. A hole the size of a small pumpkin had been punched in the passenger's side of the windshield. It seemed far too small for a person to fit through, even a child. There were blood scrapes across the Packard's bubble nose hood.

"Now let me look in your eyes. Good. Oh sweetie, you're gonna be fine. Just fine."

Bob could hear the girl's mother sobbing behind him, so for her benefit he repeated louder, "Just fine."

He reached in his inside pocket. "Here—cigar for you." He slipped it into the girl's hand, and when she giggled and gripped it he knew her nervous system was undamaged.

"What? You don't smoke?"

She giggled again, a tiny sound, as if she were fearful of too much laughter, and moved her head no, small, quick movements.

"Don't smoke, huh? Smart girl. Actually, I don't smoke either, ever since this colleague of mine back east began to make discoveries linking lung disease with tobacco smoke. I'm giving these things out in honor of the birth of my first grandchild." Bob put it in one of her pockets. "You go ahead and keep it. Just don't smoke it."

"What's the baby's name?"

"Patricia Jean Wright. She lives down in California. That's where my son and his wife have settled."

"That's a pretty name."

"She was named after my own little girl."

"How old is your own little girl? Is she all grown up like your son?"

Bob gave a slight pause, like he was going to answer, then just smiled and touched her cheek.

There had been changes since Jean left them. Many changes. Almost two decades had passed. The age of innocence was gone, blasted apart by the Great War. Nothing in the world remained the same. Even music had changed, from Ragtime to the smoky melodies of the orchestras and big bands.

Replacing monarchs and kings were well meaning systems of social reform that somehow went terribly wrong. Adolf Hitler and his Nazi Party Congress rose in Germany and issued the Nuremberg Laws, depriving Jews of their civil rights. Joseph Stalin continued with his "purge" trials. Mao Tse Tung was gaining power in China. Italy invaded Ethiopia, and Mussolini and Hitler would soon meet to sign the "Rome-Berlin Axis."

The economic depression was worldwide, the afterwash of the enormous amounts of money spent on the war, creating an even greater need for political saviors, deepening the dependency people had on these extremists.

There were also changes in medicine. An Englishman by the name of Sir Alexander Fleming discovered, quite by accident, a fungus that attacks and destroys bacteria. Penicillin. And scores of heretofore deadly diseases became no more than household nuisances.

Walt Disney paused in creativity when a mouse scampered across his drawing board, and Mickey Mouse was born.

Benny Goodman put together a band and shocked everyone by hiring colored musicians. Then came Artie Shaw, with Billie Holliday as vocalist.

And Jean, of course, got her wish. In the very year of her death full women's suffrage was granted on a federal level, and made a part of the Constitution.

The injured girl was loaded in the snowmobile, a mutant truck with skis in front and tread on the back, and was cradled in blankets.

With the precious cargo safe inside, engine idling, Bob took a few moments to speak with the mother, whose expression had turned frantic after the snowmobile door was shut. Bob reassured her that her daughter was not in danger of dying. He told her she could ride in the snowmobile too, explaining that there was plenty of room in the back. Then he noticed she too had injuries, cuts and bruises. But she wouldn't allow the doctor's attention to be diverted. "No, really, I'm fine," she kept saying. "Just take care of my little girl."

"All right then," said Bob. "Let's get her back to the office and stitch her up. Then we'll have a look at you." He opened the snowmobile's door and settled the woman beside her daughter. Then he paused to converse a moment with the men who had saved the child's life, the stranger and the three others who had appeared with him. They had been the first upon the scene, materializing at almost the very moment of the accident, as if they had been angels in watch, on a road upon which no one should have been traveling. Among them was someone Bob recognized, Matt Johnson, district highway engineer from Shoshone. Had it not been for the stranger in particular and the protection his coat had given the little girl from the wet chill of her own blood, she most decidedly would have died. Someone had also placed three silk handkerchiefs into the gaping wound. That too had been critical.

"Doc," greeted Matt, shaking Bob's hand. "What in the name of blazes do you suppose a woman with a child was doin' out here in this storm?"

"Don' know Matt. What were *you* doing here? I thought the road was closed between Shoshone and Bellevue."

"We opened 'er up for these 'ere gentlemen." Matt was a stiff talking Irishman, with an accent so thick one sometimes wondered if maybe he wasn't choking on a toothpick. He was so completely wrapped in clothing, a fur Czar's hat and parka hood, that his round cherub face could hardly be seen, like a squirrel poking out to test the safety of the outside world. He turned to one of the other men. "Mr. Hynes 'ere insisted he had to get through." Then Matt twisted the side of his mouth so as to speak privately to Bob. "Railroad muckety-muck. Supp-OS-edly. Sent by Averill Harriman hisself. Supp-OS-edly. I get this call from the governor's office, tells me that this fellow Hynes and his yahoos are out stuck in the snow and I'm to pull them out and take them as far north as they want to go."

Hynes, a polite fellow of medium height, also bundled in a parka, was wagging his mittened hands back and forth to keep warm, slapping them together. "We started out in the bus there," Hynes said, pointing up the road to a brown and white passenger coach, gopher-like, low to the ground with swept and louvered body lines. "Got stuck up on Tim-merman Hill." Bob was surprised they made it that far. "Had to hike into a farmhouse and call for help, have the road opened up for us. Then we ran into this poor lady. Hiked back to the farmhouse to have word sent to you, Doc." Up ahead of the bus was an orange colored snowplow supporting a blade that must have been fifteen feet tall at its highest point. Behind it was a clean cut, single swath of unblemished white roadway.

Matt gestured toward the stranger, who was leaning forward expecting an introduction. "This gentleman is—." He paused awkwardly. He had forgotten his name, or couldn't remember how to pronounce it.

The stranger, wearing nothing more than a white long sleeve shirt, stepped in to the rescue. "Felix Schaffgotsch," he announced, and briskly shook Bob's hand. "Pleased to meet you." His words had an Austrian charm about them, clean and crisp, politely spoken, heavily accented.

Schaffgotsch was a man in his late twenties or early thirties, with slicked back hair, no hat, and a sun-bronzed face that was chopped off to white at the neckline.

"We had better get you that coat of yours," said Bob, "Or I'll be treating another patient. My God, man, you don't even have on a hat. You do have shoes don't you?"

"I would like the little one to keep my coat," Schaffgotsch said.

"She doesn't need it," assured Bob. "We have her good and bundled up in there. You go on back to the bus and I'll bring you the coat. Get inside outa this cold."

Schaffgotsch started back up the road toward the bus, but stopped and started to look around, in a curious fashion, like he was lost and looking for his way, or like he was expecting somebody to come walking out from somewhere.

"Who *is* this guy?" whispered Bob to Matt.

"CLAIMS he's workin' for the railroad," said Matt. "CLAIMS he's been hired to find a place to build a fancy European hotel for rich folk." Johnson's eyes got wider each time he spoke, and his voice softer. "CLAIMS he's been lookin' all over the entire U. S. of A."

Matt moved his eyes back and forth to make sure Schaffgotsch was out of earshot, then stumbled on laughter with what he whispered next. "CLAIMS he's an Austrian Count."

Schaffgotsch hadn't heard, or if he had he was thoroughly uninterested. His attention was still focused on the wide valley and its gentle hills, all visible beneath the dispersing storm ceiling. Schaffgotsch said, after looking it over one more time, "We can turn around and go back,

Mr. Hynes. I won't trouble you anymore. I don't think we're going to find what I'm looking for here."

"You haven't seen Ketchum yet," said Hynes, with a tone as if in protest.

"I think I've seen enough."

Bob offered up what he thought was good advice. "You don't want to go any further this time of year, sure enough. There's no place up there to put a fancy hotel. Nothing up there but mountains. Mountains and snow."

Schaffgotsch gazed into the horizonless distance, shivering in his shirt-sleeves. "Maybe we will go on ahead a bit."

Just then the snow ceased and the sun broke through, as if someone had waved a wand. In minutes Schaffgotsch stopped shivering, in fact rolled up his sleeves and took off his gloves. "Does it always get this warm when the sun shines?" he mused.

Hynes and Matt Johnson looked at each other and shrugged.

"It must be seventy-five degrees," Schaffgotsch said, and picked up a clump of snow. "And still the stuff doesn't melt."

He looked northward again. The clouds had parted enough to show shining peaks of white. The foothills of the Sawtooths.

He set his jaw in satisfaction. "I think we will journey on. Indeed." He nodded toward the snowmobile. "Tell the child she can keep the coat. Tell her to keep it as a gift. Tell her to get well. Tell her that perhaps I shall return and teach her how to ski."

He finished walking toward the bus, and Matt eyed Bob sideways and made a looping motion next to his ear, a gesture that nearly brought laughter from Bob's mouth.

"You just keep him healthy," said Bob instead. "Otherwise I'll have to fix him for free, if he does work for the railroad."

Bob had the little girl on his office table in less than a half hour. Dott was there waiting for them. With Dott there to assist—she assisted in all his cases now—Bob stitched layer by layer, folding each set of stitches inside the next. He did it with such finesse that the girl barely reacted. The only hint of pain was when he drew the thread through. She healed so well that there was only a pencil line scar.

And Schaffgotsch, Hynes, and Matt Johnson did continue on, through Bellevue, where the snow got a little deeper, through Hailey, where it became deeper still, where the sun seemed even warmer, and its shine always made the triangular Conoco sign above the filling station a brighter shade of red, the metal Quaker State reader-board out front a deeper green, and the gasoline in the glass pumps more golden. They drove through a single lane plowed out of the middle of Main Street, past plowed-in side streets and the high-center marks of cars that had broken through, past brick buildings painted on the sides with signs like *Owyhee Candies* and *Mallory Clothing Co.*, heat pouring from their chimneys—and on into deeper snow still—and on into Ketchum.

"An Austrian Count, huh?' mused Jack Lane. "Just don't cash any of his checks."

A few months later the railroad bought the Brass Ranch a mile east of Ketchum, unprofitable and overrun with larkspur, for ten dollars an acre, and began construction of a 220-room hotel, virtually in the middle of nowhere. It was money from heaven for the Brasses, and for the Depression-ravaged Wood River Valley. Many of the locals were hired on. Bob was kept busy too, due to his Union Pacific contract, caring for employees top to bottom, from Chairman Averill Harriman to families of the workers housed in converted boxcars.

The Count was good to his word. When Sun Valley opened nearly a year later in December he looked up the little girl to personally give her ski lessons. But she would have none of it. All she wanted was a ride on the resort's imaginative mode of transportation, the "flying chairs," as she called them, developed by Union Pacific engineers back in Omaha—the first of their kind in the world—chairs suspended from cables. The last the folks of the Wood River Valley saw of the man who saved them from financial ruin, who saved that sweet little girl from freezing to death, was when he went off to fight for his country. He died an officer and a patriot when his jeep was strafed from the air…an officer and a patriot in Hitler's Third Reich.

And Union Pacific introduced a new train, the diesel powered "streamliner," yellow and sleek. It was named the City of Los Angeles. Its exhibition voyage was a run from New York to Sun Valley loaded with wealthy guests and celebrities, after which it settled into its regular route between Chicago and Los Angeles. Though changed, the valley had found rebirth in travel and tourism.

Bob and Dott Wright at their fiftieth wedding anniversary.

Chapter 21

A Barren Wonderland

Hailey, Idaho

1967

T HE UNITED STATES AND HANOI had begun peace talks. Thurgood Marshall, the first black to sit on the U.S. Supreme Court, was beginning his first term. Dr. Christiaan Bernard had successfully transplanted a human heart. And in a small Idaho town an eighty-six-year-old doctor was making his way across the back lawn to his car, like he had done every morning for decades. His strides were half as long, his footfalls carefully placed, but he stood straight as ever. In the lapel of his suit was a fresh yellow flower. His long top coat was open in front, unbuttoned.

Wendy and I pulled up with Mom and Dad just as O'You was reaching to grasp the door handle. Mom and Dad had picked us up at the train station in Shoshone where we'd come from the University of Idaho. It was a good feeling to be home for the holidays. A warm smile spread across O'You's face and he opened up his arms. "Well, let's take a look at this girl," he belted out, and embraced Wendy like she'd been a part of the family for years.

She was so touched tears came.

"Looks like you've come prepared," he said. "—logging boots—you must be going up into the high country." On O'You's face was a sly smile, a giveaway that he knew full well the trend in women's clothing was mini skirts and boots. He'd seen nearly a hundred years of change. He'd seen clothing styles roll through a half-dozen variations—the stylish formality of hoop skirts, the gentle simplicity and innocence of the Gibson Girl, the wildly suggestive costumes of the Roaring '20s, the lost flower look of the '30s, the conservative '40s, the more expressive, more courageous '50s...but nothing was quite as silly as this one, said the sly smile. And it all amused him, how clothing styles seemed to mirror social patterns and circumstances.

Nanna came out and folded her arms across her chest, a gesture that showed she was a little irritated at not being introduced. I seized on the expression and walked over and gave her a hug. "Nanna, I'd like you to meet Wendy Warner."

Nanna nodded her head, looked Wendy up and down, and smiled with approval. Wendy's full and sensitive eyes left no doubt as to her sincerity.

Wendy was shivering noticeably in the mid-December air, and O'You stripped off his topcoat and put it around her. Her blonde hair, flipped up at the shoulders, looked delicate in the cold, and her words hung in front of her in tiny clouds.

As she stood in the Idaho cold within the shelter of O'You's long and heavy coat, could she have known the future? That her legacy would be his legacy, that the blood pulsing in his veins was the same blood that would pulse in her children, that the expression of jutting boldness ever present on his face would form itself into the faces of her children and grandchildren.

The bright sun, try though it might to warm things, was no help at all, maybe because there was no snow on the ground. The lack of snow always seemed to make the cold colder. Barren winter soil simply didn't fit in Sun Valley. Dad said, "If we don't get some snow pretty soon there are some folks who won't be able to feed their families."

Nanna opened the back door. "We'll put her upstairs in Jean's room."

And I'd be sleeping in my room in the little house across the alley. My room was untouched, except for the newly washed sheets and comforter, and the meticulous dusting and care from Mom's loving hands, as if with them she could wind back the clock—she wasn't prepared for me to walk away into the world, not just yet—and it almost worked, for a moment, because it did almost seem like I was walking backwards in time instead of moving forward, as any young man should do.

There was something different about the place. It had lost some of its luster. The bamboo curtains were parched and gray. The barbecue barrels were beginning to rust. The alley was uncommonly overgrown. It was as though when I left, so did the splendor. Dead vines hung on the latticed trestle in Nanna's backyard, and stubs of what used to be flowers pocketed her rock garden—but then it was wintertime, and things die in wintertime, and there was no snow to cover it all up. Maybe that was all there was to it. A difference of perception.

But then I noticed that one of the rocks in the rock garden was twinkling in the sunshine, a broken-in-two egg shaped rock Dad and I had found one day in the riverbed up Greenhorn Canyon, hollowed on the inside and studded with tiny spiring crystals, twinkling as if to say everything was OK.

The next morning the sun shone again, brighter than before, with no clouds in sight, no sign of snow. "If this keeps up there's going to be hard times, that's for sure," said Dad again at breakfast. "Eat up now."

No one could eat all of one of Nanna's breakfasts—a sliced grapefruit half, steaming cream of wheat, golden waffles browned a touch, strawberries, giant glasses of orange juice, sizzling sausages. Afterward Nanna made me wash my hands in the kitchen sink, like she used to do when I was growing up, water running at only a trickle so as not to waste electricity. They had the money now. They didn't have to be so conservative, but it was a habit hard to break from the old days, from the Depression, from days when patients wouldn't, couldn't pay their bills.

It was Sunday morning. The sun streaming through the double kitchen window was warming things inside. But outside the cold air still snatched away the heat because there was no snow. Without the snow there was no paradise. After breakfast we went to church, and Nanna played the caralonic bells, chimes mounted way up in the bell tower with music that floated through the valley. You could hear it even up beyond Sun Valley, ringing and bouncing off the peaks. We were there a good hour early, and Nanna took some of that time to play for us on the piano, just for me and Wendy, making up songs for us, hammering out Jazz and Ragtime like something I'd never heard before. Wendy and I were dumbfounded. How could I have not known this about my own grandmother, that she was so talented? We begged her to keep playing. Finally she had to quit because people were beginning to come in and take their seats. The service would soon start, and it just wouldn't do to have the stately organist with the white hair pounding away like Jerry Lee Lewis.

During the service Reverend Yates made an unusual request, speaking from his pulpit below a redwood cross Dad had made years ago. We thought at first it was going to be about Nanna's music, asking her to play some of what had been heard prior to the service, but I guess everybody knew how good Nanna was, everybody but me. "As most of you know, or should know by now," he began, "Sun Valley has been purchased by the Janns Corporation. Bill Janns called me yesterday. It seems he heard the story about how back in the days when Pat Rodgers was Sun Valley's manager, Pat once asked Joe Fuld to pray for snow. And, as you know, Joe obliged. And, as you know, it started snowing. It snowed so hard and fell so long that Pat had to ask Joe to pray for it to *stop* snowing. All the lifts were closed because of avalanche danger." The congregation laughed and looked at Joe. Joe blushed.

"Well, Mr. Janns asked that we have Joe give it another go. So Joe, if you would…"

Everyone laughed again. Except Joe. Joe lifted his aged and stooped frame and shuffled to the front. There was something that looked like a smirk on his face. "Father in Heaven," he began, "we thank you, because we realize you hear us always. As your Son reminded us in scripture, you have knowledge of what we need before we ask. In remembrance of what you told us when you taught us to pray, by giving us the ultimate prayer, we seek only that *your* will be done. We open ourselves to your will, understanding in the process that you will give us our daily bread, that which we need to survive and be comfortable and provide for our families' security. We say this only to acknowledge to you that we understand. Truly we give it no more thought than that, because we know it is taken care of. What we seek is not what we need, for we know it is taken care of. What we seek, Lord, is your guidance, and forgiveness for our sins, as we forgive those that have sinned against us. What we seek is for you to show us even those sins we are not aware of, and forgive us for them, and guide us in your will so that we can attain the strength to resist all temptation. What we seek truly, Father, is the opening of ourselves to your will and guidance, so that we may grow closer to you, and to each one of your children, our brothers. For Thine is the Kingdom. And the Power. And the Glory. Forever. A-Men."

After church, as always from spring through to the first fall of snow, Bob and Dott brought flowers and trimmed the grass around the grave.

The next day as we were preparing to leave, New Years Day, little flickers of white were beginning to dance about in the air. And the sky was covered with white, beautiful white.

Chapter 22

A Powerful Man

Hailey, Idaho

1969

Among the barrenness of germ-free walls and stainless-steel handrails, amidst the pervasive odor of stale antiseptics, there existed a room apart from the rest, a room with sofas and chairs, and curtains for the windows, a well-meaning attempt at giving the people inside a piece of home.

The people inside moved about like they were caught in time, halfway between yesterday and today, like they were attempting to pass through a sort of viscous fluid. Most were assisted by walkers and wheelchairs. For some, to negotiate a glass of milk to their mouths required a massive effort of will. They were people without hope, gathered together waiting to die, as if being collected in some kind of bizarre way station. The echo of a wailing could be heard from somewhere down the tile corridor.

Those who came to pay their respects couldn't get out fast enough.

On a certain day in November, in that room with the chairs and sofas, curtains, and year old magazines, sat a man in a wheelchair. There was a scowl upon his face. He was thin and gaunt. His bathrobe was half tied and on his feet were slippers that were way too big.

He was well treated—just not in the way he was before. No one called him Doc anymore. To them he was just Mr. Wright, an old man with a scowl on his face. They were good to him, but in a way that wasn't quite real, speaking in voices a little louder, the way people do with the elderly, a little more forced, kindhearted but as far away from real talk as the earth is to the stars.

He seemed to be waiting for someone, the way he fidgeted with his arms and hands, like he was trying to decide the most respectable way to place them. He used his arms to help him cross one leg over the other in an effort to look stronger, more confident. Once settled, he tried not to move, because whenever he did he would shake.

And he waited.

Minutes later, hours maybe—there was no clock in the room and he had misplaced his wristwatch—the two people he had been waiting for walked in. Wendy hugged him so hard I thought he was going to tip over, and placed the baby in his lap.

O'You held the child in his shaking hands…and the scowl became a smile, a smile familiar from a long time ago, a smile of pride and confidence. And he kissed the child, not seeming to worry much about how he shook as he bent his head to do so.

The child's eyes were full of wonder as he looked up at his great-grandfather. Like his great-grandfather's, his head shook too—he was just beginning to gain muscular control over it.

For a few moments O'You was complete again. This was his legacy, his lineage, his name to be carried into the twenty-first century. Though he was old and frail, the look he bestowed upon the child was powerful, as if carrying a blessing that the child would be strong, and that things would be well with him.

A year and a half later O'You died.

On the way back from O'You's funeral I stopped at his office to fill the stove, and to sit at his desk for awhile, in the swivel tilt-back chair on the worn out cushion, and wonder what it would have been like to have been him. The roll up top of his desk was open—unusual for O'You—he must have left in a hurry.

I picked up a dust covered newspaper, very likely the last one he'd read. *NEIL ARMSTRONG WALKS ON THE MOON*, blazed the lead story in headlines that took up almost the whole front page. And I read all over again how *"hundreds of millions from all backgrounds thrilled to the feat,"* and how the Dalai Lama had predicted, *"Man's limited knowledge will acquire a new dimension of infinite scope."*

Buried under a back page column called Science and Technology there was a throwaway story—about the development of a magnetic device capable of storing information on tiny "bubbles" and retrieving it all within a hundred microseconds, and about how hundreds of thousands of these bubbles could be placed on a single tiny chip.

I folded up the newspaper and put it back in just the same way it was before, on the same part of the desk. It seemed the right thing to do.

But something was wrong.

Something was out of place, and I couldn't for the longest time figure out what it was. It's just a feeling you have, that something you've seen a million times suddenly doesn't look right, and you don't know why.

Then I noticed it—something on his desk, or rather something that *wasn't* on his desk, something that never had been there, but should have been. Something that was on my desk, on every man's desk.

Chapter 23

The Doctor's Final Victory

Shoshone, Idaho

1980

H
E DIDN'T HAVE A PICTURE of his wife on his desk. That was what was missing. He never did have one. But then why should he? He saw her every day of every year for over eighty years. That's over thirty thousand days. I couldn't think of a day they weren't together. She went with him even on the trips back to the Mayo Clinic and Cook County Hospital for surgical residency and training. Why bother having a picture of someone on your desk that you see every day, that's more a part of you than you are of yourself? She was his bonded heart and soul, and he hers.

Nor did she have a picture of him, not even in her wallet. But now that he was gone, she began amassing them by the score, placing several in prominence on her dressing table, putting the one taken by Chuck Ensign of their 50th wedding anniversary on the living room fireplace mantle, clipping out a smaller one to carry with her. She began organizing a scrap book about their accomplishments, and finally found the time to respond to the American Medical Association's request for information about his life.

For the next decade Nanna went on without O'You, working in her garden, protecting and beautifying living things, making intricate quilts for children and grandchildren with arthritic fingers, though splinters of pain accompanied every stitch. Her life wasn't so very different, in many ways, except that O'You wasn't there, she was no longer involved in medicine, and little things that had been autonomic now required thought and effort, like walking up a flight of stairs or stepping into the bathtub. She continued with her Eastern Star activities, and she and Mom kept up their involvement with PEO, a secret sisterhood whose very name was once shrouded in mystery. Many a young girl can thank the anonymous benefactors of the Philanthropic Educational Organization for college educations they otherwise wouldn't have been able to afford.

225

Of course Dad was there for Nanna, for awhile, until emphysema took him, carved out the inside of his lungs until nothing was there to metabolize the oxygen needed to feed his internal organs. That's how the end comes with emphysema, piece by piece, organ by organ, until finally the paper thin heart quits. I was the one who told Nanna. She was sitting in her wheelchair when I walked into the room, her hands on each of the chair's arm rests, bracing herself for what she knew was about to come out of my mouth. She could see it in my face as I approached.

I knelt and took her hands. I told her quickly, straight out. There is no kind way to tell a loving old woman that she has outlived her only remaining child. To tell her in any other way would be more of a cruelty. "He's dead." That's exactly how I said it, looking with impassioned empathy into her pained eyes.

Her mouth quivered. She must have been thinking of speaking, but held it back. She looked up toward the ceiling, as though chastising Almighty God for his ineptness. It should have been her. It was she who wanted to die.

It was a full year before I saw Nanna again, in the nursing home down in Shoshone.

I remember dripping water into her open mouth with a wash rag. There was no expression in her glazed eyes, but I knew she was grateful. I held her tiny boned hand, for the longest time, then said goodbye. "Sweet little lady—sweet, sweet lady—this is going to be the last time I'll be able to see you," I told her, then kissed her, pressed my lips firmly and gently on her forehead. But that didn't seem to be enough. So I kissed her on the lips, firmly, gently, on the lips of her open mouth, her jaw agape, rasping in and out air like a bellows. She didn't respond, but I knew she knew. Inside I could feel it. I could feel a connection. I could feel that she felt it. "I love you sweet lady. Sweet, sweet little lady. Thanks for everything. More than I can express."

That night, back in Seattle, I had the strangest dream. I dreamed I got up out of bed to get a glass of orange juice. When I reached the kitchen the entire house began to melt around me, dripping from the walls and sagging beneath my feet. The walls, the floor, the cabinets and cupboards, the cookie jars on the counter—all were melting, and giving off as a byproduct anesthetizing gasses, paralyzing me with odd pulsating sensations. For some reason, instead of fighting to wake up from the nightmare, I allowed, even aided the gas in its work. And, as the house around me was dissolving, I floated up and out of it.

Then I shot, at seeming light speed, to somewhere, pulled by a powerful force. Funny, the dreaming mind can manufacture its scenarios with such realism that reality itself can be turned upside down, and the thing that is unreal becomes the thing that is real.

The force pulling me was the power of love, for I found myself to be at Nanna's bedside. To those that might have watched from the physical side, the thing happening was a death. To those witnessing on the other side, the side I was on, the event was a long awaited birth. Attending at her bedside was my father and grandfather. And cradled in Dad's arms was Little Baby, my Siamese cat, my childhood pet. The animal's death had been the most painful experience of my childhood. "Look here what I've got for you," was the first thing Dad said upon seeing me, holding up the cat. Dad's voice was full of excitement. But most puzzling, and disappointing, was the fact that Dad was not at all astounded by this ability of mine to crack the barrier of death. Both Dad and O'You seemed to take for granted that I had succeeded in accomplishing this feat of the impossible. They seemed in fact to be expecting me.

I reached over to pet the cat. Could it be?

The cat responded in the same way as she had done in life, by rubbing up against my hand.

I bent over.

Again the animal responded as in life. She bumped me on the cheek with her tiny head. Dad was beside himself with excitement. "Dad, look at this," he said to O'You. "She remembers. I knew she would."

But O'You was not watching. His attention was fixed fast to the old lady in the bed, as well it should be. The metal railing on the side was pulled up high. On a table in a corner was a bedpan and a half filled glass of water.

Nanna's hair was thin, and it stuck straight out of her head in stiff clumps. Her jaw was sunken. She had no teeth in her mouth. And her breaths were being taken quickly, one a second it seemed. Her eyes—that was the worst of what I saw in my dream. They were monstrous in their expression, in their frantic attempts to communicate what apparently her mouth would not allow, that she was in pain, or that she was desperately thirsty from having to draw air through her mouth, or that she was lonely in her solitary existence, or that she was frightened of death, or angered at not being able to die, something.

O'You was calm during the ordeal, as if he'd seen what was about to happen a thousand times. He acted like the doctor he was in life, watching, observing, waiting to assist. But there was nothing to be done. There was nothing that could be done in this most natural of nature's unseen wonders. He simply stood by the bedside and watched, radiating confidence to Dad and me. Yet the professional calm, the projected peace a good doctor gives to a patient, could not conceal the excitement of the moment for which he had waited nearly fifteen years, since his own death.

The human soul of my grandmother came slowly from the useless prison her fetally contorted body had become, slowly, with a kind of quivering about it. She came only inches at a time, hardly separating herself, then popped back in again, as a baby's head first appears in childbirth. Out and in she moved, several times, until finally she stood completely free from the still breathing, unrecognizable thing that for ninety-four years had served her well. She was wobbly on her feet, unable to coordinate herself in her new weight free environment. O'You led her to a chair by the corner, where she sat with a bewildered face that still carried the mask of death on it. She recognized no one. It was as if she had brought senility with her. The only words from her mouth were nonsensical. Still O'You seemed unconcerned, and in a moment I saw why. The birth process was not yet complete. Again, this time for the final time, she was drawn back to her body.

The last emergence was strange indeed. As she came, the body she left behind, still breathing and refusing to die even with no essence in it, began to wither. Her skin shriveled on its skeleton, drawing the unanimated form hideously ugly—not something that happened on the physical side, obviously—but in my dream, from the side of my observation, that's what I saw. Again O'You led Nanna to the chair. This time she was radiantly beautiful, not young, just beautiful, with a beauty that carried in it vitality and the full awareness of the senses. And instead of the night smock she until a moment ago had been wearing, she was clothed in an attractive pink bathrobe, like one I had given her for Christmas. Odd, since the bathrobe could in no way have been upon her back. Then I noticed something else. Dad and O'You were also fully clothed, Dad in a casual shirt and an old leather army flight jacket, World War II era, O'You in a suit and tie. Perhaps here one sees oneself in a way that is most comfortable in life, projecting that image to others. Or could it be I was simply seeing them as was most comfortable to me?

Nanna was speechless as she looked unbelievingly around at the three people she had loved so dearly in life. "My heavens," was all she said.

I knelt reverently and took her hands, just as I had done a year earlier when telling her that Dad had died. "Hi Nanna," I said. "Do you recognize me? Do you know who I am?"

She said she did.

I felt a familiar touch. I stood up and allowed O'You to acknowledge me, the first he had done so, with a firm shoulder grip and a healthy pat on the back, same way he used to do years ago.

We all talked together, for a brief time, about what I can't remember. That part of the dream is lost. Nor do I remember clearly their faces, other than that there seemed to remain from life the countenance of age, just enough to make them recognizable. But it was an age marked more by maturity than chronological years, for their features were vibrant with the spirit of youth, with a spirit unburdened, a spirit carrying no physical limitations.

"Come on," said O'You. "Let's go eat." A strange statement for one to make who no longer has a body to be fueled. But that's what he said.

They walked out a set of open double doors into an explosion of light. It was much more than light, much brighter, much more radiant. Like others who have told of this moment of transition, I find it is beyond what words can describe.

Memories are vague, but it seemed there had been someone else there as well, someone who had also knelt beside Nanna, someone with glowing hair the color of a sunset. Jean? Because as the light was enveloping them I thought I saw O'You waltzing with somebody.

And—could it have been?—jumping and spinning at their feet was the shadow of what looked like a flop-eared black dog.

I tried to follow. But as I walked through the door I found myself in darkness, staring at the ceiling. I looked at the clock. 4:14 a.m.

That morning, about ten, Mom called. "I'm sorry," she said. "Your grandmother died last night."

A rose is a rose is a rose.

Sun Valley doesn't remember Dr. Robert Henry Wright. No road bears his name. There are no schools or hospitals named after him. Yet the old-timers remember, those that are left. They'll tell you. They've all got a story or two about the doctor who never lost a patient.

Not much is known about O'You's life as he aged. The stories were all about the early days. It is the same with the history books that told of the Wood River Valley—they generally focus only on the turn of the century period. One thing we do know: he guided new lives into the world—thousands of them—with skill and precision. If something went wrong in those critical moments, he was the doctor you wanted. That was his specialty, in the days before doctors specialized. I guess today he would be known as an OB/GYN. Aunt Lillian, who to this day lives down in Bellevue, told me that after Jean died O'You never performed surgery again. It was the hurt that couldn't be repaired, the mountain that couldn't be climbed. Sometimes seagulls just can't fly.

Glenn's little girl, the girl in the picture on the wall, the baby in the picture on O'You's desk, married her high school sweetheart, and began a legacy far more important than that carved into stone or memorialized somewhere on a placard and more lasting. From her descended O'You and Nanna's three great-grandchildren, eight great-great-grandchildren, and seven great-great-great-grandchildren. I eventually found Patricia. She looks just like in the picture, same engaging smile, same pretty face. Neither of us knows what happened way back then. We don't talk about it, because it would only bring hurt. We just move forward.

From a second marriage Glenn had a son—that of course would be me—and the legacy grew larger still: eight great-grandchildren and five great-great-grandchildren.

In point of fact there is a monument that bears O'You's name. It is in the Hailey cemetery, in the Masonic section on the airport side, by the road, right next to the little girl's grave by the little bush—a big bush by now.

Notes

Chapter 1
(page)

1   *Alturas County*   Today Hailey and Sun Valley are located in Blaine County, created by the state legislature in 1895. Prior to that date they were part of Alturas County.

3   *abdominal cavity*   Dr. Isamu Kawabori, pediatric heart surgeon at Children's Hospital in Seattle, provided the surgery detail. Interview February 25, 2001.

5   *Halsted*   William Stewart Halsted, 1852–1922, was one of the founding professors of Johns Hopkins Hospital, and though addicted to cocaine and morphine throughout his professional career, was a brilliant surgeon and was instrumental in establishing modern surgical techniques and anesthesia procedures. The first successful gallstone operation was performed by Halsted on his kitchen table. The patient was his mother. Much of what Halsted learned about anesthesia came from experimentations he did on himself, which some believe was responsible for his drug addiction. Gerald Imber, M.D., *Genius on the Edge: The Bizarre Double Life of Dr. William Stewart Halsted* (New York: Kaplan Publishing, 2010); Richard A. Leonardo, *History of Surgery* (New York: Froben Press, 1943), 313–4.

7   *for-real doctor*   Dr. Durham was one of Idaho's most unique and controversial personalities, and was the subject of not only many a story from my grandmother and grandfather, but is also referenced in George A. McLeod, *History of Alturas and Blaine Counties, Idaho*, 3rd ed. (Hailey, Idaho: *Hailey Times*, 1950), 188–92.

8   *chloroform vapors*   Information on turn of the century anesthesia and the effects of chloroform vapors from Arthur E. Hertzler, M.D., *The Horse and Buggy Doctor* (New York: Harper & Brothers, 1938), 219.

9   *kitchen surgery skills*   Dr. James Whorton, Professor Emeritus, Department of Bioethics and Humanities at the University of Washington School of Medicine, was of immense help in pulling back the cloak of time and helping me step into that fascinating world of medicine over a century ago when superstition and magic were being blasted into oblivion by the quantum leaps being made in medical science. Jim spent countless hours on the phone with me, and I thank him. Surgeons did indeed operate while smoking big fat cigars. And the operating theory was "in and out fast." They didn't know why tissues deteriorated after exposure to the air, but experience had taught them it was so. Also of great help was Nancy Rockafellar, *Saddlebags to Scanners: The First 100 Years of Medicine in Washington State* (Seattle: Washington State Medical Association, 1989).

10   *Rube Robbins*   Orlando "Rube" Robbins may very well have been the toughest lawman in the Old West. Rube's grave can be viewed as a part of the walking tour of Boise's Pioneer Cemetery. Many of his exploits, good and bad, are contained in a fascinating book called *True Tales and Amazing Legends of the Old West, from the Editors of True West Magazine* (New York: Clarkson Potter, 2005). One such legend is the following: In 1864, after a crowd of Confederate sympathizers in a Boise saloon announced they wouldn't allow any Yankee to sing the "Star Spangled Banner," Robbins strode into their midst and hopped up on a pool table and drew his two pistols, and blared out in a deep baritone, "Oh say can you see…" He finished the song untouched, and holstered his pistols and walked out without a hand being laid on him (65–6). He later became a scout for the army.

10   *diphtheria*   Dean Merchant, "History in Focus: Diphtheria Epidemic," *Hampton Union*, June 27, 2008. Article available at www.hampton.lib.nh.us/hampton/history.

11 *word is from back East*   The discoveries of Klebs, Lister, and Pasteur were filtering throughout the country, but were frighteningly experimental. Some of the more avant-garde doctors were trying them out and finding success. Word was spreading. German physician Edwin Klebs, along with Friedrich Loffler, discovered the diphtheria bacillus in 1884. J. Bruyere, "Medicine: Its Progress, Problems, and Prospects," *The Journal of the American Medical Association* 33, no. 6 (August 5, 1899): 463–67; Andrew W. Artenstein, *Vaccines: A Biography* (New York: Springer, 2009).

Chapter 2

13 *3rd of July*   According to George A. McLeod, *History of Alturas and Blaine Counties, Idaho*, 3rd ed. (Hailey, Idaho: Hailey Times, 1950), 188, Dr. Durham first rolled into town with his sideshow in October of 1894, but my grandmother's story, as I recall her telling it, included the mid-summer merriment of the statehood celebrations. I tell the story as it sits in my mind, because therein lies the charm. I was as young as four when some of these tales were told, and it's possible that my mind combined several stories into one.

14 *electric belts*   The Fall 1900 Sears Catalogue, No. 110, p. 38, shows an advertisement for an electric belt. Electric belt therapy was common in late nineteenth century medicine, and was even practiced by physicians. The explanation of what it was and what it was supposed to have done was supplied by Dr. Whorton. It is believed they actually contained stored electricity, an early type of battery that was worn around the waist. Some belts included testicle enclosures and penile receptacles, complete with electrode extensions. Even today a therapeutic device is being marketed by Nuskin called a Galvanic that passes a mild electric current through the body.

Chapter 3

24 *wacky marriage proposal*   My grandmother kept all my grandfather's letters, neatly tied with pink ribbons in a cigar box. There was no indication in any of them that he was pulling away from her. Just the opposite. He was worried about her; she was becoming distant. The only woman he ever kissed was the child with him at the window that day in 1894 when they observed a doctor at work, the beautiful young lady with the flowing red hair who stood beside him at the altar in 1906 and vowed a lifetime of love and loyalty, the white haired elderly woman who sat beside him in 1970 and held his hand as he took his last breath.

Chapter 4

29 *fragile lungs*   J. Dougal Bissell, M.D., "A Contribution to the Study of the Nature, Cause, and Treatment of Suspended Animation in the Newborn," in George Frederick Shrady and Thomas Lathrop Stedmen, eds., *Medical Record: A Weekly Journal of Medicine and Surgery* 48, no. 21, whole no. 1307 (November 30, 1895): 763–68.

30 *American Medical College*   American Medical College was located at 407 S. Jefferson Avenue in St. Louis. It was founded in 1873 and was unique in its approach to education, in that it incorporated herbal medicine into its standard medical curriculum. It also was one of the few medical schools in the country to admit women. In my grandfather's graduating class of 1906 there were three women. American merged with Barnes Medical College in 1911 and was renamed the National University of Arts and Sciences. Today the combined campuses of Washington University School of Medicine in St. Louis and Barnes Jewish Hospital, both on the leading edge of medical research and discovery like their predecessors,

stand within blocks of the original site of American and Barnes Medical College. Bernard Becker Medical Library Archives are available at beckerarchives.wustl. edu. More information about early medical education for women is available at beckerexhibits.wustl.edu/mowihsp/health/mededucstl.htm.

32   *My Own Darling*   The letters have been transcribed exactly as written. Blank spaces indicate illegible words.

35   *Rosebud*   My grandfather never talked much about his days at American. Most of what I learned I discovered from his letters. I do remember him making references to the Rosebud, with a glimmer of humor in that hidden smile he'd sometimes get. At the time I thought the look was there because he was talking about some fancy restaurant. He knew how boring I thought fancy restaurants were. He used to tease me about it, about how some day I'd change my mind when I wanted to take a girl to one. Now I know why the smile was there. The Rosebud was a "sporting house," a house of prostitution, and a well known one at that. The Rosebud Bar in St. Louis, at 2222 Market Street, is renovated and stands as an historic landmark. It's owned by the Missouri Department of Natural Resources and is rented out for parties and various gatherings. It is within walking distance of the original 1902 site of American Medical College, and is recognized by historians as the spot where Ragtime began its world-wide explosion. Any student at American would have known of it by reputation. It was billed as the "Headquarters for Colored Professionals and Sports." Located in the heart of Chestnut Valley, an early twentieth century red light district, the Rosebud consisted of two barrooms, a large room for gambling, and a hotel upstairs where the rooms were rented by the hour. It was a sprawling entertainment complex, taking up close to an entire city block. The Rosebud closed in 1906, probably shortly after the young Dr. Robert Henry Wright took that walk, and right before his graduation. See aaregistry.org/historic_events/view/rosebud-bar-spot-ragtime for more information.

Chapter 7

56   *dogs were hitched single file*   Tim Jones, *The Last Great Race: The Iditarod* (Harrisburg, PA: Stackpole Books, 1988), 40. Unlike today's duel tandem racers, in the early days of dog team travel the dogs were hitched up single file, with the harnesses fitted over their front quarters and the lines attached at the sides.

66   *incredible process of mending itself*   The story of the Warfield Hotsprings placenta previa case is recorded on the Cynthia B. Wright Oral History Tapes, Ketchum Library, Ketchum, Idaho. I have Dr. Anita Connell, a gynecologist, to thank for the detail of a placenta previa birth. My grandmother gave me the story, but not the particulars.

Chapter 8

71   *fightin' Scotsman*   Cynthia B. Wright Oral History Tapes, Ketchum Library, Ketchum, Idaho. When my grandmother would tell this particular story she'd use Scotty's stiff accent, and she'd mimic the way he'd swish his cane back and forth in the air. It was beyond charming. She tells the tale on the oral history tapes, but she doesn't use the accent, I'm sure because she was inhibited by the presence of the microphone and tape recorder.

78   *copperosity sagaciating*   This phrase, possibly originating from African-American roots in the nineteenth century South, loosely means *How are you doing?*

80   *abdominal walls rigid*   Interview with Dr. James Whorton, June 25, 1999. See also Hertzler, *The Horse and Buggy Doctor*, 219.

Chapter 9

90   *how old Dot Allen was*   It was my grandmother's belief that Dot Allen was around thirty, give or take, and the description comes from her.

91   *hole the size of a fountain pen*   *The Wood River Times*, Friday, October 13, 1911, page 1, "The Crowley Murder." One of the other doctors in town, Dr. Kleinman, did the autopsy, and in his testimony he explained that the fatal bullet had entered the left upper side and had struck the second rib and broken apart, one fragment piercing the lung, the other rupturing the larynx. Succeeding issues of the paper carried extensive news, reports, and transcripts from the trial that followed. See issues of Friday, September 22, 1911, Friday, October 13, 1911, and Wednesday, November 1, 1911, through Monday, November 6, 1911.

91   *been after the sheep money*   Newspaper accounts made no mention of the fact that Dot Allen acted as banker to the Basque sheepherders. Apparently it was not common knowledge, my grandmother and grandfather being among those few that knew. Whether the murderers knew it or not is unknown. According to trial testimony, they were after the money that flowed from the gambling tables. Nor was Dot Allen's necklace taken, though according to trial testimony that had been the motive for the shot that was fired at her.

94   *most unimaginable of conditions*   Michael Rutter, *Upstairs Girls: Prostitution in the American West* (Helena, MT: Farcountry Press, 2005).

94   *charged them all with murder*   Reece Clevenger was Charles Allen's brother. Reece had been adopted by a family with the last name of Clevenger, according to the *Wood River Times*. The brochure "Historic Old Hailey," available at haileycityhall. org/historicpreservation/walkingtour.asp, has the following to say about the incident: "Just before midnight September 21, 1911, during an attempted robbery, Dot Allen's piano player, M.J. Crowley, was shot dead. After an ugly investigation, compromising many stalwarts of the town, Charles Allen and Reece Clevenger were found guilty of murder and Charles Crawford and Lorenzo Swift were convicted as accomplices. Dot Allen continued in business for some years, but no one ever knew what finally became of her." See also McLeod, *History of Alturas and Blaine Counties, Idaho*, 165–66. Both accounts leave more questions than answers. My grandmother, curiously, said in the oral history tapes at the Ketchum Library that the men were never caught, which is more confusing still, since the trial attracted so much attention, and since my grandfather himself was retained as a witness. Crawford and Swift acted as witnesses for the prosecution, and claimed that they acted merely as lookouts. Defense attorneys for Allen and Clevenger claimed just the reverse, maintaining that it was really Lorenzo Swift who had fired the fatal shot.

Chapter 10

101   *C.T.'s was a Chinese restaurant*   The signs, including the C.T.'s Restaurant sign, are seen in early photos of Hailey. References to C.T.'s being a Chinese restaurant can be found in the Hailey, Idaho, *Wood River Times*, September 22, 1911, "A Mid-Night Tragedy" and October 13, 1911, "The Crowley Murder."

110   *expose the obstructing cartilage*   My grandmother told the story, but I needed surgical details. Thanks to Dr. Stanley Hirschberg, M.D., ear, nose, and throat surgeon of Seattle, Washington, for reading the manuscript and suggesting revisions and specifics.

111   *to look like a goat*   From a 1981 NPR interview with Gustav Henningsen, author of *The Witches Advocate: Basque Witchcraft and the Spanish Inquisition 1609–1614* (Reno: University of Nevada Press, 1980).

Chapter 12

119 *Squaw Tit Mountain*   Although now called Squaw Butte Mountain, the name my grandmother used in all her stories was "Squaw Tit." For a good discussion of this topic, see Mark Monmonier, *From Squaw Tit to Whorehouse Meadow: How Maps Name, Claim, and Inflame* (Chicago: University of Chicago Press, 2006).

121 *make fun of them as they tripped over words*   Pat Bieter, *The Basques in Idaho* (Boise: Idaho State Historical Society, 1980), 5–6.

122 *hope is given, just before death*   My grandmother described in graphic detail the symptoms of Rocky Mountain Spotted Fever and the progression of this one-time fatal disease. This was verified and augmented in Sherwood L. Gorbach, John G. Bartlett, and Neil R. Blacklow, *Infectious Diseases* (Philadelphia: Lippincott, Williams and Wilkins, 2004), 1473.

122 *whiskey treatments*   Background information supplied by Dr. James Whorton. Giving children whiskey, especially sick children, makes no sense to us today, but Dr. Whorton's explanation of the medical reasoning behind it—at least the medical reasoning commonplace in those days—helped clarify the issue. My grandfather's journals and my grandmother's letters and writings contain a number of instances of whiskey treatments, among them the stories of the Spotted Fever episodes.

128 *vaccine was developed*   In 1978, two years before her death, my grandmother came to Seattle for a visit, and I had the foresight to sit her down for several hours and ask about those days, thinking that I would write a book someday. I sat cross-legged on the floor next to her while she talked, recording her recollections. My fingers flew. I tried not to miss a single word, a single emotion. Most of what she talked about is also found on her oral history tapes, Ketchum Public Library.

Chapter 13

136 *quoting a famous Indian woman*   Sarah Winnemucca, *Life Among the Piutes: Their Wrongs and Claims* (New York: G.P. Putnam Sons, 1883), 51.

Chapter 16

145 *an avalanche at the North Star Mine*   Louise Shadduck, *Doctors with Buggies, Snowshoes, and Planes: One Hundred Years and More of Idaho Medicine* (Boise: Tamarack Books, 1997) 375; McLeod, *History of Alturas and Blaine Counties, Idaho*, 114–16. Both books have sections about the North Star Mine Tragedy.

Chapter 17

162 *Spice cake*   ½ cup butter, 1 cup sugar, ½ cup sweet milk, 2¼ cups flour, 2 eggs, 1 teaspoon cream of tarter, ½ teaspoon each baking soda, cinnamon, cloves, allspice, nutmeg, and mace, bake until fluffy. Dated 8-8-1894.

164 *influenza epidemic*   Gina Kolata, *Flu: The Story of the Great Influenza Pandemic of 1918 and the Search for the Virus That Caused It* (New York: Simon & Schuster, 1999), 4–7. This book reads more like a cold case whodunit than a medical history. Also, Rockafellar, *From Saddlebags to Scanners*, 144.

166 *trip out to the Brass Ranch*   The Brass Ranch is known world wide, though by a different name. People today call it Sun Valley. Dorice Taylor, *Sun Valley* (Sun Valley: Ex Libris Sun Valley, 1980), 26.

Chapter 20

213   *Felix Schaffgotsch*   As Dorice Taylor points out on page 5 of *Sun Valley*, "After
sixteen years as the head of the Sun Valley publicity department, twenty-three years
as a member of the staff of that department, and forty-three years as a guest and/
or employee, I have yet to tell a tale of this fantastic valley and the fantastic people
involved and not have someone say, 'That's not the way it was at all.'" This was
my mother's version, and I have no reason to doubt it, with the exception of my
grandfather boasting about Patricia, his new grandchild. That wasn't part of the
story she told me. But it's a fair assumption that he would have mentioned her. Pat
would have been a newborn when the Count appeared, and my grandfather kept her
picture on his desk his entire life.

214   *only a pencil line scar*   This was one of my grandmother's favorite stories. She always
told it while shaking her head in amazement, commenting that she was surprised at
how much muscle there was in the human neck, that she could look right into its
anatomy and see its complexity, and see the blood surging through the carotid artery.
An example of the brilliance of the creator, she would say. And a miracle in itself that
the accident had opened the neck with near surgical precision, yet sparing all vital
parts.

215   *chairs suspended from cables*   Taylor, *Sun Valley*, 95. Taylor was Sun Valley's publicity
agent. In her research for this pictorial work, the author spoke extensively with my
mother and grandmother. They were very close friends. In fact, Taylor's husband
Phez was O'You's attorney.

215   *an officer and a patriot*   Taylor, *Sun Valley*, 66, 67,119. Taylor writes that she,
along with many in the Wood River Valley, was slow to accept the fact that Count
Schaffgotsch was a Nazi, thinking at first that he was one of the many Austrians who
professed loyalty to their homeland simply out of necessity, because of property being
held there and for fear of repercussions against family members. However, the actor
David Niven, in his autobiography, *The Moon's a Balloon* (New York: Putnam, 1971),
tells of meeting the Count on an ocean liner in 1936, and of how the Count spoke
of his allegiance to a new political party rising up in Europe, whose leader was an
economic genius by the name of Adolf Hitler—a man who would weld the various
governments together in long overdue financial and social stability.

Chapter 23

230   *in the days before doctors specialized*   In the days following the opening of Sun Valley,
hospitals were prevalent. Home deliveries were becoming things of the past. The
third floor of the Sun Valley lodge became the hospital for the area. There were also
hospitals in Twin Falls and Boise, within hours of Hailey, Ketchum, and Sun Valley,
now that automobile travel was the norm. My grandfather worked closely with Dr.
John Moritz and Dr. Earl Fox. If Aunt Lillian was correct in saying that he never
again performed surgery after Jean died, it was probably Moritz or Fox, assisting, that
did the cesarean section, were one required. Aunt Lillian is my grandfather's brother's
son's wife. She gave me needed encouragement when I told her I was thinking of
writing this book.